Lecture Notes in Computer Science　　10375

Commenced Publication in 1973
Founding and Former Series Editors:
Gerhard Goos, Juris Hartmanis, and Jan van Leeuwen

More information about this series at http://www.springer.com/series/7408

Sebastian Gabmeyer · Einar Broch Johnsen (Eds.)

Tests and Proofs

11th International Conference, TAP 2017
Held as Part of STAF 2017
Marburg, Germany, July 19–20, 2017
Proceedings

 Springer

Editors
Sebastian Gabmeyer ⓘ
Technical University of Darmstadt
Darmstadt
Germany

Einar Broch Johnsen
University of Oslo
Oslo
Norway

ISSN 0302-9743   ISSN 1611-3349   (electronic)
Lecture Notes in Computer Science
ISBN 978-3-319-61466-3   ISBN 978-3-319-61467-0   (eBook)
DOI 10.1007/978-3-319-61467-0

Library of Congress Control Number: 2017943084

LNCS Sublibrary: SL2 – Programming and Software Engineering

Printed on acid-free paper

This Springer imprint is published by Springer Nature
The registered company is Springer International Publishing AG
The registered company address is: Gewerbestrasse 11, 6330 Cham, Switzerland

Foreword

Software Technologies: Applications and Foundations (STAF) is a federation of leading conferences on software technologies. It provides a loose umbrella organization with a Steering Committee that ensures continuity. The STAF federated event takes place annually. The participating conferences may vary from year to year, but they all focus on foundational and practical advances in software technology. The conferences address all aspects of software technology, from object-oriented design, testing, mathematical approaches to modeling and verification, transformation, model-driven engineering, aspect-oriented techniques, and tools.

STAF 2017 took place in Marburg, Germany, during July 17–21, 2017, and hosted the four conferences ECMFA 2017, ICGT 2017, ICMT 2017, and TAP 2017, the transformation tool contest TTC 2017, six workshops, a doctoral symposium, and a projects showcase event. STAF 2017 featured four internationally renowned keynote speakers, and welcomed participants from around the world.

The STAF 2017 Organizing Committee would like to thank (a) all participants for submitting to and attending the event, (b) the Program Committees and Steering Committees of all the individual conferences and satellite events for their hard work, (c) the keynote speakers for their thoughtful, insightful, and inspiring talks, and (d) the Philipps-Universität, the city of Marburg, and all sponsors for their support. A special thanks goes to Christoph Bockisch (local chair), Barbara Dinklage, and the rest of the members of the Department of Mathematics and Computer Science of the Philipps-Universität, coping with all the foreseen and unforeseen work to prepare a memorable event.

July 2017   Gabriele Taentzer

Preface

This volume contains the papers presented at TAP 2017, the 11th International Conference on Tests and Proofs. The TAP conference promotes research in verification and formal methods that targets the interplay of proofs and testing: the advancement of techniques of each kind and their combination, with the ultimate goal of improving software and system dependability. As in the four previous editions, TAP 2017 was part of STAF (Software Technologies: Applications and Foundations), a federation of leading conferences in software technology.

TAP 2017 took place in Marburg during July 16–20, 2017. The Program Committee (PC) received 16 paper submissions, each reviewed by three PC members. After two weeks of lively discussion and careful deliberation, we selected nine contributions for inclusion in this proceedings volume and presentation at the conference. The combination of topics highlights how testing and proving are increasingly seen as complementary rather than mutually exclusive techniques, and confirms TAP's commitment to bringing together researchers and practitioners from both areas of verification.

The program of TAP was nicely completed by a keynote talk by Reiner Hähnle (Technical University of Darmstadt, Germany), who also contributed an invited paper for this volume, and a tutorial by Achim D. Bruckner and Burkhart Wolff. We would like to thank the invited speaker for contributing an exciting presentation to the participants of STAF 2017.

We also thank the PC members and the additional reviewers for their timely and thorough reviewing work, and for contributing to an animated and informed discussion. Their names are listed on the following pages. The EasyChair system provided flawless technical support.

The organization of STAF made for a successful and enjoyable conference in a wonderful location. We thank all the organizers, and in particular the general chair, Gabriele Taentzer, and the organization chair, Christoph Bockisch, for their hard work; and we also thank the Technologie- und Tagungszentrum Marburg for hosting us.

July 2017

Sebastian Gabmeyer
Einar Broch Johnsen

Organization

Program Committee

Bernhard K. Aichernig	TU Graz, Austria
Elvira Albert	Complutense University of Madrid, Spain
Bruno Blanchet	Inria Paris-Rocquencourt, France
Jasmin C. Blanchette	Inria Nancy and LORIA, France
Achim D. Brucker	University of Sheffield, UK
Stijn de Gouw	Open University, The Netherlands
Catherine Dubois	ENSIIE-Samovar, France
Gordon Fraser	University of Sheffield, UK
Carlo A. Furia	Chalmers University of Technology, Sweden
Sebastian Gabmeyer	TU Darmstadt, Germany
Angelo Gargantini	University of Bergamo, Italy
Alain Giorgetti	LIFC, University of Franche-Comte, France
Christoph Gladisch	BOSCH, Germany
Martin Gogolla	University of Bremen, Germany
Arnaud Gotlieb	SIMULA Research Laboratory, Norway
Marieke Huisman	University of Twente, The Netherlands
Bart Jacobs	Katholieke Universiteit Leuven, Belgium
Einar Broch Johnsen	University of Oslo, Norway
Nikolai Kosmatov	CEA List, France
Laura Kovacs	Chalmers University of Technology, TU Wien, Sweden/Austria
Martin Leucker	University of Lübeck, Germany
Panagiotis Manolios	Northeastern University, USA
Karl Meinke	Royal Institute of Technology (KTH) Stockholm, Sweden
Andreas Podelski	University of Freiburg, Germany
Andrew Reynolds	University of Iowa, USA
Martina Seidl	Johannes Kepler University Linz, Austria
Martin Steffen	University of Oslo, Norway
Martin Strecker	Université de Toulouse, France
T.H. Tse	The University of Hong Kong, SAR China
Luca Viganò	King's College London, UK
Burkhart Wolff	University of Paris-Sud, France

Additional Reviewers

Bentkamp, Alexander
Caballero, Rafael
Herzberg, Michael
Jaroschek, Maximilian

Rojas, José Miguel
Scheffel, Torben
Schmitz, Malte

Contents

Invited Contribution

Abstraction Refinement for the Analysis of Software Product Lines

Ferruccio Damiani[1], Reiner Hähnle[2(✉)], and Michael Lienhardt[1]

[1] University of Torino, Torino, Italy
{ferruccio.damiani,michael.lienhardt}@unito.it
[2] University of Darmstadt, Darmstadt, Germany
haehnle@cs.tu-darmstadt.de

Abstract. We generalize the principle of counter example-guided data abstraction refinement (CEGAR) to guided refinement of Software Product Lines (SPL) and of analysis tools. We also add a problem decomposition step. The result is a framework for formal SPL analysis via guided refinement and divide-and-conquer, through sound orchestration of multiple tools.

1 Introduction

A *Software Product Line* (SPL) is a set of similar programs, called *variants*, with a common code base and well documented variability [23]. An SPL can be described by a triple consisting of a feature model, an artifact base, and configuration knowledge. The *feature model* defines the set of variants in terms of *features*: each feature represents an abstract description of functionality and each variant is identified by a set of features, called a *product*. The *artifact base* provides language dependent reusable code artifacts that are used to build the variants. *Configuration knowledge* connects feature model and artifact base by describing how to derive variants from the code artifacts given the products.

Tool-based analysis of software [12] is becoming more and more feasible and, therefore, common. This includes functional verification [1], resource analysis [2], safety verification [15], information flow [36], deadlock detection [30], to name just a few. It is still a challenge, however, to lift such analyses from the level of individual variants to whole SPLs. There are lifting approaches that, by making analyses and tools variability aware (i.e., to operate directly on the code of the SPL, not on the code of the variants) work for type systems [24,26] or lightweight static analyses [17]. For more complex scenarios, such as formal verification, relatively restrictive assumptions must be made [32] (see also [18,25]). There is no general theory of lifting software analysis from individual products to SPLs [42].

This work has been partially supported by: EU Horizon 2020 project HyVar (www.hyvar-project.eu), GA No. 644298; ICT COST Action IC1402 ARVI (www.cost-arvi.eu); Ateneo/CSP D16D15000360005 project RunVar (runvar-project.di.unito.it); project FormbaR (formbar.raillab.de), Innovationsallianz TU Darmstadt-Deutsche Bahn Netz AG.

© Springer International Publishing AG 2017
S. Gabmeyer and E.B. Johnsen (Eds.): TAP 2017, LNCS 10375, pp. 3–20, 2017.
DOI: 10.1007/978-3-319-61467-0_1

An alternative to making the analyses and the tools variability aware, is to generate, for a given SPL, a *meta variant* or *variant simulator* (see, e.g., [45]). This is an artifact, expressed in the same language as the variants are written in, that takes as input any product and simulates the behavior of the corresponding variant. A meta variant has the advantage that it can be analyzed with standard tools for the implementation language of its variants. To ensure that this approach is efficient, *variability encoding* (i.e., the process of transforming an SPL into a meta variant) must avoid to duplicate code that is common to different variants. Depending on the given SPL, its meta variant can be significantly more complex than any of the variants, challenging the capabilities of available tools [43]. Indeed, it has not yet been demonstrated that variability encoding provides a scalable approach to family-based analysis of large SPLs.

In this paper we present a novel and systematic approach that permits to apply software analyses to the meta variant of an SPL. We take our cue from *Counter Example-Guided Abstraction Refinement* (CEGAR) [22], a well-known and highly successful verification strategy to handle programs that are too complex to be verified directly. We generalize the CEGAR principle to guided refinement of SPLs and of analysis tools. We also add a problem decomposition step. The result is a framework for formal SPL analysis via guided refinement and divide-and-conquer, through sound orchestration of multiple tools.

Paper Organization. In Sect. 2 we briefly recall the main approaches to implement SPLs and introduce the running example of the paper. In Sect. 3 we recall the CEGAR principle and explain our proposal to generalize it to the refinement of SPLs and of tools. In Sect. 4 we recap the workflow of the running example and outline how our framework can be instantiated to other scenarios. In Sect. 5 we discuss related work and in Sect. 6 we conclude.

2   Implementation of Software Product Lines

Currently, there exist three main approaches to implement SPLs [40]: *annotative approaches* expressing negative variability (all variants are represented by a single artifact); *compositional approaches* expressing positive variability (features are associated to artifacts, possibly describing refinements to a base artifact); and *transformational approaches* expressing both positive and negative variability (feature combinations are associated to artifacts describing changes to a base artifact to obtain other system variants).

A prominent example of an annotative approach is based on C preprocessor directives (`#define FEATURE` and `#ifdef FEATURE`). *Delta-Oriented Programming* (DOP, see [13,38] and [6, Sect. 6.6.1]) is a flexible transformational approach in which the artifact base consists of a *base program* (that might be empty or incomplete) and of a set of *deltas*, which are containers of modifications to a program (e.g., for Java programs, a delta can add, remove or modify classes and interfaces), while configuration knowledge associates to each delta an *activation condition* over the features and specifies an *application ordering* between deltas.

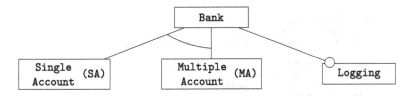

Fig. 1. Visual representation of the feature model of the Bank Account SPL example

```
data Operation = Withdraw(Int) | Deposit(Int);    Bool newOperation(Operation op) {
class Client() implements IClient { }               Bool check_needed = case op {
class Account() implements IAccount {               Withdraw(i) => i > 10000 ;
  Int amount;                                        _ => False ;
  Int getAmount() { return this.amount; }          };
}                                                   Bool apply_accepted = case check_needed {
                                                     True => this.checkAccounts();
class Bank() implements IBank {                       _ => True;
  List<IClient> clients;                            };
  Unit applyOperation(Operation op) { ... }         if(apply_accepted)
                                                       this.applyOperation(op);
                                                     return apply_accepted;
                                                  }}
```

Fig. 2. Base program

DOP supports the automatic generation of variants based on a selection of features: once a user selects a product, the corresponding variant is derived by applying the deltas with a satisfied activation condition to the base program according to the application ordering. DOP can be seen as a generalization of *Feature-Oriented Programming* (FOP) (see [11] and [6, Sect. 6.1]), a compositional approach to SPL implementation, where deltas correspond one-to-one to features and do not contain remove operations [39].

Our running example is a simple product line modeling a bank with different features, depicted in Fig. 1. The feature Single Account (or SA) associates one account with each client of the bank, while feature Multiple Account (or MA) allows a client to maintain several accounts. Finally, the feature Logging adds logging capabilities to the banking operations. Features SA and MA are *alternative* (i.e., exactly one of them must be selected), while feature Logging is *optional*. The code base of our example, presented in Figs. 2, 3, 4 and 5, is written in the modeling language ABS [35], which realizes DOP.

Figure 2 contains the *base program* that implements the core functionalities of our example. The data type Operation describes the possible banking operations, Withdraw and Deposit, respectively for withdrawing or depositing a specified amount. The Client class is empty, as its content depends on whether feature SA or MA is selected, while the Account class, that implements an account, simply stores the balance of the account.

The Bank has a list of clients and declares three methods: applyOperation performs a banking operation in the bank, without any check; newOperation is a wrapper around applyOperation that executes some checks in case the operation is a withdrawal of a large amount of money; finally, checkAccounts

```
delta dSA {
 modifies class Client {
  adds IAccount account;
  adds IAccount getAccount() { return this.account; }
 }
 modifies class Bank {
  adds Bool checkAccounts() {
   List<IClient> tmp = this.clients;
   Int total_amount = 0;
   while(!isEmpty(tmp)) {
    total_amount = total_amount + head(tmp).getAccount().getAmount();
    tmp = tail(tmp);
   }
   return total_amount > 1000000;
}}}
```

Fig. 3. Delta for the SA feature

```
delta dMA {
 modifies class Client {
  adds List<IAccount> accounts;
  adds List<IAccount> getAccounts() { return this.accounts; }
 }
 modifies class Bank {
  adds Bool checkAccounts() {
   List<IClient> tmp1 = this.clients;
   Int total_amount = 0;
   while(!isEmpty(tmp1)) {
    List<Account> tmp2 = head(tmp1).getAccounts();
    while(!isEmpty(tmp2)) {
     total_amount = total_amount + head(tmp2).getAmount();
     tmp2 = tail(tmp2);
    }
    tmp1 = tail(tmp1);
   }
   return total_amount > 1000000;
}}}
```

Fig. 4. Delta for the MA feature

performs the checks and is not part of the base program, as its implementation entirely depends on the selected features.

Figure 3 presents the delta dSA implementing the SA feature. Here, the class Client is defined, and simply contains an account (with a getter method). The method checkAccounts of the class Bank is also implemented, and simply iterates over all the accounts of the bank, to ensure that its overall balance is big enough to allow the requested withdrawal.

Figure 4 presents the delta dMA implementing the MA feature. Here, the class Client contains a list of accounts. The implementation of the checkAccounts method still iterates over all the accounts of the bank to check that its overall balance is large enough, but to do so, it now contains an inner loop that iterates over all the accounts of a client.

Figure 5 contains the delta dLog that implements the feature Logging. This delta redefines the method newOperation of the class Bank, surrounding the original implementation (modeled with the keyword **original** in place of the method call) with two calls to print. These calls simply register which operation was requested and whether it was performed.

```
delta dLog {
  modifies class Bank {
    modifies Bool newOperation(Operation op) {
      print("Managing the new operation \"" + op + "\"");
      Bool result = original(op);
      if(result) print("\tOperation successful");
      else print("\tOperation Failed")
      return result;
}}}
```

Fig. 5. Delta for the Logging feature

Finally, the configuration knowledge required to describe the Bank Account SPL is straightforward and we omit the corresponding ABS declaration—it simply specifies that each delta is activated exactly by the feature that it realizes (since for each product applying the activated deltas in any order yields the same variant, no application ordering needs to be specified).

3 Counter Product-Guided Refinement

3.1 Counter Example-Guided Abstraction Refinement (CEGAR)

Assume we want to establish that a property P holds for any run of a program m with an analysis tool t, denoted by $m \vdash_t P$. For example, m could be an ABS program, P a safety property saying that certain bad states are unreachable, and t might be a model checker: it can happen that $m \vdash_t P$ cannot be established because t times out or runs out of memory.

To render verification feasible, the CEGAR verification strategy (illustrated in Fig. 6) executes t not with m, but with an *abstraction* of m, written $A(m)$: for example, all datatypes are initially abstracted to booleans which greatly reduces the number of reachable states. Note that the chosen abstraction must be sound in the sense that $A(m)$ preserves all possible behaviors of m. Now we can assume that the—simplified—problem $A(m) \vdash_t P$ terminates. If $A(m) \vdash_t P$ holds, then also $m \vdash_t P$ holds (because the abstraction is sound) and we are done. If $A(m) \vdash_t P$ doesn't hold, then we extract a counter example, i.e., an input c of m such that $A(m)(c)$ violates P. If $m(c)$ violates P as well, then the counter example exhibits a real bug of m and we are done (i.e., we can try to fix the bug and restart the process). If $m(c)$ does not violate P, then we use c to refine A to a more precise abstraction A' so that $A, (m)(c)$ does not violate P, and we re-enter the CEGAR loop with the refined abstraction.[1] A concrete example of a CEGAR-style refinement is presented below in Sect. 3.3.

---

[1] This abstract description of CEGAR leaves many issues open: how to make sure that the refinement loop terminates? How to select a counter example? How to compute the refinement? On each of these questions a considerable literature exists, but this is not the focus of this paper.

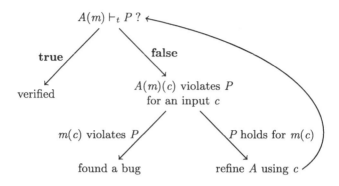

Fig. 6. Work flow of CEGAR

3.2   Counter Example-Guided Product Line Refinement (CEGPLR)

In the context of Software Product Lines, another kind of refinement can be considered: CEGAR looks at one program at a time and performs refinement on that program's data abstraction, however, Software Product Lines add the dimension of having to analyze different program variants at the same time. We observe that the meta variant of an SPL is compatible with the CEGAR approach in the following sense: A meta variant of an SPL by definition encompasses the behavior of each of its variants. Hence, a meta variant constitutes a behavioral abstraction of each variant or set of variants of a given SPL. Consequently, a meta variant might be refined to the behavior embodied in any subset of its variants.

For instance, the SPL presented in Sect. 2 defines four different variants identified by the four following products: $\{\text{Bank}, \text{SA}\}$, $\{\text{Bank}, \text{SA}, \text{Logging}\}$, $\{\text{Bank}, \text{MA}\}$ and $\{\text{Bank}, \text{MA}, \text{Logging}\}$. In this context, one can apply a CEGAR-like iteration to the SPL: first one runs an analysis tool t on an abstraction that comprises all variants. If t succeeds then, as with CEGAR, we are done. Otherwise, a counter example consisting of an input c and a *subset of the variants* exhibiting the error for c can be extracted. This triggers a *decomposition step* that consists of splitting the input SPL into two parts: one that has c as a possible counter example, and one that has not. Both parts can then be analyzed independently, as they don't exhibit the same behavior. If the part where c is no counter example has no other counter example, then that part of the SPL is verified.

To illustrate this approach to Product Line Refinement with a concrete example, let us consider the Bank SPL presented in Sect. 2, simply called L from now: assume we want to ensure the property P stating that the execution time of the newOperation() method is at most linear in the number of accounts in the bank. The analysis tool we consider is SACO [2], which is a state-of-art cost analysis tool that abstracts every non-boolean datatype by its size.

For the abstraction of the variants of an SPL, we use its meta variant, i.e., a program that contains each behavior in each variant of L (cf. Sect. 1). There are different techniques to obtain it, and here we use the 150% test model of [29,31]

```
data Product = Product(Bool fBank, fBool SA, Bool fMA, Bool fLogging);
def Bool isValid(Product p) = fBank(p) && (fSA(p) || fMA(p)) && !(fSA(p) && fMA(p));
def Bool dLogging(Product p) = fLogging(p);
...

Bool newOperation(Operation op) {
  Bool result = False;
  if(dLogging(p)) {
    print("Managing the new operation \"" + op + "\"");
    result = this.newOperationCore(op);
    if(result) print("\tOperation successful");
    else print("\tOperation Failed");
  } else {
    result = this.newOperationCore(op);
  }
  return result;
}

Bool newOperationCore(Operation op) { ... }
```

Fig. 7. Excerpt of meta variant for the Bank SPL

which is an instance of a sound *variability encoding* [45]. An excerpt of our meta variant is depicted in Fig. 7. The first two lines encode product selection and what a valid product is. The third line relates the code delta dLog to the feature Logging. This has to be completed for the remaining features and is not necessarily one-to-one like here. The meta variant selection mechanism can be seen in the method newOperation(). When the logging delta is requested, then the main **if** condition executes the code from Fig. 5, otherwise the core product version of the method is executed (that version is stored in a new method with a new name, to disambiguate the calls).

Running SACO on our meta variant yields an interesting result: it validates the property P when the feature MA is not selected, but fails to prove it when MA is selected. An analysis of the obtained counter example shows that during its abstraction step, SACO replaced lists by integers corresponding to their size, thus ignoring essential information about the accounts when the feature MA is activated, as these are stored inside a list of lists. In the following decomposition step the meta variant is split in two parts. The first of these contains all variants that do not have the behavior required by feature MA. We write this as $L[\{SA\}, \{SA, Logging\}]$ and call it a *partial meta variant*. SACO guarantees that its two variants validate P. The second partial meta variant, where MA is activated (written $L[\{MA\}, \{MA, Logging\}]$), does not have this guarantee. Of it we know that to prove P, we must not abstract away the list of lists structure.

The general form of a partial meta variant is $L[F_1, \ldots, F_n]$ where L is the SPL from which the meta variant is generated and $F_1, \ldots, F_n$ are the products of L available in this meta variant.

We can now define (illustrated in Fig. 8) a CEGAR-like loop for refining and decomposing a Software Product Line. The loop is started with the (full) meta variant of the input SPL, i.e. initially $\bar{F} = F_1, \ldots, F_n$ are all the products of the SPL. Note that we work with an abstraction $A(L[\bar{F}])$ of the meta variant, implying that standard CEGAR and SPL refinement can be interleaved.

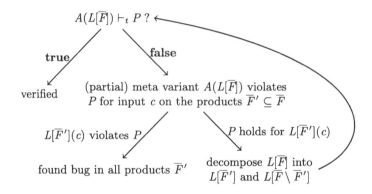

Fig. 8. Work flow of CEGPLR

Like before, if we manage to verify the property, then we are done. If not, then the counter example does not only consist of a concrete input c, but also of a set of products $\bar{F}'$ exhibiting this counter example. Like in CEGAR one checks now whether the counter example is real: we test it against the partial meta variant $L[\bar{F}']$. If $L[\bar{F}'](c)$ violates P, we found a bug. Otherwise, we attempt to refine the current meta variant $L[\bar{F}]$ into $L[\bar{F} \setminus \bar{F}']$, i.e., we assume that the selected features were critical for the counter example to manifest itself, and, therefore exclude them.[2] If we manage to verify at some point $A(L[\bar{F} \setminus \bar{F}']) \vdash_t P$ for some $\bar{F}' \subseteq \bar{F}$, then we have refined the original verification problem to $L[\bar{F}']$. We call this process *counter example-guided product line refinement* (CEGPLR).

In fact, CEGPLR goes beyond CEGAR, because it provides not only a problem refinement, but also a *problem decomposition* (into $L[\bar{F}']$ and $L[\bar{F} \setminus \bar{F}']$). Therefore, it is a combined abstraction refinement and *divide-and-conquer* approach.

3.3   Tool Refinement

Existing CEGAR-like approaches work with a single verification or analysis tool, for example, a model checker or symbolic execution, but this constitutes no principal limitation. In fact, there is growing evidence that huge efficiency gains can be obtained from systematic combination of different analysis tools [5,14,20]. One can even hypothesize that *only* the systematic combination of different tools and methods will make it feasible to attack complex problems [12]. Hence, in addition to abstraction and product line refinement, we suggest *tool refinement*. This term is justified, as long as the refined tool analyzes at least as many behaviors as the old one.

In Fig. 9 we present yet another variant of the CEGAR loop (Fig. 6), this time based on tool refinement. The difference lies in the analysis of the failed proof.

---

[2] This is a coarse-grained refinement step. Alternatively, one could branch into $|\bar{F}'|$ many refinements of the form $L[\bar{F}'']$ with $\bar{F}'' \subseteq \bar{F}'$.

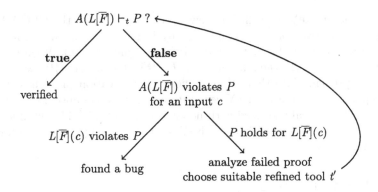

Fig. 9. Work flow of CEGTR

Instead of looking for ways to refine the abstraction A or the partial meta variant $L[\bar{F}]$, we now look for a verification tool t' that refines the analysis performed by t in a manner such that $A(L[\bar{F}]) \vdash_{t'} P$ (or a refinement thereof) becomes provable. Obviously, this is in general a step that requires deliberation by an expert, in contrast to CEGAR, where abstractions are computed automatically. Nevertheless, it is beneficial: (i) one obtains guidance in choosing an appropriate tool, (ii) behavioral refinement of the tools preserves overall soundness, and (iii) the input and instrumentation of tool t' can be obtained from A and $L[\bar{F}]$. The third point is, in principle, automatable.

We illustrate tool refinement with our running example. In the previous section, SACO failed to analyze the partial meta variant $L[\{\texttt{MA}\}, \{\texttt{MA}, \texttt{Logging}\}]$: SACO abstracted away lists into integers, and was unable to find a bound for the nested loop in dMA (Fig. 4). SACO can, in principle, deal with nested loops, but it has limited support for reference types (like lists) which are abstracted by their size. For this reason, the tool doesn't know enough about the structure of type List<IAccount> to perform the analysis. The tool also cannot express separation conditions (e.g., that the Account objects in a list are unaliased).

The abstraction of SACO cannot be further refined and we did the product line refinement already, so the only possibility now is to refine the tool. In the paper [3] a formal link between resource analysis tools and formal verification tools is described. This makes it possible to use a formal verification tool such as KeY [1] to reason about resource properties. Of course, KeY is an interactive tool and might require input from a verification expert. But thanks to product line refinement, we managed to reduce the problem already. In addition, all the invariants derived by SACO are automatically imported into KeY, such that only the *additional* annotations to prove the correctness of the meta variant $L[\{\texttt{MA}\}, \{\texttt{MA}, \texttt{Logging}\}]$ need to be supplied. A further reason to use the KeY tool in the experiment is that it can be instrumented with user-defined data type abstractions [46].

We first attempt to prove $A(L[\{\texttt{MA}\}, \{\texttt{MA}, \texttt{Logging}\}]) \vdash_{KeY} P$, where A is the abstraction embodied in SACO. As A still abstracts the inner Account lists away, this fails in KeY as well, but now we can again enter the CEGAR loop and refine the abstraction, based on the analysis above: we now model lists precisely, but we can still abstract completely away from Account. With this new abstraction, denoted A', the statement $A'(L[\{MA\}, \{MA, Logging\}]) \vdash_{KeY} P$ was successfully proven. Note that A' simplifies the verification problem considerably compared to the normal KeY verification workflow, because, in contrast to CEGAR, KeY is usually started with no abstraction at all.[3] The integration of KeY into a CEGAR framework allows KeY to profit from a previously computed abstraction.

3.4   Other Abstractions

Behavioral Abstraction. CEGAR is based on datatype refinement, but with SPL and tool refinement we introduced behavioral refinement already. Therefore, it is natural to look at further possibilities for the *behavioral abstraction* of a given program. For example, if we are interested in deadlocks (i.e., we are out to prove deadlock-freedom), it might be useful to abstract a program away to merely its call and synchronization points and completely ignore datatypes.[4] Even more drastic abstractions, e.g., occurring in type-based analyses [30], abstract completely away from object creation. This fits perfectly well into our framework. We simply extend the meaning of A to include behavioral abstractions as well.

Property Abstraction. It is also possible to abstract or refine the *property* to be proven. Please note that both directions can be useful. If we have proven P, by abstraction soundness, we have also proven $A(P)$. In this case, it might be worth trying to prove a *stronger* property. An example of a situation, where this is useful is given in Sect. 4.3 under *Formal Verification*.

Vice versa, if we do not manage to prove P, a possible strategy is to prove a weaker property $A(P)$. For example, in Sect. 3.3 we proved with KeY a linear bound for $L[\{MA\}, \{MA, Logging\}]$. However, this requires a suitable modification of the loop invariant. If we weaken P to prove just termination with no concrete bound, then it is sufficient to provide *termination witnesses* for both loops which are completely straightforward: `length(clients)-length(tmp1)` and `length(accounts)-length(tmp2)`, respectively.

4   Abstraction Refinement for Software Product Lines

4.1   An Abstraction Layer in the Analysis of SPLs

In the previous section we proposed two new CEGAR-like loops in the context of static analysis of SPLs: CEGPLR (Fig. 8) realizes SPL refinement and decomposition, based on the observation that the meta variant of a product line

---

[3] In the standard workflow of KeY abstractions are computed on demand and are mainly used for loop invariant generation and state merging.

[4] Another way to view this is to abstract all data to a single value.

Problem Space: Feature Model		
feature description language		
Configuration and Abstraction Layer		
configuration knowledge	implementation/property abstraction	tool instrumentation
Solution Space: Implementation		
annotative / compositional / transformational		

Fig. 10. SPL implementation with explicit abstraction layer

constitutes a behavioral abstraction of each partial meta variant and, in particular, of each single product variant; CEGTR (Fig. 9) realizes refinement of the underlying analysis tool with a tool that can distinguish more behavior. In addition, it can also be useful to abstract or refine the properties to be proven and to work with behavioral abstractions (not mere data abstractions) of the system under verification.

The central role that is played by abstraction and refinement, both data-level and behavioral, both of the target system and the target property, suggests to maintain an explicit configuration and abstraction layer when analyzing SPLs to achieve a clean and flexible separation between the problem space and the solution space, see Fig. 10. To work out the details and to formalize such an abstraction layer is the topic of future work.

4.2 Workflow in Abstraction Refinement for SPL

It is worth to recap the workflow of our example in Sects. 3.2 and 3.3: from a failed attempt to prove a linear worst-case runtime bound with the tool SACO we decomposed via SPL refinement the problem into two partial meta variants and showed the desired property for all products in one of them (Sect. 3.2). No further abstraction refinement in SACO is possible, so the only option (except to weaken the targeted property) was to refine the tool. The verification tool KeY offers more precision than SACO. It was instrumented with the data abstraction of SACO and the invariants computed by it. After a standard CEGAR step, KeY managed to prove the desired property (Sect. 3.3).

It is worth to note that (i) after the first refinement step, the exhaustion of other options drove the choice to perform tool refinement and (ii) that the output of the analysis in the first step provided the instrumentation of the next tool in the chain. This suggests that our framework is suitable to orchestrate the combination of static analysis and verification tools that work at different levels of precision.

For our example, only one refinement loop of each kind was necessary, but this is not true in general. For example, with a larger product line, after refinement abstraction in KeY, probably another round of product line refinement makes sense. It would be premature to speculate about concrete meta refinement loops while a robust implementation of our framework is lacking, so we refrain from it.

Having said that, it seems a good idea to always attempt to refine and decompose the product line as much as possible.

4.3   More Usage Scenarios

In the previous section we illustrated our framework with a usage scenario about resource analysis. In fact, our approach is applicable to a wide range of analyses and we want it to be understood as a general framework for the sound and systematic combination and orchestration of software analysis tools. To substantiate this claim, we instantiate our framework with three more scenarios. In each case we assume that we have an SPL over ABS programs specified with DOP following [21]. While this is not necessary in general, it makes it possible in what follows to provide concrete examples of analysis methods and tools.

Feature Interference. With feature interference we mean feature interaction within an SPL that has undesired effects. It is a practically important and intensely studied problem [34]. Denote with $f \notmid f'$ that features f and f' from a given valid product F interfere with each other, for example, they both have write access to the same memory location. To analyze a given SPL for feature interference, one may start with an obvious, but coarse abstraction: Assume that for any method m required to implement $f \in F$ and m' required for $f' \in F$, such that both m and m' share a critical resource r, it is the case that m can never be executed in parallel to m' (where both $m = m'$ and $f = f'$ is possible). This is a typically sufficient criterion to exclude feature interference.

As a first verification tool we choose a may-happen-in-parallel (MHP) analysis: the predicate $MHP(m, m')$ holds for a given ABS program if it contains methods m, m' that can possibly be executed in parallel. An efficient over-approximation of MHP is available for ABS [4]. Now we enter the product line refinement loop of Fig. 8, where P is the absence of feature interference, t is MHP, and A the not-in-parallel abstraction of the meta variant $L[\bar{F}]$. As most features tend not to interact, we can assume that the CEGPLR loop refines and decomposes the problem into a much smaller partial meta variant $L[\bar{F}']$, where absence of feature interference was proven for $L[\bar{F} \setminus \bar{F}']$.

An analysis of the failed proof for $L[\bar{F}']$ now might show that certain methods m, m' actually *do* interfere, but not in a safety-critical manner. This is not provable with MHP, but one may use deductive verification with KeY instead. To this end, one refines P so as to express that for any m, m' such that $MHP(m, m')$ holds, their common resources r satisfy a safety invariant. It is possible to encode this property in a program logic with the help of self composition [27] and use KeY to prove it. However, one might abstract away from most datatypes in that proof, because they are likely to be irrelevant for feature interaction. Hence, we would instrument KeY to implement a CEGAR loop over symbolic execution with abstraction [16,46].

Formal Verification. Deductive verification tools (e.g., KeY [1]) as well as safety verification tools (e.g., CPAchecker [15]) have impressive, yet complementary strengths. KeY was used for functional verification of SPL's using variability encoding [43], but it quickly becomes very expensive in terms of runtime and user interaction [19]. This indicates that variability encoding is not a scalable strategy for formal verification of SPLs.

Instead, one could start formal verification of a property P for an SPL L with a CEGAR-based safety verification tool [16], where P is abstracted to a weaker property $A(P)$ that is expressible in it and the initial program is of the form $Boolean(L[\bar{F}])$ (where $Boolean$ abstracts all data to booleans). A combination of CEGAR and CEGPLR decomposes and reduces the problem to a partial meta variant $L[\bar{F}']$ and computes a refinement $A'(L[\bar{F}'])$ from where no further progress seems possible. Only then one uses a deductive verification tool such as KeY, instrumented with A'. Once $A(P)$ has been shown for some $A''(L[\bar{F}'])$, one can perform property refinement from $A(P)$ to P, followed by further product line and abstraction refinement loops. This scenario shows that it can make perfect sense to (i) work with different abstractions for programs and properties and (ii) not just abstract from a property, but also refine it.

Information Flow. Information flow control is the problem to analyze whether a program allows an attacker to deduce information about secret values by manipulating its public interface. There is a wide variety of analysis tools and methods for this problem with complementary strengths: type-based approaches [37] and lightweight static analyses [33] scale well, even to SPL [17], but yield many false positives and can only express limited security policies. Deductive approaches [27,41] are expensive and often require manual annotation. As a consequence, information flow is a natural usage scenario for our framework and it can be developed in a similar manner as the previous scenarios.

5   Related Work

There are a number of verification approaches that decompose or transform a complex analysis problem such that different tools can be used in combination to solve it. CPAchecker [15] is a flexibly configurable tool framework for fully automatic verification of safety properties that allows to integrate other tools in a sound manner. Specifically, Beyer and Lemberger [16] applied CEGAR in the context of symbolic execution within CPAchecker. However, it is not designed to express complex functional properties. Ahrendt et al. [20] use the result of a partial verification attempt of a given program to generate an optimized run-time assertion checker that only monitors those properties that could not be proven. Küsters et al. [36] combine static analysis and deductive verification for information flow proofs: they transform the given program and prove with KeY preservation of behavior, then use the static analyzer on the simplified program. This corresponds to manual computation of a suitable program abstraction, whereas we propagate abstraction refinement. None of these papers is concerned with the analysis of SPLs.

Clafer [9] is a modeling language that is designed as an extension of Alloy and has a unified representation of features as well as OO models. It has been used to model and analyse Software Product Lines [8], however, it is not directly connected to executable code.

Batory [10] developed a theory of modular composition and decomposition of software that has been used also in the context of SPLs and that has been extended to verification proofs. It is also based on refinement, but requires a theoretical framework that makes it not straightforward to apply to existing languages and tools. To the best of our knowledge, it does not contain a CEGAR-like strategy. Proof composition [44] relies on creating partial correctness proofs for certain features that are then combined into proofs for a desired product. However, this approach becomes problematic when properties of feature implementations depend on each other.

The 150% model technique [29,31] originates from model-based testing and was then also employed in software analysis, e.g., [7,43]. All of these approaches are an instance of *variability encoding*, as classified and formalized in [45].

Bodden et al. [17] lift static analysis of control flow properties from product variants to software product lines, essentially by a form of variability encoding into a somewhat more expressive static analysis framework. This approach, however, does not work for more complex properties.

Independently of our work, Dimovski and Wąsowski [28] recently implemented what seems to be the first product line refinement approach for LTL model checking. It follows the same pattern as ours, employing a notion of *partial meta variant* containing all nodes and transitions of the included variants. Like in our approach, the meta variant is a standard product, in their case an LTS, that allows to use the SPIN model checker. As we do, upon finding a spurious counter example, they split the meta variant, with the help of Craig interpolation.

6   Conclusion and Future Work

In this paper we drafted an SPL analysis framework based on the principle to perform as much work as possible with lightweight, efficient, and automatic methods: this means to start analyzing product lines at a high level of abstraction, possibly with an abstract version of the targeted property. Then we apply the main lesson behind the CEGAR principle: don't throw away failed proof attempts, but carefully analyze the information contained in them to improve the analysis.

Based on the insight that a meta variant is a behavioral abstraction of each subset of its variants, we designed a CEGAR-like loop to perform *product line refinement* and, made possible through an extensional, feature-based representation of products, extended it to a *divide-and-conquer* approach that provides product line decomposition. Crucially, even when neither CEGAR nor CEGPLR are successful, this is not the end of the line: one refines the analysis tool and uses a more precise, but also more heavyweight method, but benefits from the refinement and decomposition made in the previous steps. Indeed, all four usage scenarios we discussed—resource analysis, feature interference, formal verification, information flow—offer a variety of analysis tools working at differing levels of abstraction. The concept of *tool refinement* soundly integrates these tools, where a CEGAR-style refinement analysis guides the *selection* of the chosen tool and helps to *instrument* it.

Overall, our framework implements a version of the *subsidiarity principle* in the realm of software analysis: a subtask should be solved at the highest possible level of abstraction, with the least expensive method.

CEGAR loops are normally part of a single, fully automated tool, but this is an unnecessary limitation. Our work shows that manual abstraction refinement for guiding the selection of a new tool makes perfect sense. Another important lesson that can be drawn is that it is extremely useful to have tools that can be flexibly instrumented with data abstraction. This is the case already, for example, for CPAchecker [15] and KeY [1].

The next step is to provide a robust implementation of our framework, including a suitable abstraction layer (see Fig. 10) and to conduct larger case studies.

Acknowledgment. The authors gratefully acknowledge the help of Antonio Flores Montoya who ran a number of experiments with SACO for us and helped with their analysis.

References

1. Ahrendt, W., Beckert, B., Bubel, R., Hähnle, R., Schmitt, P., Ulbrich, M. (eds.): Deductive Software Verification—The KeY Book: From Theory to Practice. Programming and Software Engineering, vol. 10001. Springer, Heidelberg (2016). doi:10.1007/978-3-319-49812-6
2. Albert, E., Arenas, P., Flores-Montoya, A., Genaim, S., Gómez-Zamalloa, M., Martin-Martin, E., Puebla, G., Román-Díez, G.: SACO: static analyzer for concurrent objects. In: Ábrahám, E., Havelund, K. (eds.) TACAS 2014. LNCS, vol. 8413, pp. 562–567. Springer, Heidelberg (2014). doi:10.1007/978-3-642-54862-8_46
3. Albert, E., Bubel, R., Genaim, S., Hähnle, R., Díez, G.R.: A formal verification framework for static analysis – as well as its instantiation to the resource analyzer COSTA and formal verification tool KeY. Softw. Syst. Model. **15**(4), 987–1012 (2016)
4. Albert, E., Flores-Montoya, A., Genaim, S., Martin-Martin, E.: May-happen-in-parallel analysis for actor-based concurrency. ACM Trans. Comput. Log. **17**(2), 11:1–11:39 (2016)
5. Albert, E., Gómez-Zamalloa, M., Isabel, M.: Combining static analysis and testing for deadlock detection. In: Ábrahám, E., Huisman, M. (eds.) IFM 2016. LNCS, vol. 9681, pp. 409–424. Springer, Cham (2016). doi:10.1007/978-3-319-33693-0_26
6. Apel, S., Batory, D.S., Kästner, C., Saake, G.: Feature-Oriented Software Product Lines: Concepts and Implementation. Springer, Heidelberg (2013)
7. Apel, S., Speidel, H., Wendler, P., von Rhein, A., Beyer, D.: Detection of feature interactions using feature-aware verification. In: Alexander, P., Pasareanu, C.S., Hosking, J.G. (eds.) 26th IEEE/ACM International Conference on Automated Software Engineering (ASE), Lawrence, KS, USA, pp. 372–375. IEEE Computer Society (2011)

8. Bak, K.: Modeling and analysis of software product line variability in clafer. Ph.D. thesis, University of Waterloo (2013)
9. Bak, K., Diskin, Z., Antkiewicz, M., Czarnecki, K., Wasowski, A.: Clafer: unifying class and feature modeling. Softw. Syst. Model. **15**(3), 811–845 (2016)
10. Batory, D.S.: A theory of modularity for automated software development. In: France, R.B., Ghosh, S., Leavens, G.T. (eds.) Companion Proceedings of 14th International Conference on Modularity, Fort Collins, CO, USA, pp. 1–10. ACM (2015)
11. Batory, D.S., Sarvela, J.N., Rauschmayer, A.: Scaling step-wise refinement. IEEE Trans. Softw. Eng. **30**(6), 355–371 (2004)
12. Beckert, B., Hähnle, R.: Reasoning and verification. IEEE Intell. Syst. **29**(1), 20–29 (2014)
13. Bettini, L., Damiani, F., Schaefer, I.: Compositional type checking of delta-oriented software product lines. Acta Inform. **50**(2), 77–122 (2013)
14. Beyer, D., Dangl, M., Dietsch, D., Heizmann, M.: Correctness witnesses: exchanging verification results between verifiers. In: Zimmermann, T., Cleland-Huang, J., Su, Z. (eds.) Proceedings of 24th ACM SIGSOFT International Symposium on Foundations of Software Engineering, FSE, Seattle, WA, USA, pp. 326–337. ACM (2016)
15. Beyer, D., Keremoglu, M.E.: CPACHECKER: a tool for configurable software verification. In: Gopalakrishnan, G., Qadeer, S. (eds.) CAV 2011. LNCS, vol. 6806, pp. 184–190. Springer, Heidelberg (2011). doi:10.1007/978-3-642-22110-1_16
16. Beyer, D., Lemberger, T.: Symbolic execution with CEGAR. In: Margaria, T., Steffen, B. (eds.) ISoLA 2016. LNCS, vol. 9952, pp. 195–211. Springer, Cham (2016). doi:10.1007/978-3-319-47166-2_14
17. Bodden, E., Tolêdo, T., Ribeiro, M., Brabrand, C., Borba, P., Mezini, M.: Spl[lift]: statically analyzing software product lines in minutes instead of years. In: Boehm, H., Flanagan, C. (eds.) ACM SIGPLAN Conference on Programming Language Design and Implementation, PLDI, Seattle, WA, USA, pp. 355–364. ACM (2013)
18. Bubel, R., Damiani, F., Hähnle, R., Johnsen, E.B., Owe, O., Schaefer, I., Yu, I.C.: Proof repositories for compositional verification of evolving software systems. In: Steffen, B. (ed.) Transactions on Foundations for Mastering Change I. LNCS, vol. 9960, pp. 130–156. Springer, Cham (2016). doi:10.1007/978-3-319-46508-1_8
19. Bubel, R., Din, C., Hähnle, R.: Verification of variable software: an experience report. In: Beckert, B., Marché, C. (eds.) Pre-Proceedings International Conference on Formal Verification of Object-Oriented Software (FoVeOOS), Paris, France (2010)
20. Chimento, J.M., Ahrendt, W., Pace, G.J., Schneider, G.: STARVOORS : a tool for combined static and runtime verification of Java. In: Bartocci, E., Majumdar, R. (eds.) RV 2015. LNCS, vol. 9333, pp. 297–305. Springer, Cham (2015). doi:10.1007/978-3-319-23820-3_21
21. Clarke, D., Diakov, N., Hähnle, R., Johnsen, E.B., Schaefer, I., Schäfer, J., Schlatte, R., Wong, P.Y.H.: Modeling spatial and temporal variability with the HATS abstract behavioral modeling language. In: Bernardo, M., Issarny, V. (eds.) SFM 2011. LNCS, vol. 6659, pp. 417–457. Springer, Heidelberg (2011). doi:10.1007/978-3-642-21455-4_13
22. Clarke, E., Grumberg, O., Jha, S., Lu, Y., Veith, H.: Counterexample-guided abstraction refinement. In: Emerson, E.A., Sistla, A.P. (eds.) CAV 2000. LNCS, vol. 1855, pp. 154–169. Springer, Heidelberg (2000). doi:10.1007/10722167_15
23. Clements, P., Northrop, L.: Software Product Lines: Practices and Patterns. Addison Wesley Longman, Boston (2001)

24. Damiani, F., Lienhardt, M.: On type checking delta-oriented product lines. In: Ábrahám, E., Huisman, M. (eds.) IFM 2016. LNCS, vol. 9681, pp. 47–62. Springer, Cham (2016). doi:10.1007/978-3-319-33693-0_4
25. Damiani, F., Owe, O., Dovland, J., Schaefer, I., Johnsen, E.B., Yu, I.C.: A transformational proof system for delta-oriented programming. In: SPLC (2), pp. 53–60 (2012)
26. Damiani, F., Schaefer, I.: Family-based analysis of type safety for delta-oriented software product lines. In: Margaria, T., Steffen, B. (eds.) ISoLA 2012. LNCS, vol. 7609, pp. 193–207. Springer, Heidelberg (2012). doi:10.1007/978-3-642-34026-0_15
27. Darvas, Á., Hähnle, R., Sands, D.: A theorem proving approach to analysis of secure information flow. In: Hutter, D., Ullmann, M. (eds.) SPC 2005. LNCS, vol. 3450, pp. 193–209. Springer, Heidelberg (2005). doi:10.1007/978-3-540-32004-3_20
28. Dimovski, A.S., Wąsowski, A.: Variability-specific abstraction refinement for family-based model checking. In: Huisman, M., Rubin, J. (eds.) FASE 2017. LNCS, vol. 10202, pp. 406–423. Springer, Heidelberg (2017). doi:10.1007/978-3-662-54494-5_24
29. Dziobek, C., Weiland, J.: Variantenmodellierung und -konfiguration eingebetteter automotive Software mit Simulink. In: Giese, H., Huhn, M., Nickel, U., Schätz, B. (eds.) Dagstuhl-Workshop MBEES: Modellbasierte Entwicklung eingebetteter Systeme V. Schloss Dagstuhl, Germany. Informatik-Bericht, vol. 2009-01, pp. 36–45. TU Braunschweig, Institut für Software Systems Engineering (2009)
30. Giachino, E., Laneve, C., Lienhardt, M.: A framework for deadlock detection in core ABS. Softw. Syst. Model. 15(4), 1013–1048 (2016)
31. Grönniger, H., Hartmann, J., Krahn, H., Kriebel, S., Rothhardt, L., Rumpe, B.: View-centric modeling of automotive logical architectures. In: Giese, H., Huhn, M., Nickel, U., Schätz, B. (eds.) Dagstuhl-Workshop MBEES: Modellbasierte Entwicklung eingebetteter Systeme IV, Schloss Dagstuhl, Germany. Informatik-Bericht, vol. 2008-2, pp. 3–12. TU Braunschweig, Institut für Software Systems Engineering (2008)
32. Hähnle, R., Schaefer, I.: A Liskov principle for delta-oriented programming. In: Margaria, T., Steffen, B. (eds.) ISoLA 2012. LNCS, vol. 7609, pp. 32–46. Springer, Heidelberg (2012). doi:10.1007/978-3-642-34026-0_4
33. Hammer, C., Krinke, J., Snelting, G.: Information flow control for Java based on path conditions in dependence graphs. In: IEEE International Symposium on Secure Software Engineering (ISSSE), pp. 87–96. IEEE, March 2006
34. Jackson, M., Zave, P.: Distributed feature composition: a virtual architecture for telecommunications services. IEEE Trans. Softw. Eng. 24(10), 831–847 (1998)
35. Johnsen, E.B., Hähnle, R., Schäfer, J., Schlatte, R., Steffen, M.: ABS: a core language for abstract behavioral specification. In: Aichernig, B.K., Boer, F.S., Bonsangue, M.M. (eds.) FMCO 2010. LNCS, vol. 6957, pp. 142–164. Springer, Heidelberg (2011). doi:10.1007/978-3-642-25271-6_8
36. Küsters, R., Truderung, T., Beckert, B., Bruns, D., Kirsten, M., Mohr, M.: A hybrid approach for proving noninterference of Java programs. In: Fournet, C., Hicks, M.W., Viganò, L. (eds.) IEEE 28th Computer Security Foundations Symposium, CSF, Verona, Italy, pp. 305–319. IEEE Computer Society (2015)
37. Sabelfeld, A., Myers, A.C.: Language-based information-flow security. IEEE J. Sel. Areas Commun. 21(1), 5–19 (2003)
38. Schaefer, I., Bettini, L., Bono, V., Damiani, F., Tanzarella, N.: Delta-oriented programming of software product lines. In: Bosch, J., Lee, J. (eds.) SPLC 2010. LNCS, vol. 6287, pp. 77–91. Springer, Heidelberg (2010). doi:10.1007/978-3-642-15579-6_6

39. Schaefer, I., Damiani, F.: Pure delta-oriented programming. In: Apel, S., Batory, D., Czarnecki, K., Heidenreich, F., Kästner, C., Nierstrasz, O. (eds.) Proceedings of 2nd International Workshop on Feature-Oriented Software Development (FOSD 2010), Eindhoven, The Netherlands, pp. 49–56. ACM Press (2010)
40. Schaefer, I., Rabiser, R., Clarke, D., Bettini, L., Benavides, D., Botterweck, G., Pathak, A., Trujillo, S., Villela, K.: Software diversity: state of the art and perspectives. Int. J. Softw. Tools Technol. Transf. **14**(5), 477–495 (2012)
41. Scheben, C., Greiner, S.: Information flow analysis. In: Ahrendt et al. [1], chap. 13, pp. 453–472 (2016)
42. Thüm, T., Apel, S., Kästner, C., Schaefer, I., Saake, G.: A classification and survey of analysis strategies for software product lines. ACM Comput. Surv. **47**(1), 6:1–6:45 (2014)
43. Thüm, T., Schaefer, I., Hentschel, M., Apel, S.: Family-based deductive verification of software product lines. In: Ostermann, K., Binder, W. (eds.) Generative Programming and Component Engineering, GPCE 2012, Dresden, Germany, pp. 11–20. ACM (2012)
44. Thüm, T., Schaefer, I., Kuhlemann, M., Apel, S.: Proof composition for deductive verification of software product lines. In: Proceedings of International Workshop Variability-Intensive Systems Testing, Validation and Verification (VAST), pp. 270–277. IEEE Computer Society (2011)
45. von Rhein, A., Thüm, T., Schaefer, I., Liebig, J., Apel, S.: Variability encoding: from compile-time to load-time variability. J. Log. Algebr. Methods Program. **85**(1), 125–145 (2016)
46. Wasser, N., Bubel, R., Hähnle, R.: Abstract interpretation. In: Ahrendt et al. [1], chap. 6, pp. 167–189 (2016)

Regular Contributions

Hybrid Information Flow Analysis
for Real-World C Code

Gergö Barany[1(✉)] and Julien Signoles[2]

[1] Inria Paris, Paris, France
gergo.barany@inria.fr
[2] Software Reliability and Security Laboratory,
CEA, LIST, 91911 Gif-sur-Yvette Cedex, France
julien.signoles@cea.fr

Abstract. Information flow analysis models the propagation of data through a software system and identifies unintended information leaks. There is a wide range of such analyses, tracking flows statically, dynamically, or in a hybrid way combining both static and dynamic approaches.

We present a hybrid information flow analysis for a large subset of the C programming language. Extending previous work that handled a few difficult features of C, our analysis can now deal with arrays, pointers with pointer arithmetic, structures, dynamic memory allocation, complex control flow, and statically resolvable indirect function calls. The analysis is implemented as a plugin to the Frama-C framework.

We demonstrate the applicability and precision of our analyzer by applying it to an open-source cryptographic library. By combining abstract interpretation and monitoring techniques, we verify an information flow policy that proves the absence of control-flow based timing attacks against the implementations of many common cryptographic algorithms. Conversely, we demonstrate that our analysis is able to detect a known instance of this kind of vulnerability in another cryptographic primitive.

1 Introduction

Information flow analysis models the propagation of data through a software system. It identifies unintended information leaks to guarantee confidentiality of information. For instance, secret data are often forbidden from influencing public outputs [10]. This is an instance of the non-interference property [12] which states that certain kinds of computations have no effects on others. A more precise standard property is termination-insensitive non-interference (TINI), i.e., non-interference without taking into account covert channels due to termination.

Information flow analyses for ensuring TINI can be static [15,23] or dynamic [3]. The former examine the source code without executing it, while

This work was supported by the French National Research Agency (ANR), project AnaStaSec, ANR-14-CE28-0014.

S. Gabmeyer and E.B. Johnsen (Eds.): TAP 2017, LNCS 10375, pp. 23–40, 2017.
DOI: 10.1007/978-3-319-61467-0_2

the latter check the desired properties at runtime. Dynamic monitors have neither knowledge of commands in non-executed control flow paths, nor knowledge of commands ahead of their execution. Russo and Sabelfeld [21] prove that such dynamic monitors cannot be sound with respect to non-interference, while being at least as permissive as flow-sensitive type system *à la* Hunt and Sands [15]. Flow-sensitivity means that the same variable may carry data of different security levels (e.g. secret and public) over the course of the program execution. It is particularly important in practice in order to accept more programs without jeopardizing security. This leads to hybrid information flow in which the dynamic monitors are helped with statically-computed information [19,21]. This paper describes an analysis in this category.

TINI monitoring was refined by Bielova and Rezk by introducing the concept of termination-*aware* non-interference (TANI) [7]. TANI monitors are required to enforce TINI with the additional constraint that they do not introduce new termination channels. That is, no information about secret values may be derived from the fact that the monitored program terminates normally. The authors prove that hybrid monitors such as ours do enforce this property.

Flows tracked by monitors may be either explicit or implicit. Explicit flows are propagated through assignments when assigning secret data to a memory location which therefore becomes secret. Indirect flows are usually propagated through program control dependencies. For instance, when considering a sensitive variable `secret` and the code snippet `if (secret) x = 0; else y = 1;`, both variables `x` and `y` become sensitive because the fact whether `secret` is zero leaks to the values of both `x` and `y`. In order to detect such a flow at runtime when executing the `then`-branch (resp. `else`-branch), it is required to have the knowledge of the update of `y` in the non-executing `else`-branch (resp. `x` in the `then`-branch). This information is unfortunately not available at runtime: a static analysis using points-to information [22] is necessary to pre-compute it.

In this paper, we discuss hybrid flow-sensitive information flow analysis for **C programs**. In previous work, Assaf *et al.* demonstrated that indirect flows may be carried through pointers [1,2]. They proposed a hybrid analysis through a sound program transformation which encodes the information flows in an inline monitor to detect TINI (and TANI) violations. A prototype was implemented as a Frama-C plugin named Secure Flow. The soundness of the program transformation relies on a static analysis in order to compute over-approximations of written memory locations in some pieces of code. Later Secure Flow was extended to arrays [4]. One benefit of a transformation-based approach is that it lets end-users choose their verification techniques: they can verify all execution paths of the generated program by static analysis, or some individual paths by runtime verification, or even use a combination of both.

Our contributions are threefold: **extending hybrid information flow analysis** for C programs containing many complex constructs; **improving the Frama-C plugin Secure Flow** with this extension; and **evaluating it** on an open-source cryptographic library by **combining static and dynamic techniques**.

The structure of the paper is as follows. Section 2 gives an overview of Secure Flow, while Sect. 3 details the recently added features. Section 4 evaluates our tool on LibTomCrypt, and Sect. 5 describes related work.

2   An Overview of Secure Flow

This paper concerns the design and implementation of a hybrid information flow monitor in the style of Le Guernic et al. [19] for the C programming language. In this section we set the stage by describing the underlying Frama-C framework and the constraints and goals that influenced our design. To make the paper self-contained, we also discuss the handling of various language constructs of C in our previous work [2, 4].

2.1   Frama-C

Our analysis is implemented as a plugin for Frama-C [17], an open source analysis and transformation framework for C programs. Frama-C parses the C source code to build an abstract syntax tree (AST) that represents the input code. After analyses and transformations, the AST can be pretty-printed to C source code that can be processed by other tools, or compiled with a C compiler and executed. Frama-C can be extended with plugins that implement new code analyzers and transformers.

To ease implementation of analyzers, Frama-C performs some normalizations of the AST: in particular, side effects can only occur due to assignments, function calls or assembly code, but not nested inside other expressions as in C. When needed, the frontend introduces assignments to temporary variables to hold the values of side effecting operations. In both our implementation and in the discussion below, we make use of the fact that side effects only occur at these well-defined places. Another normalization is relevant to our implementation: the control flow of the logical operators && and || is made explicit by the frontend by generating appropriate `if` and `goto` statements. Finally, all C loop constructs are normalized into infinite loops of the form `while (1) { ... }` containing `if` statements controlling the loop's exits via `break`.

Frama-C supports a rich contract-based annotation language called ACSL that can express assertions, function pre- and post-conditions, loop variants and invariants, and other attributes of data types and variables [5]. ACSL annotations are formatted as special comments with a leading @ character. Annotated programs are thus compatible with all other compilers and analyzers for C that ignore comments. Plugins may extend ACSL syntax with new kinds of annotations and new predicate symbols. Our plugin uses such custom ACSL annotations to specify initial information flow labels for variables and to express information flow policies as assertions to be verified.

Our hybrid information flow analysis needs precise information on the targets of pointers. For this we rely on Eva [8], a mature abstract interpretation based Frama-C plugin computing an over-approximation of the values of all variables in a program. Its results are accessible programmatically through its API.

2.2 Design Constraints

Our goal was to design an analysis that is as precise as possible while faithfully preserving the semantics of programs that do not violate the given information flow policy. The latter constraint was important for choosing the representation of information flow labels in the instrumented program. A straightforward idea would be to package each monitored variable x of type T in a structure with its label, such as:

```
struct x_label { label_t label; T x };
```

However, this would change the sizes of such variables and of compound types containing such members. As a consequence, programs using C's `sizeof` or `offsetof` operator would compute different values with and without instrumentation. We therefore chose to completely separate the storage of the program's original variables and the label variables introduced by our instrumentation. Other design goals were related to precision: we track information flow through pointer-based data structures as precisely as possible. We also track information flow in structures in a field-sensitive way. For example, we want to keep separate labels for the members of a structure holding a pair of a public and a private cryptographic key.

2.3 Security Lattice and Status Annotations

At the time of writing, our analysis uses a simple two-element lattice using the values 0 (public) and 1 (private). We use the `char` type for storing the labels and the bitwise-or (|) operator as the join operator over the lattice. It would be easy to extend this scheme to support any lattice isomorphic to a lattice of bit vectors up to 64 bits. More general lattices would require a more complex combination operator.

Users can use the custom ACSL annotation `/*@ private */` (specific to Secure Flow) to mark declarations of variables that have to be treated as sensitive; their label variables are initialized accordingly. All other variables are considered initially public. Custom ACSL annotations are also used to express the intended flow policy through *security annotations* at arbitrary program points e. g.,

```
/*@ assert security_status(result) == public; */
```

Similarly, functions (such as I/O functions) may be annotated with preconditions requiring their arguments to be public, e. g.

```
/*@ requires security_status(*x) == public; */
int send(char *x);
```

Such annotations are considered proof obligations to be discharged using Frama-C's static analyzers or provers, or to be turned into runtime assertions in the instrumented program. The predicate symbol `security_status` is an ACSL extension introduced by Secure Flow: its meaning is unknown to other Frama-C tools. To make the meaning explicit, our analysis translates such annotations into a reference to the corresponding label variable. The resulting predicate can then be analyzed by other Frama-C plugins as usual.

We do not predefine any flow policy: The policy is to be chosen by the user and expressed in the form of assertions. However, as an optional tool we provide a command line flag to ensure that the program's control flow always depends only on public information. The intention is to verify the absence of a certain class of timing-based attacks against cryptographic software. The same policy may be used to guard against denial-of-service attacks by users able to control the iteration counts of loops. This policy is implemented by inserting an assertion before every branching statement (if or switch) requiring the condition expression's label to be public.

2.4 Overview of Information Flow Monitoring

We briefly summarize the basics of the instrumentation done by Secure Flow. These operations follow the literature [1,2,4,19].

For every variable x of arithmetic type, we add a label variable $\underline{x}$ of type char. These are initialized to 1 (secret) for /*@ private */ annotations, to 0 (public) otherwise. An expression's label is obtained by mapping variables to labels and replacing every operator by the combination operator |. Constants are public (label 0). Every assignment in the program is instrumented with a corresponding label assignment, e.g., for x = a + b we add $\underline{x} = \underline{a} \mid \underline{b}$.

In a branching statement like if(c) x = 0; else y = 1; the final values of x and y depend on the path taken and thus on the condition. This is an *implicit* information flow. We model it by introducing a label variable $\underline{pc}$ for the *program counter context* in each branch or loop, initializing it from the conditional expression's label ($\underline{pc} = \underline{c}$) and using it in each label assignment controlled by the branch, e.g., $\underline{x} = 0 \mid \underline{pc}$. This handles dependencies in the branch that is actually executed, but the other branch must also be modeled. In the running example, we therefore add an update $\underline{y} \mathbin{|=} \underline{pc}$ in the true branch and the same for $\underline{x}$ in the false branch. Thus, no matter which branch is taken, all variables updated in the entire if statement have the implicit flow from the condition tracked correctly.

Pointers p that can be dereferenced n times are treated by introducing n corresponding label pointers p_d1 to p_dn [2]. We maintain the invariant that whenever p points to some object x, its label pointer p_d1 points to $\underline{x}$, and analogously for multiple dereferences. As the number of label pointers depends on p's type, pointer type casts are not supported in general. Reads/writes of *p are instrumented with corresponding label reads/writes of *p_d1. If p may refer to several targets, say x and y, the actual choice of a target at run time may depend on secret data (e.g., if (secret) p = &x; else p = &y;). An assignment to *p has an information flow from p to all of its targets because inspecting the targets after the assignment may allow inferences on p and thus the secret data. We use pointer analysis to resolve a safe overapproximation of the set of targets and insert appropriate label updates $\underline{x} \mathbin{|=} \underline{p}, \underline{y} \mathbin{|=} \underline{p}$.

Arrays introduce information flows from indices to any element the index may refer to [4]. The labels for distinct elements must therefore be shared; we use a single summary label arr_summary to model all elements of an array arr. Due to sharing, writes to the array must be modeled using monotonically non-decreasing *weak updates* of the summary label, e.g., arr_summary |= i | v for an assignment arr[i] = v. Pointers to array elements must be modeled by two label pointers: One to the array's summary label and one to the exact array element, which is needed to preserve the above pointer invariant.

3   New Features of Secure Flow

We now move on to the main contributions of this paper by presenting the way Secure Flow handles other features occurring in numerous C programs.

3.1   Structures and Unions

Our analysis treats structures in a field-sensitive way: for every struct type s defined by the program, we define a corresponding label struct type s. The members of this struct are the labels of the members of s computed in the usual way; that is, if s has a member m of a pointer type, s has the appropriate number of label pointer members m_d*i* and m_d*i*_summary. Arrays of structures have a corresponding summary structure.

We could, in principle, treat C's union types in exactly the same field-sensitive way as structs. In practice, there are problems with the precision of our current implementation: mapping the results of the pointer analysis to our symbolic lvalue representation may identify too many overlapping fields and thus track too many information flows that are not present in the actual program.

3.2   Unstructured Control Flow: goto Statements

The use of the goto statement is widespread in systems software written in C: it is frequently used in functions that check a series of conditions and jump to cleanup code at the end of the function in case of an error. The goto statement may also appear in Frama-C's AST due to some normalizations: Frama-C introduces goto statements to model early returns from the middle of a function, for continue statements in for loops, and to model short-circuit evaluation of the logical && and || operators. We must therefore be able to treat programs with gotos, at least in these restricted forms.

A problem with goto is the propagation of information flows to objects that might be modified if the branch containing the goto were not taken. This is similar to the label updates we insert in if statements for the objects modified in the other branch, but in the case of goto the effects are not local.

Consider the following example:

```
    x = 1;
    if (cond) { goto end; }
    x = 0;
end:
    return x;
```

At the **return** statement, the value of x is 0 iff the value of cond is 0. There is an information flow from the branch condition, via the **goto** statement, to x, whose assignment is skipped when the **goto** is taken. We instrument this example as follows:

```
    x = 1;
    x̲ = 0 | p̲c̲;
    p̲c̲ |= c̲o̲n̲d̲ | p̲c̲;
    if (cond) { goto end; }
    x = 0;
    x̲ = 0 | p̲c̲;
end:
    x̲ |= p̲c̲;
    return x;
```

In general, we handle **goto** statements by ensuring that the program counter label captures the condition controlling the **goto** no matter which path is taken. We identify the branch controlling the **goto** and propagate its condition's label to all the program counter labels that may be traversed by the jump, including the label for the **goto**'s target. In the example, the condition controlling the **goto** is c̲o̲n̲d̲, and the only block possibly affected has the label p̲c̲ (containing both the controlling branch and the jump target). The update p̲c̲ |= c̲o̲n̲d̲ | p̲c̲ performs the propagation. Now, whether or not the jump is taken, subsequent assignments in any affected block will take place in a context including the condition's label. For the case when the **goto** *is* taken, we also insert label updates at the target statement. These update the labels of any variable whose assignments may have been skipped by the **goto**. For simplicity, we just use the set of all variables that may be modified anywhere in the target block (in the example, only x̲).

We handle not only **goto** statements from inner blocks to enclosing ones, but also from outer blocks into more deeply nested ones. We omit the details, but they follow the same principles as explained above. Our current implementation only allows forward **goto**s, i.e., all **goto** statements must appear textually before the corresponding target. This is just an artifact of the particular implementation strategy we chose, but there are no theoretic difficulties with treating backwards jumps the same way as forward jumps.

The analysis also handles **break** and **continue** statements in a similar way as gotos: It propagates the program counter label of the branching statement that controls the jump to the corresponding loop or **switch** statement.

3.3   Function Calls

Our analysis handles function calls in different ways, depending on whether the call is direct or indirect (i.e., through a function pointer) and whether the call's target has a definition in the same program or is external.

For direct calls to defined functions, we instrument both the caller and the callee. The function's parameter list is transformed by adding extra label parameters for the original parameters as well as a parameter for the program counter label of the callee's calling context. We also add global variables for the labels of all defined functions' return values; these labels are assigned before the function returns. That is, a functionto add two numbers is instrumented as follows:

```
char add_return;
float add(char local_pc, float x, char x, float y, char y) {
    float sum;
    char sum;
    sum = x + y;
    sum = x | y | local_pc;
    add_return = sum;
    return sum;
}
```

At the call site, the function call is transformed accordingly to pass in all the required labels. If the function's return value is assigned to some object, we insert corresponding assignments from the function's return label variables to the target object's labels. This is the only case we need to handle because function calls embedded in larger expressions are first transformed by Frama-C into assignments to temporary variables.

Library functions which do not have definitions in the target program must be treated separately. ACSL provides a syntax to express the side effects of such functions using (possibly several) annotations of the form

```
assigns x1, ..., xn \from y1, ..., ym
```

meaning that the function *may* only modify the lvalues x1, ..., xn by using *at most* the lvalues y1, ..., ym (but might not necessarily modify all the xi or use all the yi).

We require such annotations for all functions without visible definitions; Frama-C includes annotations for the C standard library functions. The analyzer emits a warning for external functions without annotations and continues with the (unsound) assumption that the called function has no visible side effects. If a function is defined but has an assigns annotation, the analyzer trusts the information from the annotation and does not use its own analysis of the function's body to model the function's externally visible effects. This improves the analyzer's efficiency while remaining safe since it is still possible to verify that the function body satisfies this annotation thanks to other tools (for instance Eva). Such annotations must be provided for recursive functions.

For a call to an external function with an annotation of

```
assigns x₁ \from y_{1,1}, ..., y_{n,1};
...
assigns x_k \from y_{k,1}, ..., y_{n,k};
```

we insert the corresponding label updates:

$$\underline{x_1} \mathrel{|}= \underline{y_{1,1}} \mathrel{|} \ldots \mathrel{|} \underline{y_{n,1}} \mathrel{|} \underline{pc};$$
$$\ldots$$
$$\underline{x_k} \mathrel{|}= \underline{y_{k,1}} \mathrel{|} \ldots \mathrel{|} \underline{y_{n,k}} \mathrel{|} \underline{pc};$$

This approach works even for functions taking `void *` parameters, such as the standard `memcpy` function, whose `assigns` annotation expresses that it assigns bytes in its output buffer from its input buffer. At the call site we use the points-to analysis to resolve the pointer arguments to the underlying objects of concrete types and are able to generate well-typed label updates.

However, the approach does not work for functions whose `assigns` annotations include modifications to pointers. The semantics of `assigns` is that it models all assignments that *might* be performed by the called function. As we cannot be sure that these assignments will indeed take place, there is not enough information to insert the label pointer assignments needed to maintain our pointer invariants (Sect. 2.4). In such cases the analysis must reject the input program with an error message. For example, we allow `memcpy` on objects of the type `struct foo {int a; float b[10];}` but not on objects of the type `struct bar {int a; float *b;}`. In the latter case, the analysis would conclude that it is not able to track all the pointer-based flows that may be performed by the function. However, the practical impact of this restriction is low: `memcpy` calls can often be rewritten as assignments if needed, and not many other standard C functions may have side effects on pointer-based structures.

For indirect function calls, we require that the points-to analysis is able to resolve the function pointer's target to a fixed set of candidate functions. The transformation generates a `switch` on the function pointer's value that dispatches to the appropriate direct function call.

Functions with variable argument lists are not handled directly. Instead we first invoke another Frama-C plugin named Variadic that transforms variable-argument functions into functions that take a fixed number of arguments. The resulting program can then be treated as usual by the information flow analysis.

Finally, functions introduce the issue of visibility of identifiers. Functions may refer to other functions' local variables via pointers, as in a call like `f(&a)`. Inside the function `f` we must be able to refer to `a`'s label variable $\underline{a}$. By default, we allocate every variable's label in the same scope as the original variable. However, for such locals that may be referenced from other functions (as determined by the points-to analysis), we make the corresponding label variables global instead.

3.4 Dynamic Memory Allocation

Our information flow analysis has special handling for the dynamic memory allocation semantics of the standard C functions `malloc`, `calloc`, and `realloc`, as well as the `free` function. These functions operate on pointers of type `void *`, which we do not allow in general. However, we do allow them in the context of dynamic allocation, as long as the type conversions (made explicit as casts by Frama-C) to or from more concrete types take place immediately at the place of the function call. Otherwise (e.g., if the program assigns the result of `malloc` to a pointer to `void` and only converts it at a later point), we reject the program.

We can thus obtain the concrete type of the allocated memory buffer. From the expression specifying the size of the allocation, and knowing the target type, we can compute the number of allocated elements. We insert calls to `calloc` to dynamically allocate the same number of labels of the appropriate types:

```
float *q = (float *) malloc(42 * sizeof(float));
char *q_d1 = (char *) calloc(42, sizeof(char));
char *q_d1_summary = ...;   // see text below
```

The information flow in dynamically allocated data structures is thus tracked via dynamically allocated labels, which allows us to track pointers with maximal precision. However, there is a problem related to label updates in branches for dynamically allocated memory areas. Consider the following program:

```
p = malloc(sizeof (int));
if (...) { *p = 1; } else { ... }
```

As before, in the `else` branch we must insert updates for the summary labels of all objects that may be referenced by `p`. This is easy if `p` may only point to variables (say, `x`): We can insert an update `x |= if_pc`. However, in the case where `p` points to dynamically allocated memory, we have no simple way of naming and enumerating the correct summary label to insert the necessary updates. We must therefore introduce an approximation. Our analysis introduces one statically allocated summary label (i.e., a global variable) per dynamic allocation site. At each such call site, label arrays are allocated dynamically, but the target's summary pointer is pointed to the call site's shared summary label. The example above is instrumented as follows:

```
p = malloc(sizeof (int));
p_d1 = calloc(1, sizeof (char));
static char dynalloc_site_1_summary = 0;
p_d1_summary = &dynalloc_site_1_summary;
if_pc = cond | global_pc;
if (cond) {
    *p = 1;
    *p_d1 = 0 | if_pc;
} else {
    dynalloc_site_1_summary |= if_pc;
    ...
}
```

This approach thus introduces aliasing between the summary labels of different buffers allocated at the same site. Raising the information flow label of one object allocated at a certain call site automatically raises the labels of any other object allocated at the same site. In the extreme, if a program contains only a single static allocation site (e.g., because it uses a wrapper function around malloc), *all* dynamically allocated objects share one summary. This is a source of imprecision in our current implementation.

The simplest way to resolve this issue is to turn an allocation site that may be used in different contexts into explicitly different allocation sites. This could be done by automatic inlining of functions performing dynamic allocation. In our experiments with cryptographic software, we manually duplicate an allocation function, introducing a special variant for the allocation of secret keys.

3.5   Summary of Restrictions

We briefly summarize the restrictions on input programs that can be analyzed by Secure Flow.

- Most kinds of type casts between pointer types are forbidden; casts to and from void * related to dynamic memory allocation are allowed, as are casts between void * and character pointer types.
- The program must contain assigns annotations for all external functions (provided by Frama-C for the C standard library) and recursive functions.
- Calls to external functions may not have side effects on pointers, but may have side effects on their targets.
- No backwards jumps with goto are allowed (this is only an artifact of the current implementation).
- The analysis is imprecise (i.e., overly conservative) if logically separate memory areas are allocated at the same call site of malloc. This can be avoided by inlining/specializing functions that perform dynamic allocation.

Overall, these conditions do not impose disproportional restrictions on well-written systems code, as long as the entire program is available for whole-program analysis, or annotated with assigns annotations for the missing parts.

4   Evaluation

We evaluate our hybrid information flow analysis by checking an information flow policy to protect against timing attacks on a cryptographic library. This verification also illustrates one of the main benefits of our hybrid approach: combining static and dynamic verification.

4.1   Background on the Chosen Flow Policy

Timing attacks and other side-channel attacks are an important class of vulnerability in the implementations of cryptosystems; a recent article by Genkin et al. gives a good overview of a wide range of techniques and targets [11]. The class of timing attack that interests us is caused by conditional branching on data derived from the cryptosystem's secret key. This type of vulnerability typically occurs in asymmetric (also known as public-key) cryptosystems such as RSA, where the core of the algorithm loops over the bits of the secret key and decides based on the value of each bit which mathematical operation to perform.

In general, the two branches of an if statement take different amounts of time, and an attacker who is able to measure a cryptographic operation's execution time may use this to deduce information about the secret key. Such attacks are known against implementations of several cryptosystems in common use, including both RSA and elliptic curve cryptography [6,11]. Even if timing differences cannot be measured directly, attackers on the same machine may be able to observe instruction cache misses that allow them to deduce the same kind of information [20].

We therefore chose a flow policy forbidding control flow based on secret information; this is a useful property to verify on real-world cryptographic code. We note in passing that there are also timing attacks based on the order of accesses to lookup tables and the corresponding data cache misses. These are independent of control flow and outside of the scope of our current analysis.

In the following sections we discuss our analysis of the cryptographic implementations in the LibTomCrypt library (http://www.libtom.org/).

4.2 Symmetric Cryptosystems

LibTomCrypt includes implementations of 14 different symmetric cryptosystems. This class of system typically works by breaking the input into fixed-sized blocks, then performing permutations and substitutions of the bytes in each block based on look-up tables indexed by the key and a loop counter. The number of operations per block is fixed by the algorithm, and the number of blocks to be processed depends only on the length of the message (which we do not consider secret information). Thus we did not expect to find timing attacks against this class of system. As these programs are safe with respect to our flow policy, they are a good test to ensure that our analysis does not introduce imprecisions.

We use a separate driver program for each of the cryptosystems. The driver calls LibTomCrypt's initialization routines for the given system, then encrypts 10 megabytes of random data, decrypts the encrypted data, and quits. We perform whole-program analysis, applying Frama-C to each driver program and the entire LibTomCrypt source code. However, the (fixed) key and data to be encrypted are not exposed to Frama-C to avoid the possibility that Eva specializes its results to a given key or input.

Our analyzer was able to instrument and analyze all of the programs with only one significant change to LibTomCrypt: the internal states of all the different systems are stored in a union, only one member of which is used at a time. As discussed in Sect. 3.1, our analysis is currently unable to analyze accesses to unions precisely. We therefore changed the type of this union to struct. After this change, we can successfully instrument each of the 14 different symmetric cryptosystems. On the instrumented program, Eva successfully statically verifies for each of the systems that the flow policy is satisfied, i.e., no branch condition in the program depends on the key.

We next turned to dynamic analysis of the instrumented programs to evaluate instrumentation overhead. We compiled both the original driver program and the program instrumented by our hybrid information flow analysis with GCC version 4.8.4 at optimization level -02 and ran them on an Ubuntu Linux system on an 8-core Intel Core i7 CPU clocked at 2.30 GHz. Table 1 shows the execution times of the programs in seconds. We ran each program five times and report the median of the runs. We report execution times of the original program and the instrumented version in seconds as well as the slowdown due to instrumentation.

Table 1. Execution time of symmetric cryptographic algorithms with and without instrumentation and with additional E-ACSL instrumentation.

Program	Original	Instrumented	Slowdown	+E-ACSL	+Slowdown
aes	0.11 s	0.33 s	3.0×	6.87 s	20.8×
anubis	0.13 s	0.36 s	2.8×	6.84 s	19.0×
blowfish	0.19 s	0.44 s	2.3×	6.99 s	15.9×
cast5	0.26 s	0.50 s	1.9×	8.46 s	16.9×
kasumi	0.42 s	0.76 s	1.8×	11.24 s	14.8×
khazad	0.15 s	0.33 s	2.2×	7.26 s	22.0×
kseed	0.30 s	0.53 s	1.8×	7.60 s	14.3×
noekeon	0.22 s	0.41 s	1.9×	6.69 s	16.3×
rc2	0.42 s	0.61 s	1.5×	7.42 s	12.2×
rc5	0.15 s	0.35 s	2.3×	7.76 s	22.2×
rc6	0.18 s	0.36 s	2.0×	7.41 s	20.6×
saferp	0.28 s	1.97 s	7.0×	27.66 s	14.0×
twofish	0.15 s	0.36 s	2.4×	6.97 s	19.4×
xtea	0.30 s	0.47 s	1.6×	7.04 s	15.0×

Slowdowns for most of the programs are below or near a factor of 2. This is the order of magnitude we expected, inserting one or more assignment statements for every assignment in the program. We have not yet been able to determine the reason for the large slowdown factor of 7.0 for the one outlier, saferp.

The last two columns in Table 1 show the additional instrumentation overhead when using Frama-C's E-ACSL plugin [18]. Indeed Eva proves all security assertions, but must leave some memory safety properties unproved due to approximations made during the analysis. E-ACSL instruments the program to dynamically monitor accesses to memory blocks to ensure memory safety at runtime. This is needed because the correctness of the information flow analysis is only guaranteed if the program is memory safe. We report the absolute execution time in seconds for each benchmark instrumented with information flow tracking and memory safety monitoring. The last column shows a slowdown of 10 to 20 which is typical of this monitoring for E-ACSL version 0.8 [24].

The table does not show the memory use of the programs, which behaves fairly regularly: All of the original programs use about 32 MB as they are linked statically to the same library containing the lookup tables for all the different algorithms, and to the same buffer of random input data. These programs do not use dynamic memory allocation. For the instrumented programs memory use increases to about 52 MB, a factor of 1.6. This, too, is as expected: These algorithms perform byte-oriented processing, and we currently monitor each byte in the various byte arrays and lookup tables with a 1-byte label of type char. That is, we essentially double the memory used by monitored data. The relative overhead would be smaller for programs that mainly use larger types than char. With E-ACSL, memory use grows to about 190 MB, an additional factor of 3.7.

This combination of Eva and E-ACSL demonstrates the ability of our hybrid approach to combine static and dynamic analyses. Here Eva proves the security assertions, while E-ACSL validates at runtime the remaining safety properties. Both together ensure that our programs are safe with respect to our flow policy.

4.3   Elliptic Curve Cryptography

As a representative of the class of public-key (asymmetric) cryptosystems, we chose to analyze LibTomCrypt's implementation of elliptic curve cryptography (ECC). The library offers two implementations of the underlying algorithm: one of the implementations is known to be faster but vulnerable to timing attacks, while the other is claimed to be resistant to timing attacks. The vulnerable operation is the multiplication of a point on an elliptic curve with a scalar in the function ltc_ecc_mulmod. The scalar k is part of the system's private key. In a loop, the function inspects k's bits one by one and, depending on its value, performs some arithmetic or continues to the next loop iteration.

Elliptic curve operations must be done on multiple-precision integers. LibTomCrypt is able to use one of several multiple-precision arithmetic libraries; we chose its sister project LibTomMath. Again, we perform whole-program analysis using Frama-C on a driver program, the LibTomCrypt library, and LibTomMath. Some rewrites were needed to make it possible to analyze this system with our information flow analyzer. The biggest change concerned LibTom-Crypt's interface to its math library, which needlessly uses void * pointers throughout to refer to multiple-precision integers. As discussed in Sect. 2.4, our analysis cannot deal with such programs. We manually changed the types in this internal interface to the concrete type of LibTomMath's integers.

For the information flow analysis we also had to be able to label the private ECC key as secret. In LibTomCrypt all integers are allocated by the mp_init function, which calls malloc. Due to the context sensitivity problem described in Sect. 3.4, all integers share the same dynamic allocation summary label, thus marking the secret key as secret would trivially make every number secret. To avoid this we duplicated mp_init as mp_init_secret and used this variant to allocate the numbers in the secret key. As the `malloc` call site is no longer shared, this version no longer suffers from the false sharing issue.

We also had to change a few places where backwards jumps with `goto` statements were used to implement loops. In all cases we were able to rewrite the code to avoid using a `goto`. We added ACSL annotations of the form

```
assigns result->dp[..], result->sign \from
    a->dp[..], a->sign, b->dp[..], b->sign[..]
```

to some of the basic mathematical functions in LibTomMath (addition, subtraction, multiplication) to speed up Eva. These annotations express that the sign and digits (`dp`) of the result of such an operation depend only on the sign and digits of the operands. Finally, we simplified code for parsing serialized ECC keys. The code was in principle analyzable, but its complexity caused unnecessary slowdowns in Eva, hindering our experiments.

After these changes, we were able to apply our program transformation. Subsequent static analysis using Eva has shown that the flow policy is indeed violated: The secret label is propagated from the secret key to a conditional branch as discussed above. We can thus confirm the known timing vulnerability.

However, our analysis also found essentially the same bug in the variant of the `ltc_ecc_mulmod` function that is claimed to be resistant to timing attacks by performing the same amount of work on different branches that depend on secret information. We give a simplified description of this implementation. Depending on a variable `i` (the next bit of the key, 0 or 1) and another 0–1 variable `mode` derived from `i`, the code performs a conditional branch and executes either a call `ecc_ptdbl(M[i], M[i])`, doubling some value `M[i]` and storing it back into `M[i]`, or `ecc_ptdbl(M[1], M[2])`, doubling `M[1]` and ignoring the result by storing it into a dummy location `M[2]`. This is in violation of our flow policy, as the conditional branch on secret data remains in the program. We believe that this implementation may give a false sense of security in the light of cache-based attacks, and that it should be replaced by a version that does not suffer from this problem [6, Sect. 3].

A possible solution is to replace the branch on `i` and `mode` by a lookup table to determine the arguments for the function call. The following variant of the computation sketched above is correctly accepted by our static analysis without raising an alarm about secret-dependent control flow:

```
int i1_tbl[2][2] = {{1,1},{i,i}}, i2_tbl[2][2] = {{2,2},{i,i}};
ecc_ptdbl(M[i1_tbl[mode][i]], M[i2_tbl[mode][i]]);
```

For dynamic analysis, we use a test program that performs 3000 repetitions of the basic ECC operation `ecc_shared_secret`. The original program executes in 0.73 s (median of five runs), using 1400 kB of memory. We run the dynamic analysis with instrumentation to propagate labels, but without aborting the program on policy violations (which would happen instantaneously). With instrumentation, execution time increases to 4.71 s (6.5×) and memory use to 1553 kB (1.1×). The current version of E-ACSL does not scale well to programs of several hundreds of thousands of lines of code, so we did not run it on this benchmark.

5   Related Work

As mentioned before, this paper is based on work by Assaf et al. [1,2] and Barany [4] which focused on sound hybrid information flow analysis of a subset of C including pointers, arrays and pointer arithmetics. We extend this work to a larger subset of C including structures, unstructured control flow, indirect function calls and dynamic memory allocation.

There is an abundant literature on information flow analysis. However, as far as we know, there is no hybrid information flow analysis that handles a subset of the C programming language as large as ours. To our knowledge, the only approaches that handle real-world programs target JavaScript [13,16].

First, Kerschbaumer et al. [16] handle JavaScript's arrays, structures, unstructured control flow and function calls. However, the details are omitted except for unstructured control flow. There is no mention of indirect function calls. Second, Hedin et al. develop JSFlow [14] with its extended hybrid version [13]. They track arrays, structures, function calls and dynamic allocations precisely. They also support JavaScript's closures which are usually encoded via function pointers in C. However, there is no mention of unstructured control flow. Also they target a less permissive notion of non-interference than ours: they do not allow to assign secret values to locations that previously held public values (the converse, overwriting a secret value by a public value, is allowed). In contrast, our approach only uses such constraints at user-defined program points through security annotations. However, we could encode their non-interference property by adding an assertion to every assignment statement.

Regarding the C programming language, previous work which aims at targeting a large variety of C programs is based on taint analysis, either statically [9] or dynamically [25]. However taint analysis is not appropriate for verifying non-interference properties similar to ours because it does not detect all kinds of indirect flow. The aforementioned approaches are no exception.

6   Conclusions

We have presented Secure Flow, a hybrid information flow analysis for real-world C programs. Secure Flow instruments C code with monitoring code after an auxiliary static analysis. The instrumented code tracks information flow labels for all values of interest, as determined by a flexible annotation system for expressing information flow policies. After instrumentation, the code may be analyzed statically or may be executed for dynamic monitoring. Our experiments show that the overhead of dynamic monitoring is reasonable.

Secure Flow is implemented as a plugin for the Frama-C platform. It is about 3500 lines of OCaml code, blank lines excluded. It supports a large subset of C, including important real-world features such as pointers with pointer arithmetic, dynamic allocation, `goto` statements, and function pointers. Future work includes removing current restrictions, including at least backwards jumps and several memory allocations from the same call site.

We have demonstrated Secure Flow, in combination with the static analysis tool Eva and the monitoring tool E-ACSL, on a real-world cryptographic library. Our experiments show that they can verify the absence of an important class of timing attacks in many cryptosystem implementations. It has also found a known timing vulnerability in another cryptosystem, but also a similar issue in the alternative implementation supposedly correcting the vulnerability.

References

1. Assaf, M.: From qualitative to quantitative program analysis: permissive enforcement of secure information flow. Ph.D. thesis, Université de Rennes 1 (2015). https://hal.inria.fr/tel-01184857
2. Assaf, M., Signoles, J., Tronel, F., Totel, É.: Program transformation for non-interference verification on programs with pointers. In: Janczewski, L.J., Wolfe, H.B., Shenoi, S. (eds.) SEC 2013. IAICT, vol. 405, pp. 231–244. Springer, Heidelberg (2013). doi:10.1007/978-3-642-39218-4_18
3. Austin, T.H., Flanagan, C.: Efficient purely-dynamic information flow analysis. In: Proceedings of the ACM SIGPLAN Fourth Workshop on Programming Languages and Analysis for Security, PLAS 2009, pp. 113–124. ACM (2009). http://doi.acm.org/10.1145/1554339.1554353
4. Barany, G.: Hybrid information flow analysis for programs with arrays. In: Hamilton, G., Lisitsa, A., Nemytykh, A.P. (eds.) Proceedings of the Fourth International Workshop on Verification and Program Transformation, Eindhoven, The Netherlands, 2nd. Electronic Proceedings in Theoretical Computer Science, vol. 216, pp. 5–23. Open Publishing Association, April 2016
5. Baudin, P., Filliâtre, J.C., Marché, C., Monate, B., Moy, Y., Prevosto, V.: ACSL: ANSI/ISO C Specification Language. http://frama-c.com/acsl.html
6. Bernstein, D.J., Lange, T.: Failures in NIST's ECC standards (2016). https://cr.yp.to/newelliptic/nistecc-20160106.pdf
7. Bielova, N., Rezk, T.: A taxonomy of information flow monitors. In: Piessens, F., Viganò, L. (eds.) POST 2016. LNCS, vol. 9635, pp. 46–67. Springer, Heidelberg (2016). doi:10.1007/978-3-662-49635-0_3
8. Blazy, S., Bühler, D., Yakobowski, B.: Structuring abstract interpreters through state and value abstractions. In: Bouajjani, A., Monniaux, D. (eds.) VMCAI 2017. LNCS, vol. 10145, pp. 112–130. Springer, Cham (2017). doi:10.1007/978-3-319-52234-0_7
9. Ceara, D., Mounier, L., Potet, M.L.: Taint dependency sequences: a characterization of insecure execution paths based on input-sensitive cause sequences. In: The 3rd International Conference on Software Testing, Verification and Validation Workshops (ICSTW 2010), pp. 371–380 (2010)
10. Denning, D.E., Denning, P.J.: Certification of programs for secure information flow. Commun. ACM 20(7), 504–513 (1977). http://doi.acm.org/10.1145/359636.359712
11. Genkin, D., Packmanov, L., Pipman, I., Shamir, A., Tromer, E.: Physical key extraction attacks on PCs. Commun. ACM 59(6), 70–79 (2016). http://cacm.acm.org/magazines/2016/6/202646-physical-key-extraction-attacks-on-pcs/fulltext
12. Goguen, J.A., Meseguer, J.: Security policies and security models. In: 1982 IEEE Symposium on Security and Privacy, April 1982

13. Hedin, D., Bello, L., Sabelfeld, A.: Value-sensitive hybrid information flow control for a javascript-like language. In: Proceedings of the 2015 IEEE 28th Computer Security Foundations Symposium, CSF 2015, pp. 351–365. IEEE Computer Society (2015)

14. Hedin, D., Birgisson, A., Bello, L., Sabelfeld, A.: JSFlow: tracking information flow in JavaScript and its APIs. In: Proceedings of the 29th Annual ACM Symposium on Applied Computing, SAC 2014, pp. 1663–1671. ACM (2014)

15. Hunt, S., Sands, D.: On flow-sensitive security types. In: Conference Record of the 33rd ACM SIGPLAN-SIGACT Symposium on Principles of Programming Languages, POPL 2006, pp. 79–90. ACM (2006). http://doi.acm.org/10.1145/1111037.1111045

16. Kerschbaumer, C., Hennigan, E., Larsen, P., Brunthaler, S., Franz, M.: Information flow tracking meets just-in-time compilation. ACM Trans. Archit. Code Optim. **10**(4), 38:1–38:25 (2013)

17. Kirchner, F., Kosmatov, N., Prevosto, V., Signoles, J., Yakobowski, B.: Frama-C: a software analysis perspective. Formal Aspects Comput. **27**(3), 573–609 (2015). http://dx.doi.org/10.1007/s00165-014-0326-7

18. Kosmatov, N., Signoles, J.: A lesson on runtime assertion checking with Frama-C. In: Legay, A., Bensalem, S. (eds.) RV 2013. LNCS, vol. 8174, pp. 386–399. Springer, Heidelberg (2013). doi:10.1007/978-3-642-40787-1_29

19. Le Guernic, G., Banerjee, A., Jensen, T., Schmidt, D.A.: Automata-based confidentiality monitoring. In: Okada, M., Satoh, I. (eds.) ASIAN 2006. LNCS, vol. 4435, pp. 75–89. Springer, Heidelberg (2007). doi:10.1007/978-3-540-77505-8_7. http://dl.acm.org/citation.cfm?id=1782734.1782741 http://dl.acm.org/citation.cfm?id=1782734.1782741

20. Percival, C.: Cache missing for fun and profit (2005). http://www.daemonology.net/papers/cachemissing.pdf

21. Russo, A., Sabelfeld, A.: Dynamic vs. static flow-sensitive security analysis. In: 2010 23rd IEEE Computer Security Foundations Symposium (CSF), pp. 186–199, July 2010

22. Smaragdakis, Y., Balatsouras, G.: Pointer analysis. Found. Trends Program. Lang. **2**(1), 1–69 (2015). https://yanniss.github.io/points-to-tutorial15.pdf

23. Volpano, D., Irvine, C., Smith, G.: A sound type system for secure flow analysis. J. Comput. Secur. **4**(2–3), 167–187 (1996). http://dl.acm.org/citation.cfm?id=353629.353648

24. Vorobyov, K., Signoles, J., Kosmatov, N.: Shadow State Encoding for Efficient Monitoring of Block-level Properties Submitted for publication

25. Xu, W., Bhatkar, S., Sekar, R.: Taint-enhanced policy enforcement: a practical approach to defeat a wide range of attacks. In: Proceedings of the 15th Conference on USENIX Security Symposium, USENIX-SS 2006, vol. 15. USENIX Association (2006)

Symbolic Execution of Transition Systems with Function Summaries

Imen Boudhiba[1]([✉]), Christophe Gaston[2], Pascale Le Gall[1], and Virgile Prevosto[2]

[1] Laboratoire MICS, Grande Voie des Vignes, 92195 Châtenay-malabry, France
{imen.boudhiba,pascal.legall}@centralesupelec.fr
[2] CEA LIST, Point Courrier 174, 91191 Gif-sur-Yvette, France
{christophe.gaston,virgile.prevosto}@cea.fr

Abstract. Reactive systems can be modeled with various kinds of automata, such as Input Output Symbolic Transition Systems (IOSTS). Symbolic execution (SE) applied to IOSTS allows computing constraints associated to IOSTS path executions (path conditions). In this context, generating test cases amounts to finding numerical input values satisfying such constraints using solvers. This paper explores the case where IOSTS models contain functions which are outside of the scope of such solvers. We propose to use *function summaries* which are logical formulas built from concrete values describing some representative input/output data tuples of the function. We define algorithmic strategies to solve path conditions including such functions based on techniques using and enriching function summaries. Our method has been implemented within the Diversity tool and has been applied to several examples.

Keywords: Input Output Symbolic Transition Systems · Functions summaries · Symbolic execution · Transition coverage

1 Introduction

Many testing theories and algorithms use Symbolic Execution (SE) techniques [10]. In the last decade, it has received much attention and has been incorporated in several testing tools such as NASA's Symbolic (Java) PathFinder [28], UIUC's CUTE and jCUTE [20], UC Berkeley's CREST [13], and the CEA's PathCrawler [27] and DIVERSITY tools [15]. In particular, for the latter one, SE has been adapted for models using variants of abstract labeled transition systems, namely Input Output Symbolic Transition Systems (IOSTS) [17]. Symbolic trees representing all possible execution paths of the model (up to some coverage goals) are computed by executing the model with variables instead of concrete

---

Part of this work has been conducted within the French PIA project SESAM Grids 2012–2016 [12] and the Vessedia project funded from European Union's Horizon 2020 research and innovation programme under grant agreement No. 731453.

S. Gabmeyer and E.B. Johnsen (Eds.): TAP 2017, LNCS 10375, pp. 41–58, 2017.
DOI: 10.1007/978-3-319-61467-0_3

values. For a particular path, a constraint on these variables, called path condition, characterizes concrete values ensuring its execution. Sequences of concrete test inputs exercising a given path are computed by solving the corresponding path condition. As is the case for programs, one of the main limits of this approach is that the usage of some particular functions in the model may make the process inapplicable, either because their symbolic analysis would cause combinatorial explosion in the number of paths to be considered, or because they contain operations that go beyond the capacity of the solver used, or even simply because they are black box functions from the model point of view. This latter situation occurs for example when the modeler makes a reference to an executable function without accessible source code in its model (or without source code processable by the SE tool). In this paper, we call such functions *external functions* and they are assumed to be functionally correct (*i.e.* we suppose that we have a reference implementation for each of the external functions used in the model). In the frame of Model-based Testing [32], a classical way to deal with this situation is to fully abstract external functions by considering the results of their calls as random values. This makes the model behaviors highly non deterministic and causes the test case generation process to compute test cases with a low level of controllability: the behavior of the system under test may deviate from the execution path which it is supposed to exercise without revealing an error in the system. Those situations are referred to as *inconclusive*.

In this paper we adapt to models an approach used at the code level, which is based on a representation of external functions as so-called *function summaries*. A function summary is a logical formula that can be computed from a partial knowledge of the function, represented as a table containing some representative tuples of inputs/output data. Those tuples are obtained by (concretely) executing the function on a set of inputs, either produced randomly or given by the programmer. They may also result from pre-existing unit test campaigns. Path conditions are then computed based on a joint analysis of the guards occurring in executed transitions and of the function summaries associated to external functions called in those transitions. A drawback of such an approach is of course that the tables might be too incomplete to provide input/output data to follow a given model path, meaning that their corresponding summaries are too restrictive to follow the path. The main contribution of this paper is to define a heuristic to deal with this situation by completing the function tables. The heuristic is based on the computation of new inputs by solving formulas built to avoid duplications in the tables and also to take benefits of the potential function dependencies. The overall approach can be seen as a reachability analysis based on symbolic execution techniques and an heuristic search algorithm used to solve path conditions. The resulting symbolic paths can then be used to generate test cases, in a classical model-based testing approach, for IOSTS extended with function calls. Concrete test inputs can thus be given to an existing system, in order to see if this system reacts according to its IOSTS model. This contribution has potential applications for industrial software testing practices especially integration testing, where units of code (i.e. external functions) must be taken into account while testing the whole system.

The remainder of the paper is organized as follows. Section 2 gives basic concepts about IOSTS and SE. In Sect. 3, we define function summaries. The main contribution of the paper is given in Sect. 4: it concerns the resolution of path conditions involving function calls using function summaries. The implementation and experiments of our approach are discussed in Sect. 5. Finally we conclude the paper with a discussion of related work (Sect. 6) and some concluding words (Sect. 7).

2   IOSTS

2.1   Preliminaries

A *data signature* is a pair (S, F) where S is a set of *types* and F a set of *functions* provided with a profile $s_1 \cdots s_n \rightarrow s_{n+1}$ on S. For $V = \coprod_{s \in S} V_s$ a set of variables typed in S, the set $T_F(V) = \coprod_{s \in S} T_F(V)_s$ of terms over V is defined as usual. For two sets A and B, B^A denotes the set of mappings $f : A \rightarrow B$ from A to B and id_A is the identity mapping on A. For a mapping $f : A \rightarrow B$, $f[a_i \mapsto b_i]_{i \in 1..n}$ is the mapping associating b_i to a_i for all i in $1..n$ and $f(a)$ to a not belonging to $\{a_i \mid i \in 1..n\}$.

The set $Sen_F(V)$ of *formulas* is built over Boolean constants $\top$ and $\bot$, equalities $t = t'$ for t and t' terms in $T_F(V)$ of same type and Boolean connectives $(\wedge, \vee, \neg)$. *Substitutions* over V are applications $\sigma : V \rightarrow T_F(V)$ that preserve types. Substitutions can be canonically extended to $T_F(V)$.

A *F-model* is a set of typed variables $M = \coprod_{s \in S} M_s$ provided with a function $f^M : M_{s_1} \times \cdots \times M_{s_n} \rightarrow M_{s_{n+1}}$ for each $f : s_1 \cdots s_n \rightarrow s_{n+1}$ in F. An *interpretation* is an application ν in M^V that preserves types and is canonically extended to $T_F(V)$. The satisfaction of a formula φ in $Sen_F(V)$ by an interpretation $\nu \in M^V$, denoted $M \models_\nu \varphi$, is defined as usual. A formula φ is said satisfiable or feasible if there exists an interpretation ν such that $M \models_\nu \varphi$.

In the sequel, a data signature (S, F) and an F-model M are supposed given. Moreover, when a formula φ is satisfiable and can be handled by a solver, $Sat(\varphi)$ will denote a solution computed by a solver (whatever are the solution or the solver).

2.2   IOSTS

Input Output Symbolic Transition Systems (IOSTS) represent behaviors of reactive systems as sequences of emissions or receptions of values through communication channels conditioned by guards expressed on some attribute values. An *IOSTS-signature* Γ is a couple (A, Ch), where $A = \coprod_{s \in S} A_s$ is a set of typed variables, called *attribute variables*. In the sequel, a variable v of A will be denoted either as a simple identifier (id) or as an identifier (id) and an integer (i) pair, denoted as $id[i]$. The latter case will be useful for dealing with modeling of arrays. Ch is a set of *communication channel names*.

An IOSTS communicates with its environment through actions. The set of *symbolic actions* over $\Gamma = (A, Ch)$, denoted $Act(\Gamma)$, is $I(\Gamma) \cup O(\Gamma) \cup \{\tau\}$ where:

$I(\Gamma) = \{c?(x_1,\ldots,x_n)|\forall i \in 1..n, x_i \in A, c \in Ch, \forall i,j \ (i \neq j \Rightarrow x_i \neq x_j)\}$ is the set of inputs, $O(\Gamma) = \{c!(t_1,\ldots,t_n)|\forall i \in 1..n, t_i \in T_F(A), c \in Ch\}$ is the set of outputs and τ is an internal action. If $n = 0$, (resp $n = 1$), then $c\Delta()$ (resp $c\Delta(t_1)$) with $\Delta \in \{?,!\}$ is simply denoted $c\Delta$ (resp. $c\Delta t_1$).

Values of attribute variables can be modified either by a reception from the environment or by an assignment of a value issued from some internal process.

Definition 1 (IOSTS). *An IOSTS (Q, q_0, Tr) over $\Gamma = (A, Ch)$ is a triple where Q is a set of states, $q_0 \in Q$ is the initial state and $Tr \subseteq Q \times Sen_F(A) \times Act(\Gamma) \times T_F(A)^A \times Q$ is a set of transitions tr of the form (q, ψ, act, ρ, q') where:*

- *q and q' are resp. the source (source(tr)) and target state (target(tr)) of tr;*
- *$\psi \in Sen_F(A)$ is a guard;*
- *$act \in Act(\Gamma)$ is a communication action;*
- *$\rho \in T_F(A)^A$ is a substitution.*

Example 1. Let us illustrate an example of IOSTS inspired from the Sesam-Grids project [12]: Fig. 1 describes a simple model of a Microgrid, that is, a system of interconnected and distributed smart components (smart meters, controller, ...) in connection with energy resources and energy consumption devices. Our example describes a simplified model of a controller inside a Microgrid. Electricity measurements are requested by a smart controller (*mReq!* action) and sent by a smart meter (*getmeas?Value[cpt]*). *N* measurements are stored in the array *Value* whose data can be accessed through variables of the form *Value[i]* with *i* integer. Then, they are used by the controller to compute the total electricity consumption via an integral calculation ($I \mapsto INTGR(Value)$) where $INTGR$ is an external function. If the overall consumption is greater than 200, then the function *RISE* (which is also an external function) is called to compute, according to the returned consumption I, a rate r that is added to the energy price. The new price ($(1 + r) * i$) is sent to the actuator via the (*out*) channel, together with a message indicating whether the rise is normal ("*ok*", if $r \leq 1$) or should trigger a warning ("*alarm*", if $r > 1$). Otherwise, if the consumption is lower than 200, an acknowledgment is sent (*out!*("*ok*", I)). In Fig. 1, guards of the form $t_1 \leq t_2$, $t_1 < t_2$, $t_1 > t_2$ or $t_1 \geq t_2$ are concise representations of respectively $t_1 \leq t_2 = \top$, $t_1 < t_2 = \top$, $t_1 > t_2 = \top$ or $t_1 \geq t_2 = \top$.

2.3   Symbolic Execution of IOSTS

Symbolic execution (SE) consists in executing the *IOSTS* with symbolic variables rather than numerical values. SE gathers constraints (*path condition*) over such variables that characterize under which circumstances a particular execution path is taken.

To store information concerning an execution, we use a set Fr of so-called fresh variables with $Fr \cap A = \emptyset$ and structures called symbolic states. Fr is an infinite set in which, whenever necessary, it is possible to take a variable not previously used. A *symbolic state* η is a tuple (q, π, λ) where: q (or $q(\eta)$) denotes the state in Q reached after an execution leading to η, $\pi \in Sen_F(Fr)$ (or $\pi(\eta)$)

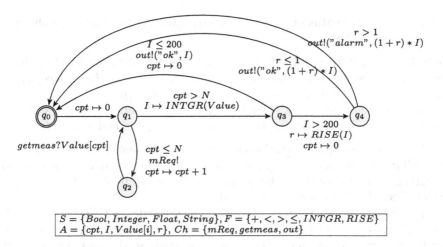

$$S = \{Bool, Integer, Float, String\}, F = \{+, <, >, \leq, INTGR, RISE\}$$
$$A = \{cpt, I, Value[i], r\}, \; Ch = \{mReq, getmeas, out\}$$

Fig. 1. Micro grid controller IOSTS

is the *path condition* that should be satisfied for the execution to reach η and $\lambda : A \to T_F(Fr)$ (or $\lambda(\eta)$) denotes terms over variables in Fr that are assigned to variables of A.

Definition 2 (SE of transitions). *Let* $\mathbb{G} = (Q, q_0, Tr)$ *be an IOSTS,* $tr = (q, \psi, act, \rho, q')$ *a transition of Tr and $\eta = (q, \pi, \lambda)$ a symbolic state.*

Let us define λ_i as $\lambda[x_1 \mapsto f_1, \ldots, x_n \mapsto f_n]$ if act is of the form $c?(x_1, \ldots, x_n)$, where each f_i is a fresh variable in Fr and as λ otherwise. The symbolic execution $SE(tr, \eta)$ of tr from η is the symbolic transition $(\eta, \lambda_i(act), \eta')$ where $\eta' = (q', \pi', \lambda')$, with $\pi' = \pi \wedge \lambda(\psi)$, and $\lambda' = \lambda_i \circ \rho$.

We denote $Fr(SE(tr, \eta))$ the set of all fresh variables of Fr occurring in its definition while not already present in η.

The symbolic execution tree associated with the *IOSTS* is then defined simply by executing all transitions from all symbolic states.

Definition 3 (SE of *IOSTS*). *Given an IOSTS $\mathbb{G} = (Q, q_0, Tr)$ over $\Gamma = (A, Ch)$, the symbolic execution $SE(\mathbb{G}) = (SS, Init, ST)$ of $\mathbb{G}$ is minimally defined by:*

- *$Init = (q_0, \top, \lambda_0)$ is the initial state. Init is in SS and we have $\forall x \in A$, $\lambda_0(x) \in Fr$, and $\forall x \neq y \in A$, $\lambda_0(x) \neq \lambda_0(y)$. We denote $Fr_0 = \{\lambda_0(x) \mid x \in A\}$ the set of variables used in Init.*
- *ST is a set of symbolic transitions such that for any $\eta = (q, \pi, \lambda)$ in SS and for any $tr \in Tr$ of source state q, there exists one symbolic execution $SE(tr, \eta) = (\eta, act_F, \eta')$ of tr from η with $SE(tr, \eta) \in ST$ and $\eta' \in SS$.*

Moreover $Fr(SE(tr, \eta)) \cap Fr_0 = \emptyset$ and for any two distinct symbolic transitions $SE(tr_1, \eta_1)$ and $SE(tr_2, \eta_2)$ in ST, $Fr(SE(tr_1, \eta_1)) \cap Fr(SE(tr_2, \eta_2)) = \emptyset$. For $st = (\eta, act_F, \eta')$ in ST, we denote $source(st) = \eta$ and $target(st) = \eta'$.

Now, we define paths of the symbolic tree resulting from the symbolic execution of an $IOSTS$:

Definition 4 (Symbolic Paths). *The set $Paths(SE(\mathbb{G}))$ of paths of $SE(\mathbb{G})$ is the set of all sequences $st_1 \cdots st_n$ with $\forall i \in 1..n$, $st_i \in ST$ such that $source(st_1) = Init$ and for any $j < n$, $q(target(st_j)) = q(source(st_{j+1}))$.*

For a path $\delta = st_1 \cdots st_n$ with $1 \leq n$, we note $End(\delta) = target(st_n)$ and $Fr(\delta) = \cup_{i \in 1..n} Fr(target(st_i))$. By convention, $End(\varepsilon) = Init$ and $Fr(\varepsilon) = \emptyset$.

By construction, path conditions accumulate constraints from all the guards of the IOSTS transitions over a path. Hence, feasibility of path pa is checked by calling a solver over the path condition of the last state of pa. In the sequel, such call will be denoted $Sat(\pi(End(pa)))$.

As already mentioned in Sect. 1, external functions such as $INTGR$ and $RISE$ have no built-in interpretations in standard constraint solvers. Thus, when path conditions contain external functions, usual constraint solving techniques cannot be applied directly. We thus propose an improved resolution method to guide the symbolic execution by checking paths feasibility up to some function calls.

3 Function Summaries

Instead of either considering external functions as purely abstract by replacing their output with a fresh variable or inserting their code (inlining) at model level quickly leading to combinatorial explosion, our approach allows to control this issue by replacing external functions with *summaries* that offer a partial and extendable view of the function within the model.

In the sequel, P will denote a distinguished subset of F, the set of all external functions.

3.1 Summaries

Values which are used to summarize an external function are taken from its concrete execution on some inputs. This can be represented and saved as a table mapping a finite set of tuples associating input and output data of the function.

Notation 3.1. *For $p \in P$ an external function of profile $s_1 \ldots s_n \to s_{n+1}$ and $p^M \in M$ its interpretation, we denote by tab_p, a set of tuples $(v_1, \ldots, v_n, v_{n+1}) \in M_{s_1} \times \cdots \times M_{s_n} \times M_{s_{n+1}}$ verifying $p^M(v_1, \ldots, v_n) = v_{n+1}$, a function table of p. If tab_p covers the entire domain of p then it will fully represent p^M.*

We associate with each external function a summary built on values in the function table. More precisely, a function call will be stored in a given symbolic state under the form

$$(p, (t_1, \cdots, t_n), x)$$

indicating that a call has been performed for the external function p with arguments $(t_1, \cdots, t_n)$ and that its result is stored in the fresh variable x.

We note $Calls(P)$ the set of all function calls.

Definition 5 (Function call summaries). *Let $Cls \subseteq Calls(P)$ be a set of function calls and $Tab = (tab_p)_{p \in P}$, where tab_p is a function table associated to p in P.*
The summary of Cls up to Tab is:

$$Sums(Cls, Tab) = \bigwedge_{\substack{cl=(p,(t_1,\cdots,t_n),x) \in Cls, \\ tab_p \in Tab}} Sum(cl, tab_p)$$

where $Sum(cl, tab_p)$ computes the disjunction of different inputs/output tuples of tab_p, i.e.:

$$Sum(cl, tab_p) = \bigvee_{(v_1,\cdots,v_{n+1}) \in tab_p} ((\bigwedge_{i \leq n} t_i = v_i) \wedge x = v_{n+1})$$

with the convention $Sum(cl, \emptyset) = \bot$.

Example 2. Let us go back to the Microgrid example (Fig. 1) with the hypothesis $N = 2$. Then, a scenario involves two measurements m_1 and m_2. For illustrative purposes, values that will be used in the summaries associated to the external functions $INTGR$ and $RISE$ are given in Table 1. Based on the values provided by Table 1, we can then compute the corresponding summaries for the set of function calls $Cls = \{cl_1, cl_2\}$ with $cl_1 = (INTGR, ([m_1, m_2]), I)$ and $cl_2 = (RISE, (I), r)$:

- $Sum(cl_1, tab(INTGR))$ is
  $(m_1 = 123 \wedge m_2 = 96 \wedge I = 228) \vee (m_1 = 148 \wedge m_2 = 141 \wedge I = 300)$
- $Sum(cl_2, tab(RISE))$ is
  $(I = 202 \wedge r = 0.7) \vee (I = 300 \wedge r = 2.42)$

Finally, $Sums(Cls, Tab)$ is simply $Sum(cl_1, tab(INTGR)) \wedge Sum(cl_2, tab(RISE))$.

Table 1. $INTGR$ and $RISE$ tables

tab(INTGR)		tab(RISE)	
[123, 96]	228	202	0.7
[148, 141]	300	300	2.42

3.2 Formula Transformation

A path condition φ is built over terms of $T_F(V)$ that may contain occurrences of external functions. Since the satisfiability of φ requires to find an interpretation ν ensuring $M \models_\nu \varphi$, the idea is to proceed in two steps:

1. φ is transformed into a formula with no occurrence of external functions and a set of function calls.
2. the satisfiability of φ is checked with a constraint solver and based on external function summaries (built on concrete executions of called functions).

For a formula φ containing a term of the form $p(t_1, \cdots, t_n)$ with $p \in P$, we will eliminate the occurrence of p in φ by introducing a new fresh variable x in charge of storing the result of the application of p to the terms $t_1, \ldots, t_n$. An interpretation will be acceptable as a solution only if it evaluates terms $t_1, \ldots, t_n$ and x so that they correspond to one of the elements of the function table tab_p. Thus, while eliminating all occurrences of external function in formulas, we also collect all tuples $(t_1, \ldots, t_n, x)$ memorizing all contexts of calls of external functions.

Let us first define a function $\chi : T_F(V) \rightarrow T_F(V \cup Fr) \times Calls(P)$ as follows:

- if t is a variable or a constant[1], $\chi(t) = (t, \emptyset)$
- if t is of form $f(t_1, \ldots, t_n)$ with $f \notin P$, then[2]
  $\chi(t) = (f(\chi(t_1)_{|1}, \ldots, \chi(t_n)_{|1}), \cup_{i \in 1..n} \chi(t_i)_{|2})$
- if t is of form $p(t_1, \ldots, t_n)$ with $p \in P$, then $\chi(t) = (x, \{(p, (\chi(t_1)_{|1}, \ldots, \chi(t_n)_{|1}), x)\} \cup_{i \in 1..n} \chi(t_i)_{|2}$ with x a fresh variable in Fr.

We assume that all fresh variables introduced by function calls (i.e. the sets $\chi(t)_{|2}$) are pairwise disjoint. Note that the term substitution is performed iteratively by starting with the innermost sub-terms in case of nested function calls. The function χ is canonically extended to formulas by preserving formula structure and accumulating all sets of function calls in a unique set. In the sequel, for a formula φ, $\chi(\varphi)_{|1}$, the formula φ without external functions, will be denoted $\overline{\varphi}$ and $\chi(\varphi)_{|2}$, the set of associated calls, will be denoted $\kappa(\varphi)$.

Example 3. Let us denote φ_0 the formula $RISE(INTGR([x+1, 0])) > 1$ defined over the external functions $INTGR$ and $RISE$ and the variable x.

Then, $\overline{\varphi_0}$ is $r > 1$ while $\kappa(\varphi_0)$ is $\{(RISE, (I), r), (INTGR, ([x + 1, 0]), I)\}$ with I and r new fresh variables.

Now that we are able to remove external functions, we will propose an algorithm to check formula satisfiability.

4   Satisfiability of Formulas up to Function Summaries

Given a formula φ possibly built over external functions, we aim at defining an algorithm that analyzes the satisfiability of φ up to summaries of called external functions. Recall that φ is transformed into a formula $(\overline{\varphi})$ with no occurrence of external functions, while we keep track of external function calls in $\kappa(\varphi)$. We also suppose that we have function tables for these external function calls in Tab.

---

[1] A constant is a function of profile of the form $\rightarrow s$.
[2] For a couple $c = (e, f)$ of elements, $c_{|1}$ is e and $c_{|2}$ is f.

Since by construction $Sums(\kappa(\varphi), Tab)$ is the formula specifying that function calls of κ match with at least a tuple of Tab, if $Sat(\overline{\varphi} \wedge Sums(\kappa(\varphi), Tab))$ returns a solution, then φ is satisfiable (i.e. there exists an interpretation ν such that $M \models_\nu \varphi$). Otherwise, either φ is not satisfiable (i.e. $\forall \nu, M \not\models_\nu \varphi$) or φ is satisfiable but the function tables (used to summarize functions) are not complete enough to exhibit an interpretation ν such that $M \models_\nu \varphi$. Therefore, in the sequel we place ourselves in the hypothesis that function tables can be enriched during the satisfiability search. Furthermore, some heuristics are proposed to help the solver finding a solution when current function summaries are not compatible with the formula, e.g. to find additional input data for external functions that could make the formula feasible. We describe these heuristics in more detail below.

4.1   Resolution Strategies

NoCorres Strategy: NoCorres computes a formula guaranteeing that the inputs of called external functions are different from those already present in the current function tables. This formula will be used later to get new inputs for the concrete executions of external functions, ensuring the enrichment of the function tables, which in turn increases chances to find a solution.

Definition 6 (NoCorres). *Let $Cls \subseteq Calls(P)$ be a set of function calls and $Tab = (tab_p)_{p \in P}$ a set of tables where tab_p is the table associated to p in P. $NoCorres(Cls, Tab)$ is defined as follows:*

$$NoCorres(Cls, Tab) = \bigvee_{\substack{cl=(p,(t_1,\cdots,t_n),x) \in Cls, \\ tab_p \in Tab}} (NoCorres1(cl, tab_p))$$

with $NoCorres1((p, (t_1, \cdots, t_n), x), tab_p)$ being defined as follows:

$$\bigwedge_{(v_1,\cdots,v_{n+1}) \in tab_p} (\bigvee_{i \leq n} t_i \neq v_i)$$

By considering the conjunction of $NoCorres(\kappa(\varphi), Tab)$ and $\overline{\varphi}$, the solver cannot compute interpretations of variables for which all function calls in $\kappa(\varphi)$ are already present in Tab.

Example 4. By applying the above *NoCorres* definition on the set of function calls and tables given in Example 2, $NoCorres(Cls, Tab)$ is the formula $NoCorres1(cl_1, Tab(INTGR)) \vee NoCorres1(cl_2, Tab(RISE))$ where:

- $NoCorres1(cl_1, tab(INTGR))$ is
  $(m_1 \neq 123 \vee m_2 \neq 96) \wedge (m_1 \neq 148 \vee m_2 \neq 141)$
- $NoCorres1(cl_2, tab(RISE))$ is $(I \neq 202) \wedge (I \neq 300)$

Dependency Heuristic: Another way to accelerate and help the solver resolution task to find new inputs, when no solution is found with the current function tables, is to take advantage of direct dependencies between function calls. Indeed when the arguments of a call to an external function f depend on the result of calls to other external functions f_i, we can indicate to the solver to search for solutions in which the inputs of f are compatible with the outputs already present in the tables of the f_i.

Definition 7 (Dep). *Let $Cls \subseteq Calls(P)$ be a set of function calls and $Tab = (tab_p)_{p \in P}$ a set of tables where tab_p is the function table associated to p in P. $Dep(Cls, Tab)$ is defined as follows:*

$$Dep(Cls, Tab) = \bigwedge_{cl \in Cls} (Dep1(cl, Cls, Tab))$$

with $Dep1(cl, Cls, Tab)$ being defined as follows:

$$\bigwedge_{cl_i = (q,(t'_1,\cdots,t'_n),x') \in Dep_{cl}} (CorresRes(cl_i, tab_q))$$

where:

- *For $cl = (p, (t_1, \cdots, t_n), x)$, $Dep_{cl} = \{cl_i = (q, (t'_1, \cdots, t'_n), x') \in Cls \setminus \{cl\} \mid x' \in \bigcup_{i \leq n} Occ(t_i)\}$ is the set of function calls on which the inputs of cl depend, i.e. the result of these function calls occurs in one or several input terms of cl.*
- *For $cl' = (q, (t'_1, \cdots, t'_n), x')$, $CorresRes(cl', tab_q)$ is the formula*

$$\bigvee_{(v_1,\cdots,v_{n+1}) \in tab_q} (x' = v_{n+1})$$

$CorresRes(cl', tab_q)$ extracts values from the tables of function calls on which cl' depends.

Example 5. Let us consider again the function calls introduced in Example 2. We have:

- $Dep_{cl_2} = \{cl_1\}$ with $cl_1 = (INTGR, ([m_1, m_2]), I)$, because I (the variable storing the result of cl_1) is an input of $cl_2 = (RISE, (I), r)$.
- $CorresRes(cl_1, tab(INTGR))$ is $(I = 228 \vee I = 300)$

Therefore, to find new inputs for $RISE$, we can give to the solver $Dep(cl_2, Cls)$, that is $CorresRes(cl_1, tab(INTGR))$ to exploit the values of I already existing in $Tab(INTGR)$.

By combining both *NoCorres* and *Dep* heuristics, it is possible to generate new sets of inputs, i.e. new rows in the tables of external functions that are relevant for the overall path constraint resolution. Indeed, *NoCorres* ensures that we will add at least one new row to a function table, while *Dep* takes care of avoiding solutions that cannot be satisfied by the current summaries of the callers, and are thus useless for the current solving process.

4.2   SolveTab Algorithm

Algorithm 1 describes our dynamic solving procedure $SolveTab(m, \overline{\varphi}, \kappa(\varphi), Tab)$. The goal of $SolveTab$ is to analyze the satisfiability up to some function tables Tab of a formula $(\overline{\varphi})$ with no occurrences of external functions, provided with a set of function calls $(\kappa(\varphi))$. The integer parameter m is used to bound the number of attempts that are made to increase the size of function tables. As explained in the previous section, we resort to this mechanism when no tuple in a function table is compatible with φ. However, since there is no guarantee that extending function tables will eventually lead to find a solution for $\overline{\varphi} \wedge Sums(\kappa(\varphi), Tab)$, we cut the search after at most m steps. If no solution is found beyond m or no possible function inputs are found, then we can deduce that the formula is unsatisfiable up to function tables. The case $m = 0$ corresponds to a purely static version where a solution is searched without modifying function tables (i.e. Tab is then a static variable).

Algorithm 1. $SolveTab(m, \psi, \kappa, Tab)$

Data: m: an integer, ψ: a formula without black-box functions, κ : a set of function calls, Tab: function tables
Result: satisfiability of ψ up to κ; Tab: updated function tables

```
1  begin
2      sol ← Sat(ψ ∧ Sums(κ, Tab));
3      TabModified ← True;
4      while TabModified and sol = NONE and m ≠ 0 do
5          In ← Sat(ψ ∧ NoCorres(κ, Tab) ∧ Dep(κ, Tab))      /* Search for new
             solutions while considering dependencies between function
             calls */ ;
6          if In = NONE then          /* no possible inputs for function */
7              In ← Sat(ψ ∧ NoCorres(κ, Tab))      /* Search for new possible
                 solutions without considering function dependencies */ ;
8          if In ≠ NONE then          /* new possible inputs for function */
9              for  each call cl = (p, (t₁, ⋯ , tₙ), x) in κ do
10                 VIns ← Ins(In, cl)  /* extract inputs for p from In */;
11                 r ← Execₚ(VIns)        /* concrete execution of p */;
12                 Tab(p) ← (VIns, r).Tab(p)  /* save new tuple in Tab */;
13             sol ← Sat(ψ ∧ Sums(κ, Tab));
14         else
15             TabModified ← False;
16         m ← m − 1;
17     return (sol, Tab);
```

Let us now give some few comments on Algorithm 1. By hypothesis, arguments $(\psi, \kappa) = \chi(\varphi)$ for some φ, so that ψ and κ share external functions and variables.

If $Sat(\psi \wedge Sums(\kappa, Tab))$ gives back a result sol, then sol directly provides an interpretation of variables that satisfies the formula φ in which external functions are interpreted according to values given in their associated tables Tab. In other words, by construction $M \models_{sol} \varphi$.

In case no solution is found with $Sat(\psi \wedge Sums(\kappa, Tab))$ in Line 2 (ψ is unsatisfiable up to current function summaries), then we try to find additional input data for external functions that could enrich Tab (and function summaries) and make the formula satisfiable. In order to guide the solver to find new inputs, Dep and $NoCorres$ heuristics can be used. $NoCorres$ is necessary to compute new inputs distinct from those already present in current tables (that failed to provide us with a solution). On the other hand, Dep is an alternative option that can facilitate the search for inputs that are compatible with dependencies among function calls. However, this might restrict the search space too much, as we may need to add a new output to the table of function f to find a suitable input for g that depends on f. Therefore, if adding the Dep condition results in an unsatisfiable formula (Line 7), we call the solver again with only the formula and the $NoCorres$ condition. Indeed, the new tuples might give us new outputs that will in turn make Dep satisfiable at next step, or even give directly a solution to the original problem.

If an interpretation (variable In) is found, then lines 10, 11 and 12 allow us to add new tuples in function tables (variable Tab), by successively extracting input values $VIns \leftarrow ins(In, cl)$ for each function call (line 10), concretely executing the function (line 11) with $VIns$ as input data, ($Exec_p$ being the reference implementation of p), to obtain the corresponding output (variable r) and finally storing new tuples in Tab_p (line 12). Then, the solver is called (line 13) to check the satisfiability of ψ, with the new summaries based on the enriched function tables.

Last, let us point out that a bigger number m of allowed attempts to search for new tuples enriching function tables gives more chances to find a solution, but will possibly take longer to compute.

4.3   Discussion: *SolveTab* for Symbolic Execution

Since path conditions are formulas built over terms that may contain occurrences of external functions, we proceed as detailed in the previous section in order to check symbolic paths feasibility according to function summaries. For that, we use the *SolveTab* solving Algorithm 1 based on concrete executions of called functions to guide the symbolic execution of $IOSTS$. Therefore, we need to extend symbolic states by accumulating function calls. An extended symbolic state is of the form $\eta = (q, \pi, \lambda, \kappa)$, where κ (or $\kappa(\eta)$) denotes the sequence of function calls of the form $(p, (t_1, \cdots, t_n), x)$. By construction, the path condition π does not contain occurrences of external functions.

A symbolic state $(q, \pi, \lambda, \kappa)$ is satisfiable according to function summaries only if there exists an integer m and function tables Tab such that the result (sol, Tab) provided by $SolveTab(m, \pi, \kappa, Tab)$ defines an interpretation sol of fresh variables ensuring the interpretation of π as true.

The symbolic execution in accordance with function tables is based on the *SolveTab* resolution algorithm which takes as arguments, in addition to the path condition and the set of accumulated function calls, the parameter m and the set of tables Tab. If we note $SE_{Tab,m}(\mathbb{G})$ the symbolic execution of $\mathbb{G}$ using *SolveTab* for building satisfiable symbolic states, then $SE_{Tab,m}(\mathbb{G})$ is highly dependent on the initial tables (Tab) specifying called functions, the chosen threshold of resolution attempts m, the choice of the solver and the strategy of traversal (in depth, in width, ...) of the symbolic tree. Thus, the construction of $SE_{Tab,m}(\mathbb{G})$ will more or less approach the ideal symbolic tree $SE(\mathbb{G})$. If elements of Tab are representative enough of the behavior of called functions, with regard to the solicitations of the $IOSTS$ or if m is large enough to find a solution for each possible path of the $IOSTS$ (by enriching function tables), then $SE_{Tab}(\mathbb{G})$ becomes closer to $SE(\mathbb{G})$ and more states become reachable.

5 Implementation and Experiments

5.1 Implementation

DIVERSITY Tool: DIVERSITY [3,14], is a multi-purpose and customizable platform for formal analysis based on symbolic execution (test generation, proof, deadlock search, etc.) that is on its way to becoming an Eclipse open-source project[3]. DIVERSITY generates a symbolic tree (for a fixed maximal height) by simulating the system specification with input symbols rather than concrete values for data. Test inputs are computed by solving the path conditions. For that purpose, DIVERSITY integrates solvers such as $Z3$[4], and $CVC4$[5].

We have implemented the *SolveTab* Algorithm 1 and the heuristics described in Sect. 4 as additional Formal Analysis Module (FAM) for checking satisfiability of path conditions within DIVERSITY. By default, constraints involving external functions are left uninterpreted (i.e. out of the scope of solvers). In addition, variable assignments within an $IOSTS$ transition contain only basic operations. Now, all such external functions can be handled with the newly implemented technique, using values recorded in function tables. The *SolveTab* algorithm allows to know whether a new execution context EC (a symbolic state) can be built in the symbolic execution tree in accordance with called functions, after the execution of a transition in the $IOSTS$. In other words, it checks if a transition of the $IOSTS$ could be fired or not according to called functions, with a possible enrichment of the function tables. Therefore, thanks to *SolveTab* we ensure the symbolic tree's construction with only feasible paths compatible with called functions while ensuring a high transition coverage of the $IOSTS$ transitions.

Microgrids Case Study: Here, we discuss the application of our technique to the Microgrid Example 1 that uses external function calls ($INTGR$ and $RISE$).

---

[3] https://projects.eclipse.org/proposals/eclipse-formal-modeling-project.
[4] https://z3.codeplex.com/.
[5] http://cvc4.cs.nyu.edu/web/.

For that, we present the resulting symbolic trees (to a depth of 6) by applying the *SolveTab* algorithm with the initial function tables of Table 1 and various values of m, the number of attempts made to increase the function tables. At first, we use the static version (static tables, $m = 0$). Result is shown in the left tree of Fig. 2. Then we progressively increase m until 196, function tables are enriched by concretely executing functions with new inputs found thanks to NoCorres and Dependency heuristics. As expected, this permits to cover more transitions of the model, reach more symbolic states and explore more feasible paths. Indeed the size of the generated tree grows with the value of m. The middle tree of Fig. 2 is obtained with $m = 1$, while the one on the right is the result of $m = 196$, where all transitions of the $IOSTS$ are covered.

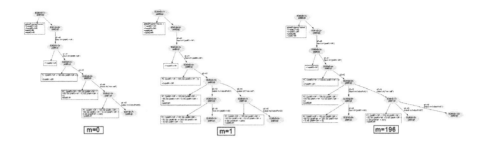

Fig. 2. Symbolic execution tree in DIVERSITY

5.2 Experiments

A summary of the main outcomes of the application of our technique to the Microgrid example is provided in Table 2. It should be noted that our results are based on the initial function tables given in Table 1 and that we dispose of the functions' implementation in order to be able to execute them with appropriate inputs in an unitary setting. For each experiment (i.e. each line), we fix "m" (maximum number of attempts for the *SolveTab* algorithm) and the maximum "*height*" allowed for the symbolic tree. Then we record results concerning the enriched tables (number of tuples) and the symbolic tree computation: the number of reachable states, the achieved $IOSTS$ transitions coverage and the execution time. Again, when $m = 196$ all possible symbolic states are covered, and there is no need to try to further enrich the function tables.

The resulting coverage rate and execution time depend on the initial function tables. In fact, the more the elements of called function tables are representative of the function behaviors and compatible with path conditions, the less attempts are needed to achieve the same level of coverage. For instance, if we now start with the initial function tables of Table 3 for the Microgrid example, all transitions of the specification are covered (in 2 s 759 ms) without doing any concrete execution ($m = 0$), as all possible outcomes are captured by one row of the tables (Table 4).

Table 2. Experiments with initial Tables 1

"m"	Height	Enriched Tab		States	Transition coverage	Time
		INTGR	RISE			
0	15	2	2	16	62.5%	638 ms
1	15	8	3	27	75%	2 s
196	**15**	**198**	**3**	**120**	**100%**	**4 m 15 s**

Micro-grid IOSTS: initial Tab (Tables 1)

Table 3. Other initial tables

tab(INTGR)	
[0, 0]	0
[12, 18]	30
[123, 96]	228
[148, 141]	300

tab(RISE)	
202	0.7
228	0.97
300	2.42

Table 4. Experiments with other initial Tables 3

"m"	Height	Enriched Tab		States	Coverage	Time
		INTGR	RISE			
0	**15**	**4**	**3**	**120**	**100%**	**2 s 759 ms**

Micro-grid IOSTS: other initial Tab (Tables 3)

6   Related Work

IOSTS and symbolic execution have been used in many works [6,10,17] for different purposes. Until now standard solvers were not capable of dealing with functions occurring in path conditions. The usage of symbolic execution and path feasibility analysis are studied in [7,34] but this is limited to the analysis of functions themselves and does not take into consideration the impact of function calls on the feasibility of the whole system.

Our work borrows the idea of mixing symbolic execution with information obtained from instrumented concrete executions, from *concolic testing*, a method that has been implemented in various settings, such as [9,18,31]. However, these frameworks are primarily directed at source code level in the objective of unit testing. Another concolic tool, PathCrawler [35] proposed an approach to encompass function calls [24], using pre/post-condition couples as a specification.

Other unit testing frameworks traditionally use stubs [25], which are built manually in an ad-hoc way, to replace external functions for which no implementation is available. Also, automatically-generated software stubs [18] are used for abstracting (over-approximating) lower-level functions during dynamic test generation [16] based on code.

[1,4,19,21], propose different techniques to conduct symbolic execution with simplified summary representations. But these techniques do not include heuristics similar to the ones (NoCorres, Dependency) we introduce in our paper.

Other techniques have been proposed to deal with constraints generated from symbolic code execution [2,29]. These techniques fall back on concrete values and use randomization to help simplify complex constraints that cannot be solved directly. Our approach based on IOSTS models is orthogonal to these code-based approaches and uses some heuristic search to solve path conditions including external function calls.

In our previous work [8], like in the work [24], we specify external functions by means of contracts (instead of tables): we unfolded the symbolic tree of an IOSTS by replacing each transition including an external function call by as many transitions as there are behaviors in the contract associated to the considered external function.

7   Conclusion and Future Work

In this work, we use the IOSTS framework extended with external functions. We adapt existing symbolic execution techniques over IOSTS to deal with such function calls, using function tables to summarize them with a formula. The construction of a symbolic execution tree is based on an algorithm *SolveTab* that permits to check path conditions satisfiability up to function summaries with the possibility of enriching function tables by concretely executing them, in order to achieve a high transition coverage of the *IOSTS*.

The proposed approach has been implemented within the DIVERSITY symbolic execution tool. The results show that symbolic execution coupled with function summaries is a practical and effective approach to take into consideration external functions for IOSTS models analysis mainly for model-based testing which is a significant motivation for our work. Nevertheless, it could probably be applied to other families of transition systems like those in [30,32,33].

References

1. Anand, S., Godefroid, P., Tillmann, N.: Demand-driven compositional symbolic execution. In: Ramakrishnan, C.R., Rehof, J. (eds.) TACAS 2008. LNCS, vol. 4963, pp. 367–381. Springer, Heidelberg (2008). doi:10.1007/978-3-540-78800-3_28
2. Anand, S., Păsăreanu, C.S., Visser, W.: JPF–SE: a symbolic execution extension to Java PathFinder. In: Grumberg, O., Huth, M. (eds.) TACAS 2007. LNCS, vol. 4424, pp. 134–138. Springer, Heidelberg (2007). doi:10.1007/978-3-540-71209-1_12
3. Arnaud, M., Bannour, B., Lapitre, A.: An illustrative use case of the DIVERSITY Platform based on UML interaction scenarios. Electron. Notes Theor. Comput. Sci. **320**, 21–34 (2016)
4. Babić, D., Hu, A.J.: Structural abstraction of software verification conditions. In: Damm, W., Hermanns, H. (eds.) CAV 2007. LNCS, vol. 4590, pp. 366–378. Springer, Heidelberg (2007). doi:10.1007/978-3-540-73368-3_41

5. Bannour, B., Escobedo, J.P., Gaston, C., Le Gall, P.: Off-line test case generation for timed symbolic model-based conformance testing. In: Nielsen, B., Weise, C. (eds.) ICTSS 2012. LNCS, vol. 7641, pp. 119–135. Springer, Heidelberg (2012). doi:10.1007/978-3-642-34691-0_10

6. Bannour, B., Gaston, C., Aiguier, M., Lapitre, A.: Results for compositional timed testing. In: 20th Asia-Pacific Software Engineering Conference, APSEC, pp. 559–564. IEEE Computer Society (2013)

7. Bjørner, N., Tillmann, N., Voronkov, A.: Path feasibility analysis for string-manipulating programs. In: Kowalewski, S., Philippou, A. (eds.) TACAS 2009. LNCS, vol. 5505, pp. 307–321. Springer, Heidelberg (2009). doi:10.1007/978-3-642-00768-2_27

8. Boudhiba, I., Gaston, C., Le Gall, P., Prevosto, V.: Model-based testing from input output symbolic transition systems enriched by program calls and contracts. In: El-Fakih, K., Barlas, G., Yevtushenko, N. (eds.) ICTSS 2015. LNCS, vol. 9447, pp. 35–51. Springer, Cham (2015). doi:10.1007/978-3-319-25945-1_3

9. Cadar, C., Engler, D.: Execution generated test cases: how to make systems code crash itself. In: Godefroid, P. (ed.) SPIN 2005. LNCS, vol. 3639, pp. 2–23. Springer, Heidelberg (2005). doi:10.1007/11537328_2

10. King, J.C.: Symbolic execution and program testing. Commun. ACM **19**, 385–394 (1976)

11. Clarke, L.A.: A system to generate test data and symbolically execute programs. IEEE Trans. Softw. Eng. **3**, 215–222 (1976)

12. The Consortium Sesam-Grids: The Sesam-Grids Project. http://www.sesam-grids.org/

13. CREST. https://code.google.com/archive/p/crest/. Accessed 04 Mar 2017

14. Deltour, J., Faivre, A., Gaudin, E., Lapitre, A.: Model-based testing: an approach with SDL/RTDS and DIVERSITY. In: Amyot, D., Fonseca i Casas, P., Mussbacher, G. (eds.) SAM 2014. LNCS, vol. 8769, pp. 198–206. Springer, Cham (2014). doi:10.1007/978-3-319-11743-0_14

15. DIVERSITY. https://projects.eclipse.org/proposals/eclipse-formal-modeling-project. Accessed 04 Mar 2017

16. Engler, D., Dunbar, D.: Under-constrained execution: making automatic code destruction easy and scalable. In: Proceedings of the 2007 International Symposium on Software Testing and Analysis, pp. 1–4. ACM, New York (2007)

17. Gaston, C., Le Gall, P., Rapin, N., Touil, A.: Symbolic execution techniques for test purpose definition. In: Uyar, M.Ü., Duale, A.Y., Fecko, M.A. (eds.) TestCom 2006. LNCS, vol. 3964, pp. 1–18. Springer, Heidelberg (2006). doi:10.1007/11754008_1

18. Godefroid, P., Klarlund, N., Sen, K.: Dart: directed automated random testing. In: Proceedings of the 2005 ACM SIGPLAN Conference on Programming Language Design and Implementation, PLDI 2005, pp. 213–223 (2005)

19. Gopan, D., Reps, T.: Low-level library analysis and summarization. In: Damm, W., Hermanns, H. (eds.) CAV 2007. LNCS, vol. 4590, pp. 68–81. Springer, Heidelberg (2007). doi:10.1007/978-3-540-73368-3_10

20. jCUTE. http://osl.cs.illinois.edu/software/jcute/. Accessed 04 Mar 2017

21. Khurshid, S., Suen, Y.L.: Generalizing symbolic execution to library classes. SIGSOFT Softw. Eng. Notes **31**, 103–110 (2005)

22. Kicillof, N., Grieskamp, W., Tillmann, N., Braberman, V.: Achieving both model and code coverage with automated gray-box testing. In: Advances in Model-Based Testing (A-MOST). ACM (2007)

23. MathWorks: The Simulink documentation. http://fr.mathworks.com/help/simulink/

24. Mouy, P., Marre, B., Willams, N., Le Gall, P.: Generation of all-paths unit test with function calls. In: International Conference on Software Testing (ICST), pp. 32–41 (2008)
25. Myers, G.J., Sandlers, C., Badgett, T.: The Art of Software Testing, 3rd edn. Wiley, New York (2011)
26. Object Management Group: The UML standard specification. http://www.omg.org/spec/UML/2.4.1/
27. PathCrawler. http://frama-c.com/pathcrawler.html. Accessed 04 Mar 2017
28. Symbolic   PathFinder.   http://babelfish.arc.nasa.gov/trac/jpf/wiki/projects/jpf-symbc. Accessed 04 Mar 2017
29. Păsăreanu, C.S., Rungta, N., Visser, W.: Symbolic execution with mixed concrete-symbolic solving. In: Proceedings of the 2011 International Symposium on Software Testing and Analysis, pp. 34–44. ACM, New York (2011)
30. Rutten, J.J.M.M.: A calculus of transition systems (towards universal coalgebra). Technical report, CWI (Centre for Mathematics and Computer Science), Amsterdam, The Netherlands (1995)
31. Sen, K., Marinov, D., Agha, G.: CUTE: a concolic unit testing engine for C. SIGSOFT Softw. Eng. Notes **30**, 263–272 (2005)
32. Tretmans, J.: Conformance testing with labelled transition systems: implementation relations and test generation. Comput. Netw. ISDN Syst. **29**(1), 49–79 (1996)
33. Tretmans, J.: Model based testing with labelled transition systems. In: Hierons, R.M., Bowen, J.P., Harman, M. (eds.) Formal Methods and Testing. LNCS, vol. 4949, pp. 1–38. Springer, Heidelberg (2008). doi:10.1007/978-3-540-78917-8_1
34. Wang, Y., Xing, Y., Zhang, X.: A method of path feasibility judgment based on symbolic execution and range analysis. Int. J. Future Gener. Commun. Netw. **7**, 205–212 (2014)
35. Williams, N., Marre, B., Mouy, P., Roger, M.: PathCrawler: automatic generation of path tests by combining static and dynamic analysis. In: Dal Cin, M., Kaâniche, M., Pataricza, A. (eds.) EDCC 2005. LNCS, vol. 3463, pp. 281–292. Springer, Heidelberg (2005). doi:10.1007/11408901_21

Unit Testing of Database-Driven Java Enterprise Edition Applications

Andreas Fuchs$^{(\boxtimes)}$ and Herbert Kuchen

Department of Information Systems, University of Münster,
Leonardo-Campus 3, 48149 Münster, Germany
{andreas.fuchs,herbert.kuchen}@wi.uni-muenster.de
https://www.wi.uni-muenster.de/

Abstract. The Java Enterprise Edition (Java EE) platform and its persistence API are widely adopted technologies to develop applications that interact with database systems. Many control flows of these applications strongly depend on a specific database state. This paper presents an automatic test-case generation approach for applications in this environment. The approach generates both test data for the application's input, as well as entity objects for the different database states that are required to cover a respective control flow. We integrate constraints from symbolically executing a control flow with constraints on a required database state. We also support typical Java EE functionalities in the symbolic execution, e.g. dependency injection. An experimental evaluation shows an increase in control-flow coverage by our approach.

Keywords: Symbolic execution · Automated unit tests generation · Java Enterprise Edition · Java Persistence API · Database applications

1 Introduction

Java is widely used to develop enterprise applications [3]. Those applications typically interact with external systems such as a database management system (DBMS) providing transaction management for a proper concurrent user access to persistent data. In such an environment, the behavior of an application can strongly depend on the state of the connected systems. Manually generating meaningful test cases for each path of an enterprise application is in most cases impractical. Each test case must include the input data to the application under test (AUT) and set up the state of each required external system for a specific execution path of the AUT. The Java Enterprise Edition (Java EE) APIs define a set of services for a typical enterprise application. There are many tools that automatically generate unit tests for Java applications [13,15,16], and some of them also target the Java EE platform [7]. These tools generate test cases for the AUT but they do not consider the state of an external database system in their test-case generation process. Other works [5] generate both input data for the AUT as well as database records required for a specific path of the AUT,

© Springer International Publishing AG 2017
S. Gabmeyer and E.B. Johnsen (Eds.): TAP 2017, LNCS 10375, pp. 59–76, 2017.
DOI: 10.1007/978-3-319-61467-0_4

but they do not specifically target the Java EE platform. In this paper, we address the challenges that arise when generating unit tests for Java EE applications that use the Java Persistence API (JPA) to interact with an external database system. The automatic generation of test cases for a database-driven Java EE application A includes (1) the instantiation of A with a proper resolution of injected dependencies, (2) the generation of input data for A, (3) the generation of a data store leading to a specific control flow of A, and (4) oracles to verify the result of a test-case execution. We have used the existing test-case generator Muggl [6,12] that did not consider the state of an external database yet. We have extended that system to dynamically generate both input data for the AUT as well as entities that must exist in a data store for a particular path to be executed. Moreover, we have implemented an initial support of important Java EE functionalities, such as dependency injection, that allows us to run the symbolic execution in a standalone environment. The test cases are stored as JUnit files that can be executed on a real application server to enable integration testing of the AUT. Our approach has been evaluated by generating test cases for a couple of example applications. The results show that we can generate more meaningful test cases compared to an approach that does not consider the state of an external database.

```
1   @Stateless
2   public class CustomerService {
3       @PersistenceContext
4       private EntityManager em;
5
6       public void incrementStatus
7           (int s, Date d, long r) {
8       String ql = "SELECT oi.order.customer "
9               + "FROM OrderItem oi "
10              + " JOIN oi.order o "
11              + " JOIN o.customer c "
12              + "WHERE o.orderDate >= :d "
13              + "GROUP BY c.id "
14              + "HAVING SUM(oi.price) >= :r";
15      List<Customer> cList =
16          em.createQuery(ql, Customer.class)
17              .setParameter("r", r)
18              .setParameter("d", d)
19              .getResultList();
20      for(Customer c : cList) {
21          if(c.getStatus() < s) {
22              c.setStatus(s);
23          }
24      }
25  }
```

(a) A Java session bean updating entities.

```
1   @Entity public class Customer {
2       @Id String id;
3       @Min(value=0) int status;
4       @NotNull String name;
5       @OneToMany
6       List<CustomerOrder> orders;

1   @Entity public class CustomerOrder {
2       @Id @GeneratedValue int orderId;
3       @Temporal Date orderDate;
4       @ManyToOne Customer customer;
5       @OneToMany
6       List<OrderItem> items;

1   @Entity public class OrderItem {
2       @Id @GeneratedValue int itemId;
3       @Min(value=0) int price;
4       @ManyToOne
5       CustomerOrder order;
```

(b) JPA entity classes used in the method incrementStatus.

Fig. 1. An Enterprise Java Bean that selects JPA entity objects of type Customer and increases the status level of these objects.

Based on a running example, we illustrate the challenges that arise when symbolically executing Java EE applications that use JPA to interact with a data store. A Java session-bean class of this example is depicted in Fig. 1a and the corresponding JPA entity classes in Fig. 1b. The method `incrementStatus` has three arguments: two numeric values s and r, and one object reference d. It selects all entities of type `Customer` that have made a revenue of at least r on all their orders from the date d. The status of such a customer is increased to s, if it is currently below s. In Fig. 1a the Java class `CustomerService` is implemented as a stateless Enterprise Java Bean (EJB). It uses dependency injection to have an instance of the JPA `EntityManager` injected into the field `em`. EJBs typically run inside a Java EE container, which ensures that the declared dependencies are resolved when an EJB is initialized. We assume that the EJB is executed in such an environment and that all dependencies are properly resolved, and hence `em` $\neq$ `null`. In the method `incrementStatus`, the string `ql` represents a select statement written in the Java Persistence Query Language (JPQL). JPQL is defined by JPA as an object-oriented query language that is independent of the way the entity objects are actually stored[1], e.g., in a relational database or in an object database. The string `ql` is used by the entity manager `em` to create a query object, set its parameters and retrieve entities satisfying the restrictions in `ql` from a data store by invoking the method `getResultList`. As a result, `cList` is a list of all those entities. Note that the elements in `cList` strongly depend on the database state at the time the method `getResultList` is executed. Finally, the method iterates over the elements in `cList` and updates the status in case the current status level of a customer is lower than the given level in s. The aim of our test-case generation approach is to increase the control-flow coverage of an EJB method that interacts with a data store via JPA. In particular, our approach generates both concrete input values for the method arguments, as well as a database state that is required for a specific path through the method. The database state is represented as a set of entity objects that must exist in the data store before the test case is executed.

In order to generate test cases for such an application, we need to address the following challenges:

(1) JPA offers many different methods to interact with a data store, e.g., `getResultList` and `find`. The result of most JPA methods depends on the state of the data store at the time the method is invoked. In order to identify a required state, we have implemented a *symbolic object data store* that tracks all changes made by the application (e.g., persist an entity), and is able to dynamically populate new entities that are required for a specific control flow of the method under test. An entry in a table of the symbolic data store is a tuple of expressions consisting of logic variables (in the sense of logic programming [1]), constants, and operation symbols. Additionally, there is a list of constraints relating these logic variables.

(2) The assumption that the dependencies of an EJB are properly resolved poses two challenges. First, executing a test case that uses an EJB must ensure that the EJB runs inside a Java EE container that supports dependency injection. Second, the symbolic execution system that we have used

---

[1] http://docs.oracle.com/html/E13946_04/ejb3_langref.html, accessed January 2017.

in this paper runs inside a standalone environment and had no support of Java EE functionalities yet. For the first challenge, we have used a JUnit integration testing framework[2] to deploy and run the EJB inside a Java EE container. The JUnit test connects to this container and invokes the method under test of the EJB via a Web-Service. For the second challenge, we have implemented support for dependency injection while symbolically executing a Java method. This avoids `NullPointerExceptions` when accessing the entity manager while symbolically executing the application.

(3) The JPQL query string can be built dynamically by the application, which makes it hard to statically extract the query string from the program [8]. However, when the method `createQuery` of the entity manager is invoked, the first parameter must be a symbolic object reference of type `String` having a field `value` which contains the string representation of the query to be executed. We use this string to get hold of the query which shall be submitted to the database. In this context, we perform a concolic execution since we operate on concrete query strings. When the query string has been extracted, we have to determine its structure in order to generate entities corresponding to this query and satisfying restrictions of the entities (e.g. `@NotNull` or `@Min(value = 0)` in Fig. 1b). We have used the ANTLR parser [14] to parse the JPQL string and deliver a tree representation of it. We also have to integrate those constraints with the constraints from the method's control flow, such that the satisfiability of the constraints collected on an explored path in the method can be determined.

(4) In order to generate an implicit test oracle, we have to distinguish between the set of entities that are required to exist in the data store before the test case is executed, and the set of entities that exist in the data store when the symbolic execution of the method under test completes. We call the first set *pre-execution required* and the second set *post-execution expected*. We have implemented a symbolic object data store that manages both sets.

In summary, our contributions are the following:

– We have extended a Java bytecode based symbolic execution system to execute Java EE applications using JPA to interact with a data store. We have integrated constraints from the entity definitions and queries with constraints originating from the application's control flow.
– By solving the resulting system of constraints for a representative set of execution paths, we can ensure that all nodes and edges of the control-flow graph will be covered (if they are reachable), even if the control flow depends on the state of the database.
– An evaluation of our approach on a set of benchmarks, including a comparison to a state of the art tool to generate JUnit tests for Java applications.

The rest of this paper is structured as follows. In Sect. 2, we explain the symbolic execution of Java bytecode and present a running example that motivates our

---

[2] http://arquillian.org/, accessed March 2017.

work. In Sect. 3, we show how we fill our symbolic data store such that it corresponds to the JPQL queries and control-flow branches occurring on an execution path of the considered program. In Sect. 4, we evaluate our approach based on a set of benchmarks. In Sect. 5, we discuss related work. Finally in Sect. 6, we conclude and point out future work. We also name the limitations of our current prototypical implementation.

2   Symbolic Execution of Java Bytecode

Symbolic execution [9] is a program analysis technique for systematically exploring paths through a program. A symbolic executor interprets the program with symbolic values (represented by logic variables) instead of concrete values as inputs. When it executes a conditional branch instruction depending on symbolic values, it forks the execution and explores all possible continuations of the control flow (in our case using backtracking with iterative deepening as search strategy). As a result, a *path condition* is the conjunction of all conditions chosen along a particular path, and it represents constraints over symbolic values that must be satisfied for that particular path.

A constraint solver can examine the satisfiability of these constraints, and thus determine whether a particular path can be triggered by any valid concrete input values.[3]

A classic algorithm [18] to generate test cases with symbolic execution takes a program $\mathcal{P}$ with a set $\mathcal{V}$ of variables, a set $\mathcal{V}_{in} \subseteq \mathcal{V}$ of input variables, and a set $\mathcal{I}$ of instructions. The aim is to find concrete values for all $v \in \mathcal{V}_{in}$, such that (in the case of control-flow coverage) every (reachable) node and edge of the control-flow graph (see Fig. 2 for an example) is covered by the execution path corresponding to at least one test case. In order to systematically explore all these paths, it is necessary to track the different states a symbolically executed program has, when it follows a particular path. Such a state includes the (possibly symbolic) values of variables in $\mathcal{V}$, the path condition, and a program counter for the currently executed instruction [9]. A *symbolic value* is an expression consisting of logic variables, constants, and operation symbols.

Since our approach must consider the state of a data store that is used by an object-oriented program, we extend this definition. We define the state S of a symbolically executed, database-driven, object-oriented program as a quintuple $S = (\Gamma, X, c, p, r)$. The database state Γ represents both the set of pre-execution required entities as well as the set of post-execution expected entities. Both sets are dynamically constructed during the symbolic execution. Each variable $v \in \mathcal{V}$ has some (possibly) symbolic value $x_v \in X$. c represents the condition of the path currently being explored. The program counter p represents the current instruction being executed, and r is the method's result value. Hence, $r = \perp$ until a path has been explored. Note that even a method without an explicit return value (void) can have a result value r, e.g., an uncaught exception. The

---

[3] If an explored path contains a bug, the input values that trigger it can be derived from the path condition.

execution of an instruction $i \in \mathcal{I}$ changes the state S and might cause the program to terminate. In that case, the exploration of the current path has been completed and c can be evaluated in order to find concrete values for the symbolic inputs in $\mathcal{V}_{in}$ that trigger the inspected path. Moreover, the path condition c can also contain constraints over the attributes of entities in the pre-execution required set of Γ. Thus, an evaluation of c also gives concrete values for attributes of the entities that are required to exist in a data store to follow a particular path in the program.

The symbolic execution of a Java program is challenging, since the Java bytecode offers a broad range of instructions[4] with possibly complex behavior. Java uses a stack to provide the operands for an instruction. If the instruction produces a result, it pushes this result onto the stack. The operand stack of a method and the values of its local variables are organized in a *frame* that is created each time a method is invoked and destroyed when it completes.

The symbolic execution that we use is based on a Symbolic Java Virtual Machine (SJVM) [6,12]. Roughly speaking, the SJVM integrates the features of a non-symbolic Java Virtual Machine [11] such as heap and frame stacks with components known from the Warren Abstract Machine (WAM) [1], which is used for the execution of Prolog programs. In particular, it includes a *choice-point stack* and *trail*. A choice-point represents an alternative computation branch, which is tried after backtracking. Backtracking happens, when the accumulated system of constraints is no longer satisfiable or when a possible computation path is finished and alternative computations shall be tried. The trail records all changes of the state of the SJVM. When backtracking, all such changes are undone that happened since the creation of the last choice point. The symbolic execution finishes, when every feasible branch of each choice point has been explored (or another termination criterion is met). In Fig. 3, the state of our SJVM after executing line 16 of the example in Fig. 1a is sketched. The corresponding picture will be explained in more detail later on.

There are variables of a primitive data type (such as `int`). All other variables refer to objects. An object may have several attributes, each of which may have a symbolic or concrete value. We write $o.a = b$ to assign the (possibly symbolic) value b to the attribute a of the object o. A *null reference* is a special object reference referring to no object.

We illustrate our extensions to that system with the class in Fig. 1a. The symbolic execution of the method `incrementStatus` starts with initializing the class `CustomerService`. After a class has been initialized, instances of it can be generated. Since the method `incrementStatus` is not static, the SJVM requires an object of type `CustomerService` to symbolically execute it. Thus, such an object is created. Each attribute of this object is initially represented by a logic variable, which may later on be bound to a (possibly structured) symbolic value and eventually to a concrete value. Some attributes may receive a value by dependency injection. In order to cope with this, we scan the respective Java

---

[4] https://docs.oracle.com/javase/specs/jvms/se8/html/jvms-6.html, accessed March 2017.

class in order to find attributes that are annotated for dependency injection, such as the attribute em in Fig. 1a. For each injectable attribute a of an object o, we generate a new reference r to an object of the type t of the corresponding attribute a, and set $o.a = r$. After an object of class CustomerService has been created, a new frame for the method under test is generated and symbolically executed by the SJVM, as explained in the following.

Figure 2 shows the control-flow graph based on Java bytecode of the method in Fig. 1a. The program address of each instruction is written before a colon and the mnemonic of the bytecode instruction after it, followed by a short comment in italic. The instruction at program address 4 loads a reference to an object o of type CustomerService onto the operand stack. The next instruction pushes the (symbolic) value of the field em of the object o onto the stack, which is by our construction a reference to an object of type EntityManager and guaranteed not to be null. The instruction at program address 8 pushes a string constant (variable ql in Fig. 1a), and the instruction at program address 10 a reference to an object of class Customer onto the operand stack. The instruction at program address 12 consumes both constants and creates a JPA query object.

At this point, we have made one of our major extensions to the system. The JPA consists of a couple of Java interfaces, and thus its methods are executed by the invokeinterface instruction. We have enhanced the symbolic execution of this instruction in order to identify the invocation of JPA methods that require a special handling. One of these methods is createQuery of the EntityManager. Instead of just symbolically executing this method, we identify the concrete query string from the first, and the concrete class type from the second argument. We use the Hibernate semantic query model (SQM) [4] to parse the JPQL query string with an ANTLR 4 parser [14] into a comprehensive Java object of type SqmStatement. We create an instance q of a wrapper class that stores the SqmStatement object, and a hashmap for its parameters. As a result, the execution of the instruction at program address 12 pushes q onto the operand stack. In block 3 and 4 of Fig. 2, q is used to set the parameters sum and date. Note that the parameters r and d will have symbolic values that have been passed as arguments to the method.

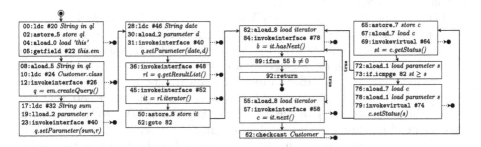

Fig. 2. Control-flow graph based on the Java bytecode of the method incrementStatus in Fig. 1a.

The instruction at program address 36 uses q to generate a result list rl for the query. At this point, the result of the method invocation depends on the state of the data store. The execution of an `invokeinterface` instruction, that invokes the method `getResultList` on an object-reference of our wrapper class, results in the generation of a *symbolic query result list* with a symbolic length l and a reference to q. Roughly speaking, this list allows to dynamically add elements to it that satisfy the restrictions in q while following a specific path of the application. The construction of this list is explained in detail in Sect. 3. In order to iterate over the elements in that list, we create a new *symbolic iterator* in the instruction at program address 45. This iterator has a concrete counter value idx for the index of the current iteration. Invoking method `hasNext` by the instruction `invokeinterface` (at program address 84) results in a (symbolic) value b. Via backtracking, we will try both possible values `true` and `false` for b. Thus, we first set b to `true` and create a choice point referring to the other alternative. Then, we push it onto the choice-point stack. In addition, we will add the constraint $l > idx$ to the constraint store making sure that the length l of the result list rl is at least idx. When backtracking to this choice point, we will set b to `false` and remove the choice point from the choice-point stack. In addition, we will replace the mentioned constraint by $l \leq idx$.

If b is true, we will enter the body of the `for`-loop (at program address 55). Otherwise, we will continue at program address 92, where the current path ends. In the body of the `for`-loop, the instruction at program address 57 pushes the element e_{idx} at position idx of the result list rl onto the operand stack. In our example, e_{idx} refers to an object of type `Customer`. Note that in general such an object has to satisfy the restrictions made in the query and the restrictions enforced by the entity class (here `Customer`). However, in our example there are no such restrictions. Thus, e_{idx}.`status` may assume any integer value. Next (at program address 69), we push the symbolic values e_{idx}.`status` and s (method argument) onto the operand stack, and check whether e_{idx}.`status` $\geq s$. Since there are no restrictions on e_{idx}.`status` and on s, we can easily generate symbolic values and corresponding constraints such that both possible results `true` and `false` of the comparison will be tried via backtracking analogously as we did it for the results of `hasNext` above. The first alternative continues with the instruction at program address 82.

The corresponding state of the SJVM is depicted in Fig. 3. Here, boxes with "?" represent logic variables. Note that also `int` variables such as `s` and `r` are represented by logic variables in the heap of the SJVM. Note also that the end of the list `cList` is represented by a logic variable. Thus, if this list needs to have more elements in order to fulfill the constraints, new elements can be appended by binding the logic variable correspondingly. Moreover note that the two operands consumed by the instruction `if_cmpge` are added to the trail such that the previous state can be reestablished after backtracking. The corresponding program address is stored in the newly created choice point on the choice point stack. Finally, the constraint $st > s$ is added to the constraint stack. If the accumulated set of constraints gets unsatisfiable, backtracking will occur and an

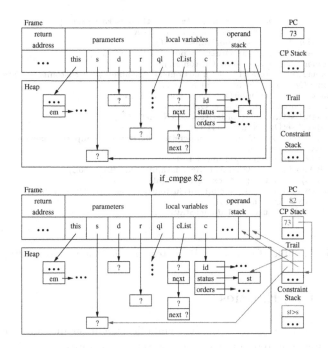

Fig. 3. State of the SJVM at instruction 73 of Fig. 2.

alternative computation indicated by the topmost choice point will be tried. Due to the lack of space, we skip the explanation of the remaining symbolic execution. Note that the potential branching due to possible exceptions thrown by the bytecode instructions `getfield` and `invokeinterface` can in fact not happen due to data dependencies. Thus, when the symbolic execution tries to reach one of the corresponding exits in Fig. 2, the constraint solver will determine that the current set of constraints is no longer satisfiable and will initiate backtracking. Since these exits are unreachable, the edges leading to them are dotted rather than solid.

For the considered example in Fig. 2, our test-case generator produces three test cases. Figure 4 shows the test case in which the query result list `cList` is expected to have one entity e_c of type `Customer` that has a lower status level than the first method parameter s. Hence, it is expected that the method under test increases the status level of e_c to s. Note that at least one entity of each JPA class `CustomerOrder`, `Customer`, and `OrderItem` is required to exist in the database before the method under test is invoked (line 15). Those entities must be joined (line 7 and 11), and some of their attributes require specific values. The next section describes the generation of those entities in detail.

```
1   @Test public void testIncrementStatus3() throws Exception {
2   //     (1) create pre−execution required data
3   transaction.begin(); em.joinTransaction();
4   CustomerOrder customerOrder1 = new CustomerOrder();
5   Customer customer1 = new Customer();
6   customer1.setCustomerId("#"); customer1.setName("#"); customer1.setStatus(0);
7   customerOrder1.setCustomer(customer1);
8   customerOrder1.setOrderDate(new java.util.Date(0));
9   OrderItem orderItem1 = new OrderItem();
10  orderItem1.setPrice(1); orderItem1.setName("#");
11  orderItem1.setOrder(customerOrder1);
12  em.persist(customerOrder1); em.persist(orderItem1); em.persist(customer1);
13  transaction.commit();
14  //     (2) execute method under test
15  testedClass.incrementStatus(1, new java.util.Date(0), −50L);
16  //     (3) check the post−execution database state
17  Customer customer1_db = em.find(Customer.class, customer1.getId());
18  assertNotNull(customer1_db);
19  assertEquals(1, customer1_db.getStatus());
20  }
```

Fig. 4. Example of generated JUnit test case for the method in Fig. 1a.

3   Generating Entities

The current database state Γ of the symbolic execution includes the set E_{req} of pre-execution required entities, and the set E_{app} representing the data store used by the AUT. At the end of the computation, E_{app} corresponds to the set of post-execution expected entities, and hence an implicit test oracle can compare it with the actual database state after a test execution. When the AUT generates a new entity e_a during its symbolic execution, e_a is added to E_{app}, and when it deletes an entity e_a, e_a is removed from E_{app}. When an entity e_r is required to exist in a data store in order to follow a specific path in the AUT, e_r is added to E_{req}. For each required entity e_r an entity e_a cloned from e_r is added to E_{app}. The AUT operates on the set E_{app}. The logic variables of the elements in the set E_{req} are used to generate path constraints. The AUT can set a new logic variable to an attribute of an element in E_{app}, but (without backtracking) never reset a logic variable for an attribute of an element in E_{req}. Therefore, in our running example in Fig. 1a, we set e_a.status $= s$ in line 22, but we retain e_r.status $= \eta$ with η being a logic variable having the constraint $\eta < s$ (see line 21). The connection between e_a and e_r is in particular useful for an auto-generated identifier, where the concrete identifier is not known, when the JUnit file is created by our symbolic execution system. For example in line 17 of Fig. 4, the identifier of the pre-execution required entity customer1 is used to find the post-execution expected entity customer1_db.

The EntityManager is a central component in JPA that allows both, to operate on a single entity as well as to create a query that operates on multiple entities. In the next two subsections, we describe how we dynamically generate entities in both cases.

3.1 Entity Manager Method Invocations

The persist(e) method of the EntityManager is a commonly used JPA method to make an entity e persistent in the data store. However, if the data store already contains an entity with the same identifier as e, the execution does not continue with the next instruction in the application, but rather the method is supposed to throw an unchecked exception that can result in a different control flow. We analyze the identifier attribute a_{id} of e and the database state Γ to decide whether we fork the control flow into (1) a branch in which e already exists in the data store, and (2) a branch in which e does not exist in the data store.

If a_{id} is a generated value (@GeneratedValue annotation, see Fig. 1b), we assume that the persistence framework (e.g. Hibernate) generates a non-existing identifier for e. We therefore add e to E_{app} and continue the symbolic execution with the next instruction. If a_{id} is not a generated value, but there already exists an entity with the same identifier as e in the data store, the execution of the invokeinterface instruction for this method throws an unchecked exception, and we continue the symbolic execution with the instruction that catches the execption. Otherwise, we create a new choice point that forks the current control flow. In the first branch, we simply add e to E_{app} and continue the symbolic execution with the next instruction. In the second branch, we create a new entity e^*, set $e^*.a_{id} = e.a_{id}$, add $e^*.a_{id}$ to E_{req}, and throw an unchecked exception, since the identifier of the entity e now already exists in the data store.

Since an entity is simply a Java object, we first create a new object o of the given entity type t having logic variables as attributes. For an attribute that has a static JPA entity constraint (e.g. @Min(1)), we add a constraint for the corresponding logic variable to the path condition.

Another commonly used method of the EntityManager is find(c,id). It returns an entity of the entity class c from the data store that has an identifier id, or it returns null if no such entity exists in the data store. First, we check whether E_{app} contains any entity of type c that has id as its identifier. In that case, we push that entity onto the operand stack and continue the symbolic execution with the next instruction. Otherwise, we push a logic variable r representing the result onto the operand stack. In case a following instruction in the program requires $r \neq$ null, we proceed as in described in the beginning of this subsection and create a new object e to which r refers, set $e.a_{id} = id$, and add e to E_{req}. If an instruction requires $r =$ null, we do not change E_{req} and simply set $r =$ null.

We currently support the following data types for entity objects: all Java primitives, String, Date, Collection, and List. As data types for identifier, we currently support numeric and string values.

Other JPA methods such as merge and remove are handled analogously.

3.2 Generating Entity Objects from a JPQL Query

The entity manager allows to create a query that selects entities from a data store. This entity generation process is more challenging, since it can include the generation of multiple entities that must have specific values as specified by the query. We support queries that are either using a JPQL string, or queries that were built using the JPA Criteria API[5].

When the JPA method `getResultList` is symbolically executed, we first generate a result list. This list initially consists of all the elements in E_{app} which have been enforced by previous constraints concerning entities of the involved entity types (i.e. database tables) and the query. The end of this list is represented by a logic variable, which may later on be bound in order to add further elements enforced by subsequent constraints. From E_{app}, we take all the elements of entity types (i.e. database tables) mentioned in the `FROM` clause of the query and perform the corresponding join (see Fig. 5). Then, we eliminate all results which violate the `WHERE` clause or `HAVING` clause. Finally, we project the remaining tuples onto the attributes mentioned in the `SELECT` clause.

Once the initial query-result list has been generated, it can happen that due to subsequent constraints the method under test requires later on more elements to exist in the list. Since the elements in that list depend on the query as well as on the state of the database, we have implemented an entity generator that is associated to the result list. The generator is dynamically executed each time a new entry in the result list is required and generates one entry at a time. Additionally, it adds all the corresponding entities, which produce the entry when joined, to E_{req} and E_{app} (see Table 1, initial entities, for an example). An overview of the generator is depicted in Fig. 5. In a first step, it creates an initial entity set E derived from the `FROM` and `JOIN` clauses. We join two (object oriented) entities e_1 and e_2 by connecting them through a constraint of the form $e_1.a = e_2$.[6]

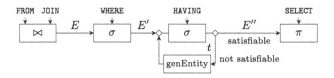

Fig. 5. Overview of the element generator for the symbolic query result list.

After these initial entities are created, we use the selection predicate in the query's `WHERE` clause to generate additional constraints on the logic variables of the attributes of the entities. We support selection predicates which are conjunctions of clauses of the form a op b, where a and b are entity attributes, constants, or symbolic values, and $op \in \{>, \geq, <, \leq, =, \neq\}$.

Similarly to the previous step, we now apply potential aggregation constraints. We support the following aggregation operations: `SUM`, `AVG`, `COUNT`. Since

---
[5] https://docs.oracle.com/javaee/7/tutorial/partpersist.htm, Chap. 40.
[6] From a database point of view, this corresponds to a constraint $e1.foreignKey = e2.primaryKey$.

each aggregation operation is applied to entities of exactly one entity type t, we know that the aggregation has failed on t, if the constraints derived from the aggregation are not satisfiable. Thus, we will generate a new entity of type t and try the aggregation again. In our running example in Fig. 1a, adding a new order item could cause the sum of prices to reach the requested minimal amount (line 14).

If the aggregation clause can be satisfied, we can apply a projection as specified in the query's SELECT clause to extract the *result-list entry* from the generated entities. Additionally, we add the generated entity references to E_{req} and E_{app} inside the data store.

Table 1. Phases of the entity object-reference generation process.

Phase	Entities			Constraint stack	
	OrderItem e_{oi}	CustomerOrder e_{co}	Customer e_c	Level	Constraint
Initial entities	order $= e_{co}$	items $= \{e_{oi}\}$	orders $= \{e_{co}\}$	1	items.length > 0
		customer $= e_c$		2	orders.length > 0
Static constraints	price $= p$		status $= s$	3	$p \geq 0$
			name $= n$	4	$s \geq 0$
				5	$n \neq$ null
Where		orderDate $= od$		6	$od \geq d$
Having				7	$p \geq r$

We illustrate the result-list generator with the JPQL query from our running example in Fig. 1a. Since we start the symbolic execution with an empty data store and the method incrementStatus does not persist any data, the result list cList is initially empty. In order to enter the for-loop in line 20, the list requires at least one element of type Customer. We generate that element as an entity object by first analyzing the FROM and JOIN clause of the query that selects data from three entity types: OrderItem, CustomerOrder and Customer. First, an entity e_{oi} of type OrderItem is generated for the specified FROM clause. Next, the query joins this entity with an entity of type CustomerOrder. We therefore generate an entity e_{co} of that type. Both entities e_{oi} and e_{co} are joined on the specified attribute order in e_{oi}, by setting e_{oi}.order $= e_{co}$. For the second join, we generate an entity e_c of type Customer, and set e_{co}.customer $= e_c$. In Table 1, the result of these three entity generations and the respective join operations is referred to as the *initial entities* in the first phase. In this phase, we add two constraints for the list items in e_{co} and the list orders in e_c as shown in Table 1.

In the next step, we apply static constraints on the entities that are derived from the entity specifications in Fig. 1b. The entity type OrderItem has a constraint the attribute price to be greater or equal to zero. We therefore add the constraint e_{oi}.price ≥ 0 to the constraint stack. For the entity of type Customer, we add the constraints e_c.status ≥ 0 and e_c.name $\neq$ null to the constraint stack.

Subsequently, we generate constraints derived from the query's WHERE clause: e_{co}.orderDate $\geq d$, with d being a logic variable passed as method argument.

Last, we generate constraints derived from the query's `HAVING` clause, which is applied to the attribute `price` of all `OrderItem` entities that have been generated so far, i.e. e_{oi}. We therefore add the constraint $e_{oi}.\texttt{price} \geq r$ to the constraint stack.

4   Empirical Study

We have implemented our test-case generation approach as an extension to the symbolic execution system Muggl [12]. As a constraint solver, we have used JaCoP [10]. For each discovered path through the method under test (MUT), the system generates a test similar to the test shown in Fig. 4. All tests for a method are stored in one JUnit file. A test case for a method is executed in three steps: (1) persist the required entities in the database, (2) execute the MUT, and (3) check the method result and the post-execution expected database state.

The test case has an instance of the session bean injected that is used to invoke the MUT. It also has an instance of the JPA `EntityManager` injected that is used to persist data in the test database before the MUT is executed, and to query for entities to check the post-execution database state. Since the test-case execution requires an implementation of this manager, we run our JUnit tests on a WildFly[7] application server that uses Hibernate as an implementation of JPA. As a data store, we use a H2 in-memory database that is started by the WildFly server. In order to deploy the AUT on the WildFly server and to run the JUnit test inside its container, we use Arquillian[8] as an integration testing framework. In order to test a complete EJB class, we generate test cases for each of the EJB's methods and combine them in a JUnit test suite file.

We have evaluated our approach with the EJBs of the Java EE projects listed in Table 2, that all use JPA to interact with a database. The methods of those EJBs create, persist, update, and remove entities from a database, as well as query for entities either via the `find` method of the `EntityManager`, or with a query that is built by either a JPQL string or with the JPA Criteria API. In our evaluation, we answer the research question:

What is the effect on branch coverage by a systematic generation of entities for test cases for Java EE applications using JPA to interact with a database?

We compared our deterministic approach with the state of the art unit-test generation tool EvoSuite [7]. Our main aim is to increase the branch coverage. However, there are a couple of business methods that select entities from a data store, and apply operations on these entities without explicitly branching the control flow (e.g., with an `if`-statement). We therefore included the line coverage in our evaluation results as well. The column headed with # shows the total number of branches and lines per class. For the evaluated methods of the EJBs, our approach generates test cases within a few seconds. We observe

---

[7] http://wildfly.org/, accessed March 2017.
[8] http://arquillian.org/, accessed March 2017.

that our test cases execute the complete MUT, and do not throw unexpected exceptions (e.g. JPA constraint violation exceptions). In order to enable the repetition of our evaluation and to reproduce the results, we have released the symbolic execution system including our extensions, as well as a couple of sample Java EE projects, as open-source on a GitHub repository[9].

We evaluated the session beans of the projects listed in Table 2. In order to measure the branch and line coverage of our approach, we have used the JaCoCo[10] code-coverage tool. Similar to the empirical study in [2], we ran Evo-Suite with a default configuration 30 times for each EJB class. We used the statistics generated by EvoSuite to compare both test-case generation tools. These statistics are very similar to the ones that JaCoCo produces.

Table 2. Comparison of generated unit tests statistics by Muggl and by EvoSuite on different Java EE projects.

Java EE project	EJB class	Branch coverage			Line coverage		
		#	Muggl	EvoSuite	#	Muggl	EvoSuite
WWU Library	BookServiceBean	9	100%	78%	21	100%	90%
	CopyServiceBean	12	100%	83%	28	100%	93%
	LoanServiceBean	10	100%	40%	25	100%	40%
	UserServiceBean	8	100%	88%	16	100%	94%
Oracle Case Study Dukes Bookstore	BookRequestBean	12	100%	67%	43	93%	63%
Oracle Case Study Dukes Tutoring	AdminBean	47	87%	100%	172	90%	92%
Oracle Tutorial Order	RequestBean	25	92%	68%	138	85%	58%
Oracle Tutorial Roster	RequestBeanNoCriteria	18	89%	56%	119	97%	58%
	RequestBeanQueries	29	55%	45%	188	83%	57%

We executed the generated test cases from EvoSuite with the `EvoRunner`. Despite the fact that the generated test cases by EvoSuite run successfully, we found that some of these tests – in contrast to our approach – do not consider JPA constraints specified in the entity classes, which results in a JPA constraint violation. We have used EvoSuite in version 1.0.4, which currently seems to have trouble initializing EJBs with a `@PostConstruct` annotated method, i.e. a method that is executed once dependency injection is done. In our evaluation, we have therefore rewritten this method in order to be able to generate test cases for the respective Java EE projects with EvoSuite as well. Some of the branches that are not covered by our approach are due to JPQL queries that are currently not supported by our approach, such as the locating of substrings (`LOCATE`); or due to an unsupported initialization of classes, such as JavaServer Faces (JSF) classes. For methods of the latter kind, EvoSuite produces test cases with a higher coverage. In the *Oracle Roster* example, we know that certain branches and lines cannot be reached for the EJB `RequestBeanQueries`, since we have previously made sure that the required entity manager has in fact been injected.

---

[9] https://github.com/wwu-pi/tap17-muggl-javaee.
[10] http://www.eclemma.org/jacoco/, accessed March 2017.

Thus, we actually cover 100% of the reachable branches and lines and refrain from generating useless test cases.

The results show that our approach generates test cases with a high branch coverage for EJBs that use JPA to interact with a database system. In particular, our approach produces a higher branch coverage on methods of an EJB that have a control flow which strongly depends on the result of a query made to a database – compared to the state of the art testing tool EvoSuite. On the other hand, EvoSuite produces better results on methods that use functionalities that we currently do not support.

5   Related Work

There are two works that are closest to our work. First, Arcuri and Fraser [2] implemented a proper bean initialization for the search-based test-case generation tool EvoSuite [7]. Their results show that a proper initialization of the bean as class under test already increases the control-flow coverage, e.g., by avoiding unexpected `NullPointerException`s. We support dependency injection typically used by EJBs that interact with a database system via JPA, such as the injection of an instance of `EntityManager`, and the invocation of a `@PostConstruct` annotated method after the initialization of a session bean has completed. In addition to that, our main contribution is the generation of entity objects that must exist in the database before a test case is executed. This is especially useful to cover control-flow paths that dependent on a specific database state, as shown by our running example in Fig. 1a. Emmi et al. [5] use a dynamic symbolic execution to generate both test input data for the program and a required database state. Similarly to our approach, they have also used a symbolic database, though our implementation of it is based on entities as objects in contrast to a relational database. In our symbolic data store, we distinguish between the pre-execution required database state and the post-execution expected state. In contrast to [5], we also support the challenging `JOIN` operation and aggregation functions (e.g. `SUM`), which require the generation of multiple entities for a required result of a query. Other works [17] mock the database-related objects instead of using an actual database.

6   Conclusions, Limitations, and Future Work

We have presented an approach which generates a set of test cases such that all (reachable) nodes and edges of the control-flow graph are covered. Our main contribution is that we not only consider the constraints occurring when passing branching statements but also consider the constraints imposed by the database. Thus, we generate database states such that the control flow is covered. Our prototypical implementation extends the test-case generator Muggl [6,12], which is based on a symbolic Java virtual machine. We have compared our tool to a state of the art test-case generator and shown that it increases the control-flow coverage for a set of benchmarks.

Currently, our prototypical implementation does not support multithreading and reflection. Also, our implementation uses in case of an inadmissably long runtime some artificial stopping criteria such as a maximal runtime or a maximal nesting depth of method calls. If these criteria cause the test-case generation to stop, a complete coverage of the control flow can no longer be guaranteed. However as our experiments show, such a loss of completeness rarely happens in practice. As future work, we would like to also support other coverage criteria such as data-flow coverage.

References

1. Ait-Kaci, H.: Warren's Abstract Machine: A Tutorial Reconstruction. MIT Press, Cambridge (1991)
2. Arcuri, A., Fraser, G.: Java enterprise edition support in search-Based JUnit test generation. In: Sarro, F., Deb, K. (eds.) SSBSE 2016. LNCS, vol. 9962, pp. 3–17. Springer, Cham (2016). doi:10.1007/978-3-319-47106-8_1
3. Diakopoulos, N., Cass, S.: Interactive: The Top Programming Languages 2016. IEEE Spectrum (2016). http://spectrum.ieee.org/static/interactive-the-top-pro gramming-languages-2016
4. Ebersole, S.: Semantic Query Model and Interpreter for HQL/JPQL and JPA Criteria Queries. Hibernate (2017). https://github.com/hibernate/hibernate-semantic-query
5. Emmi, M., Majumdar, R., Sen, K.: Dynamic test input generation for database applications. In: Proceedings of the 2007 International Symposium on Software Testing and Analysis, pp. 151–162. ACM (2007)
6. Ernsting, M., Majchrzak, T.A., Kuchen, H.: Dynamic solution of linear constraints for test case generation. In: Margaria, T., Qiu, Z., Yang, H. (eds.) 6th International Conference on Theoretical Aspects of Software Engineering, pp. 271–274. IEEE, Beijing (2012)
7. Fraser, G., Arcuri, A.: EvoSuite: automatic test suite generation for object-oriented software. In: Proceedings of the 19th ACM SIGSOFT Symposium and the 13th European Conference on Foundations of Software Engineering, pp. 416–419. ACM (2011)
8. Gould, C., Su, Z., Devanbu, P.: Static checking of dynamically generated queries in database applications. In: Proceedings of the 26th International Conference on Software Engineering, pp. 645–654. IEEE Computer Society (2004)
9. King, J.C.: Symbolic execution and program testing. Commun. ACM 19(7), 385–394 (1976)
10. Kuchcinski, K., Szymanek, R.: Jacop - Java constraint programming solver. In: Proceedings of of CP Solvers: Modeling, Applications, Integration, and Standardization (2013)
11. Lindholm, T., Yellin, F., Bracha, G., Buckley, A.: The Java Virtual Machine Specification, Java SE 8 Edion. Addison Wesley, Boston (2014)
12. Majchrzak, T.A., Kuchen, H.: Automated test case generation based on coverage analysis. In: Proceedings of the 3rd IEEE International Symposium on Theoretical Aspects of Software Engineering, pp. 259–266. Tianjin, China (2009)
13. Pacheco, C., Lahiri, S.K., Ernst, M.D., Ball, T.: Feedback-directed random test generation. In: Proceedings of the 29th International Conference on Software Engineering, pp. 75–84. IEEE Computer Society (2007)

14. Parr, T.: The Definitive ANTLR 4 Reference. Pragmatic Bookshelf, Raleigh (2013)
15. Prasetya, I.: T3i: a tool for generating and querying test suites for Java. In: Proceedings of the 2015 10th Joint Meeting on Foundations of Software Engineering, pp. 950–953. ACM (2015)
16. Sakti, A., Pesant, G., Guéhéneuc, Y.G.: Instance generator and problem representation to improve object oriented code coverage. IEEE Trans. Softw. Eng. **41**(3), 294–313 (2015)
17. Taneja, K., Zhang, Y., Xie, T.: MODA: automated test generation for database applications via mock objects. In: Proceedings of the IEEE/ACM International Conference on Automated Software Engineering, pp. 289–292. ACM (2010)
18. Yi, Q., Yang, Z., Guo, S., Wang, C., Liu, J., Zhao, C.: Postconditioned symbolic execution. In: 2015 IEEE 8th International Conference on Software Testing, Verification and Validation (ICST), pp. 1–10. IEEE (2015)

Model-Based Testing of Probabilistic Systems with Stochastic Time

Marcus Gerhold and Mariëlle Stoelinga$^{(\boxtimes)}$

University of Twente, Enschede, The Netherlands
m.gerhold@utwente.nl, marielle@cs.utwente.nl

Abstract. This paper presents a model-based testing framework for black-box probabilistic systems with stochastic continuous time. Markov automata are used as an underlying model. We show how to generate, execute and evaluate test cases automatically from a probabilistically timed requirements model. In doing so, we connect classical **ioco**-theory with statistical hypothesis testing; our **ioco**-style algorithms test for functional behaviour, while χ^2 hypothesis tests and confidence interval estimations assess the statistical correctness of the system.

A crucial development are the classical soundness and completeness properties of our framework. Soundness states that test cases assign the correct verdict, while completeness states that our methods are powerful enough to discover each discrepancy in functional or statistical misbehaviour, up to arbitrary precision.

We illustrate our framework via the Bluetooth device discovery protocol.

1 Introduction

The role of computer-based systems is ever increasing: robots, drones and autonomous cars will soon pervade our lives. Attuning to this progress, verification and validation techniques of these systems have grown to a field of crucial importance. They provide methods that show whether the actual and the intended behaviour of a system differ, or give confidence that they do not.

Conversely, the progressively intricate design of embedded systems continuously brings new challenges to the field of verification engineers. The key question of whether a system works as intended therefore has a variety of angles: Was the functional behaviour correctly implemented? Does the system continue to operate under a work overload? Is the average lifetime within safety regulations? Can requirements be met on time?

Probabilistic aspects in many computer applications naturally add one of those angles. Security protocols use random bits in their encryption methods [9], control policies in robots lead to the emerging fields of probabilistic robotics [46],

This research has been partially funded by STW and ProRail under the project ArRangeer (12238), STW under the project SEQUOIA (15474), NWO under the project BEAT (612.001.303), NWO under the project SamSam (628.005.015), and the EU under the project SUCCESS (509-18240).

© Springer International Publishing AG 2017
S. Gabmeyer and E.B. Johnsen (Eds.): TAP 2017, LNCS 10375, pp. 77–97, 2017.
DOI: 10.1007/978-3-319-61467-0_5

hidden Markov chains are used in speech recognition [39] and communication protocols are often equipped with a stochastic delay [15,44]. Therefore, there is a natural demand for a pendant in the verification and validation community that accounts for probabilistic aspects.

Testing. To investigate such questions, probabilistic verification has become a mature research field with techniques like stochastic model checking (SMC) [38] based on models like probabilistic automata [40], Markov decision processes [37], generalised stochastic Petri nets [33] or stochastic automata [12]. These techniques are complemented with tools like PRISM [29], PLASMA [27] or the MODEST toolset [20].

In practice, however, the most common validation technique is testing. The system is subjected to many well-designed test cases and the outcome is compared to a specification. A verdict, i.e. *pass* or *fail*, is then given based on the expectations.

This paper presents a model-based testing (MBT) approach that can handle probabilistic and stochastic-time aspects in systems. MBT gained a lot of traction in recent years in both academia and industry. It mirrors the faster development of systems, by providing access to faster test methods due to automation. Test cases are automatically generated, executed and evaluated based on a requirements specification. A number of industrial and academic MBT tools have been developed, such as TorXakis [35], MaTeLo [19], UPPAAL Tron [22] or SpecExplorer [51].

There is a large body of different frameworks that accommodate a variety of requirements aspects, like functional properties [50], real-time [2,6,30], quantitative aspects [3,5] and coverage [7]. Surprisingly, only few papers are concerned with the testing of probabilistic systems[1], with some notable exceptions being [24–26].

We present an applicable framework in an MBT setting, that is capable of verifying if probabilistic choices made by the system itself were implemented correctly. Furthermore, the approach also accommodates stochastic-time aspects of systems, such as specified delays, degradation rates or intended waiting periods. This is of particular interest, if only the mean duration of an activity is known.

Our Approach. The foundation of our methodology are Markov automata (MAs). MAs are equipped with both probabilistic and nondeterministic choices. The first represent choices made by the system (e.g. coin tosses or random seeds) or the environment (e.g. degradation rates or failure probabilities). The latter model choices that are not under its control. As widely agreed [40,43], nondeterminism is crucial for implementation freedom, scheduling choices and interleaving. Complementary, they are of particular interest because of their memoryless exponential distributed timed transitions. These give a highly appropriate stochastic approximation, if only the mean duration of an activity is known, as is often the case in a practical setting. Mathematically, MAs arise as the

---

[1] The topic of statistical testing, e.g. [1,52], is concerned with choosing test inputs probabilistically; it does not check the correctness of the random choices made by a system itself.

conservative extension of both probabilistic automata (PAs) [40] and interactive Markov chains (IMCs) [21].

An important contribution are our algorithms that automatically generate, execute and evaluate probabilistic test cases from a specification MA. They check the functional, probabilistic and stochastic-time behaviour of the system. Probabilities are observed via frequencies, hence, test cases need to be repeated multiple times. We use statistical hypothesis testing, in particular χ^2 testing, to assess whether a test should *pass* or *fail*.

To account for the correctness of our framework, we prove it to be *sound* and *complete*. Soundness states that each test case assigns the correct verdict, while completeness (a.k.a. exhaustiveness) guarantees that the test method is powerful enough to discover each deviation from the requirements. Phrasing these results requires a mathematical notion of conformance. We propose the **Mar-ioco** relation, an implementation relation that pins down precisely when an implementation modelled as an MA conforms to a requirements specification model. We prove **Mar-ioco** to be a conservative extension to the **ioco** relation known from MBT literature [47,50]. Lastly, we provide a case study on the Bluetooth device discovery protocol showing the applicability of our framework.

While test efficiency is essential, this paper focusses on the methodological set up and correctness. Imperative future research is to optimize the statistical verdicts we give and provide fully fledged tool support.

We summarize our key contributions:

1. The general input output Markov automata model comprising discrete probability distributions, non-deterministic choices and exponentially delayed transitions,
2. a behavioural description for Markov automata based on trace semantics,
3. solid definitions of probabilistic test cases, test execution and verdicts,
4. the treatment of the absence of outputs in a stochastically time delayed setting and
5. the soundness and completeness results of our framework.

Related Work. There is a large body of work on testing real-time systems [2,6,28,30]. Briones and Brinksma [6] extend the framework to incorporate the notion of quiescence, i.e. the absence of outputs.

Conversely, probabilistic testing preorders and equivalences are well-studied [10,14,40]. Distinguished work by [31] introduces the concept of probabilistic bisimulation via hypothesis testing. Largely influential work is given by [8], presenting how to observe trace frequencies during a sampling process. Executable probabilistic test frameworks are suggested for probabilistic finite state machines in [23,26] and Petri nets [4].

Closely related to our work is the study of Markovian bisimulation. The foundation of an observational equivalence is presented in [16] in the form of weak bisimulation for Markov automata, and was refined by introducing late-weak bisimulation [13,42] and branching bisimulation [49].

This paper is an extension of earlier work [17] that investigated the test process in the probabilistic setting and a workshop paper [18] sketching how stochastic time and exponential delays can be incorporated. Novel contributions of the current version are the complete integration of stochastic-time delays and the treatment of quiescence.

Overview Over the Paper. In Sect. 2 we recall definitions of Markov automata. Section 3 describes how Markov automata are used in the testing process and Sect. 4 shows that our framework is sound and complete. We show experimental results in Sect. 5. The paper ends in Sect. 6 with conclusions and future work.

2   Markov Automata

We recall properties of Markov automata and show how nondeterminism is resolved. We assume that the reader is acquainted with the basics of probability theory, but recall integral definitions. In particular, we borrow the standard construction of probability spaces via σ-fields. See [11] for an excellent overview and further reading.

Probability. A *discrete probability distribution* over a set X is a function $\mu : X \to [0, 1]$, such that $\sum_{x \in X} \mu(x) = 1$. The set of all distributions over X is denoted *Distr* (X) and subdistributions *SubDistr* (X) respectively.

Let Ω be a set, $\mathcal{F}$ a σ-field of Ω and $(\Omega, \mathcal{F})$ the resulting measurable space. A σ-additive function $\mu : \mathcal{F} \to [0, 1]$ is called a *probability measure*, if $\mu(\Omega) = 1$. We denote the set of all probability measures over X by *Meas* (X).

A *probability space* is a triple $(\Omega, \mathcal{F}, Pr)$, where Ω is a set, $\mathcal{F}$ is a σ-field of Ω and $Pr : \mathcal{F} \to [0, 1]$ is a probability measure, such that $Pr(\Omega) = 1$ and $Pr(\bigcup_{i=1}^{\infty} A_i) = \sum_{i=1}^{\infty} Pr(A_i)$ for $A_i \in \mathcal{F}$, $i = 1, 2 \ldots$ pairwise disjoint.

2.1   The Markov Automaton Model

Markov automata [48] comprise nondeterministic choices, discrete probability distributions and exponentially delayed transitions. They allow modelling choices made by the system (e.g. coin tosses) or the environment (e.g. degradation rates) and are an appropriate stochastic approximation, if only the mean duration of an activity is known.

Definition 1. *A* Markov automaton $\mathcal{M} = \langle S, s_0, L, \to, \rightsquigarrow \rangle$ *is a five-tuple, consisting of*

- *S a set of states, with s_0 the unique starting state,*
- *L a set of actions,*
- *$\to \subseteq S \times L \times Distr(S)$, the probabilistic transition relation and*
- *$\rightsquigarrow \subseteq S \times \mathbb{R}_{\geq 0} \times S$, the Markovian transition relation.*

An IOMA is an MA, where $L = L_i \sqcup L_o \sqcup L_\tau$ is the disjoint union of input, output, and internal actions respectively, containing a special quiescence label $\delta \in L_o$.

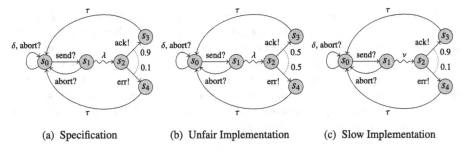

(a) Specification   (b) Unfair Implementation   (c) Slow Implementation

Fig. 1. Protocol specification IOMA and two erroneous implementations. After the input *send?* there is an exponentially delayed transition, followed by an acknowledgement or error output.

If we replace $\to$ *by* $\to' \subseteq S \times Distr\,(L \times S)$ *with the requirement that for all* $(s, \mu) \in \to'$ *if* $\mu\,(s, a) > 0$ *for an input* $a \in L_i$, *then* $\mu\,(s, b) = 0$ *for all* $b \neq a$, *the input output MA becomes* input-reactive *and* output-generative.

An action a is *enabled* in state s, if there is a distribution μ, such that $(s, \mu) \in \to$ and $\mu\,(a, s') > 0$ for some $s' \in S$. We write *enabled* $\{s\}$ for the set of enabled actions in s. A state is called *probabilistic*, if at least one action of L is enabled. A state is called *input-enabled*, if all actions of the set L_i are enabled. A state is called *Markovian*, if it has at least one transition $(s, \lambda, s') \in \leadsto$. The Markovian actions are parameters for the exponentially delayed transitions and therefore deemed invisible.

A distinctive feature of Markov automata are their exponentially distributed timed transitions, i.e. the set $\leadsto$. The *rate* to go from a state s to a state s' is the sum of all λ, such that $(s, \lambda, s') \in \leadsto$ and is denoted $\mathbf{R}\,(s, s')$. The sum of all rates in a state s is called *exit rate* of s and denoted by $\mathbf{E}\,(s)$. We require $\mathbf{E}\,(s) < \infty$ for all $s \in S$. The *delay* associated with a Markovian state is exponentially distributed with its exit rate. Multiple Markovian transitions in one state thus lead to a *race condition*. The probability to move from s to a successor s' equals the probability that (one of) the Markovian transitions leading from s to s' wins the race. This induces the *discrete branching probability distribution* $\mathbb{P}_s$ for s given by $\mathbb{P}_s\,(s') = \mathbf{R}\,(s, s')\,/\mathbf{E}\,(s)$.

A state is called *stable*, if it enables no internal action. We employ the maximal progress assumption, meaning that time is not allowed to progress in unstable states. This renders Markovian transitions in unstable states unnecessary [32].

Example 1. Fig. 1 shows three input-reactive output-generative IOMA. The model describes a protocol that associates a delay with every sent action, followed by an acknowledgement or error. Input is suffixed with "*?*" and output with "*!*". Discrete probability distributions are denoted with a dotted arc, together with the action label and corresponding probabilities. Markovian actions are presented as staggered arrows.

After the *send?* input is received, there is an expected delay indicated by the Markovian action λ. The delay is exponentially distributed, thus, the probability to go from s_1 to s_2 in T time units is $1 - e^{-\lambda T}$. In state s_2 there is one outgoing discrete probability distribution. The specification in Fig. 1a implies that only 10% of all messages should end in an error report and the remaining 90% get delivered correctly. After a message is delivered, the automaton goes back to its initial state where it stays quiescent until input is provided. This is denoted with the δ self-loop, marking the desired absence of outputs.

2.2   Paths and Traces

Let $\mathcal{M} = \langle S, s_0, L, \rightarrow, \rightsquigarrow \rangle$ be an IOMA. We define the usual language theoretic concepts. A *path* π of $\mathcal{M}$ is a (possibly) infinite sequence of the form

$$\pi = s_1\, t_1\, \mu_1\, \alpha_1\, s_2\, t_2\, \mu_2\, \alpha_2 \ldots ,$$

where $s_i \in S$, $t_i \in \mathbb{R}_{\geq 0}$, $\mu_i \in \rightarrow \cup \mathbb{P}_{s_i}$ and $\alpha_i \in L \cup \mathbb{R}_{\geq 0}$ for $i = 1, 2, \ldots$. We require that each finite path ends in a state. The sequence $s_i\, t_i\, \mu_i\, \alpha_i\, s_{i+1}$ means that $\mathcal{M}$ resided t_i time units in state s_i before moving to s_{i+1} via α_i using the distribution μ_i. The *length* of a finite path, denoted $|\pi|$, is the number of input and output actions occurring on it.

Note that measuring a single time point in continuous time results in probability zero. Hence, it is necessary to talk about time intervals instead of individual time values. An *abstract path* is a path, where each occurrence of single time values t_i is replaced by intervals $I_i \subseteq \mathbb{R}_{\geq 0}$. However, we limit our interested to intervals of the form $[0, t]$ with $t \in \mathbb{R}_{\geq 0}$. Consequently, any path can be replaced with its abstract path by changing t_i to $[0, t_i]$ or vice versa. This convention lets us use both notions interchangeably.

The *trace* of a path $tr\,(\pi)$ only records its visible behaviour, i.e. time and input/output actions. It is given by the (possibly) infinite sequence of the form

$$\sigma = tr\,(\pi) = t_1\, a_1\, t_2\, a_2 \ldots ,$$

where $t_i \in \mathbb{R}_{\geq 0}$ and $a_i \in L_i \cup L_o$ for $i = 1, 2, \ldots$. The length of a trace is the length of its corresponding paths. Note that a path fragment $s_1\, t_1\, \mu_1\, \lambda\, s_2\, t_2\, \mu_2\, a\, s_3$ collapses to $(t_1 + t_2)\, a$ if λ is a Markovian action. Technically, Markovian actions are just parameters for an exponential delay and therefore invisible. Similar to abstract paths, an *abstract trace* is given, if all $t_i \in \mathbb{R}_{\geq 0}$ of a trace are replaced by intervals $I_i \subseteq \mathbb{R}_{\geq 0}$. Again, we limit ourselves to abstract traces only using intervals of the form $[0, t]$ with $t \in \mathbb{R}_{\geq 0}$. This enables us to use traces and abstract traces interchangeably.

We denote the set finite paths $Paths^*\,(\mathcal{M})$ ($Traces^*\,(\mathcal{M})$ resp.) and abstract paths as $AbsPaths^*\,(\mathcal{M})$ ($AbsTraces^*\,(\mathcal{M})$ resp.) and omit the asterisk to include the infinite case. We use $ctraces\,(\mathcal{M})$ to denote the set of traces ending in a deadlock state. Lastly, let the operator $act\,(\pi)$ return the *action path* of π by removing all time values t_i and distributions μ_i. For traces $act\,(\sigma)$ returns visible actions only.

2.3 Traces and Their Probabilities

Similar to how the visible behaviour of a labelled transition system (LTS) is given by its traces, the visible behaviour of an IOMA is given by its trace distributions. A trace distribution is a probability space, that assigns probabilities to all traces. A trace of an LTS is obtained by removing all states and internal actions from a given path. We do the same in the IOMA case: First we resolve all nondeterministic choices via an adversary and then remove all invisible information. The resolution of nondeterministic behaviour leads to a purely probabilistic structure.

The mathematical framework for infinite abstract paths is technically more involved, but completely standard [43]. A classical result in measure theory [11] shows, that it is impossible to assign a probability to *all* sets of traces in nontrivial scenarios. To illustrate: the probability of always rolling a 6 with a die is 0, but the probability of rolling a 6 within the first 100 tries is positive. To resolve this, we use a cone construction of sets of traces.

Adversaries and Path Probability. Similar to [40,43], adversaries form the core concept of our framework. Given any finite piece of history leading to the current state, an adversary returns a distribution over the available transitions.

Definition 2. *An* adversary A *of an IOMA* $\mathcal{M} = \langle S, s_0, L, \rightarrow, \rightsquigarrow \rangle$ *is a function*

$$A : Paths^* (\mathcal{M}) \longrightarrow Distr (Distr (L \times S) \cup \{\bot\}),$$

such that for each finite path π *only available distributions are scheduled, i.e.*

$$\forall \pi \in Paths^* (\mathcal{M}) : A (\pi) (\mu) > 0, \text{ then } (last (\pi), \mu) \in \rightarrow .$$

The value $A(\pi)(\bot)$ *is the probability to* interrupt/halt *the process. An adversary* A *halts on path* π, *if* $A(\pi)(\bot) = 1$. *We say an adversary is of* length $k \in \mathbb{N}$, *if it halts for all paths* π *with length greater or equal to* k. *We denote this set by* $adv (\mathcal{M}, k)$ *and the set of all adversaries by* $adv (\mathcal{M})$ *respectively.*

An adversary resolves all nondeterministic choices of an IOMA making it possible to calculate the probability for each path via the probabilistic execution function. Probabilistic executions assign the unique starting state probability 1 and each following transition either multiplies the probability that the scheduler assigned to an action or, if no action was scheduled, the probability of a Markovian action taking place in a certain time interval.

Definition 3. *Let* A *be an adversary of an IOMA* $\mathcal{M}$, *then we define the* probabilistic execution function $P_A : AbsPaths (\mathcal{M}) \rightarrow [0,1]$ *inductively by* $P_A(s_0) = 1$ *and*

$$P_A (\Pi \cdot I\alpha\mu s) = P_A (\Pi) \cdot \begin{cases} A (\pi) (\mu) \cdot \mu (\alpha, s) & \text{if } \alpha \in L \\ \int_I \mathbf{R} (last (\Pi), s) e^{-\mathbf{E}(last(\Pi))t} dt & \text{if } \alpha \in \mathbb{R}_{\geq 0} \end{cases},$$

where $I = [0, T] \subseteq \mathbb{R}_{\geq 0}$ *and* π *is the corresponding path to the abstract path* Π.

The probability space of an adversary is constructed based on *cones* of paths [40]. The cone C_π of a path π contains all paths that have π as prefix. Given $A \in adv\,(\mathcal{M})$, let $\Omega_A := Paths\,(\mathcal{M})$ be the sample set and $\mathcal{F}_A$ be the smallest σ-field generated by the set of cones $\{C_\Pi \subseteq Paths\,(\mathcal{M}) \mid \Pi \in AbsPaths^*\,(\mathcal{M})\}$. Standard measure theory arguments [11] ensure that P_A induces a unique probability measure on the measurable space $(\Omega_A, \mathcal{F}_A)$. Hence, an adversary induces a probability space $(\Omega_A, \mathcal{F}_A, P_A)$ on a Markov automaton.

Trace Distributions. A trace distribution is obtained from (the probability space of) an adversary, in the way a trace is obtained from a path; all invisible behaviour is removed. Intuitively, the probability assigned to a set of abstract traces X, is defined as the probability assigned to all abstract paths whose abstract trace is an element of X.

Definition 4. *The trace distribution D of an adversary A is the probability space $(\Omega_D, \mathcal{F}_D, Pr_D)$ given by $\Omega_D = Traces\,(\mathcal{M})$, $\mathcal{F}_D$ as the smallest σ-field generated by the set of cones $\{C_\sigma \subseteq Traces\,(\mathcal{M}) \mid \sigma \in AbsTraces^*\,(\mathcal{M})\}$ and P_D as the unique probability measure on $\mathcal{F}_D$, such that $P_D\,(X) = P_A\,\left(tr^{-1}\,(X)\right)$ for $X \in \mathcal{F}_D$*

A trace distribution is of length $k \in \mathbb{N}$, if it based on an adversary of length k. We denote the set of all such trace distributions by $Trd\,(\mathcal{M}, k)$. The set of all trace distributions is denoted by $Trd\,(\mathcal{M})$. This naturally induces an equivalence relation, denoted $=_{TD}$, that equates two IOMAs, if they have the same set of trace distributions.

3   Testing with Markov Automata

Model-based testing entails automatic test case generation, execution, and evaluation. We formalize the notion of offline tests and show how they can be generated in batch or on-the-fly. The functional correctness of a system under test (SUT) is assessed upon test execution. To evaluate the probabilistic correctness of the system, tests are executed multiple times and recorded in a sample. The trace frequencies observed in a sample are then compared to their expectations. Consequently, an implementation is deemed correct, if these frequencies are within certain confidence intervals given by the requirements.

3.1   Test Generation

Test Cases. We consider test cases as sets of traces based on an action signature consisting of inputs and outputs (L_i, L_o). These traces describe the possible behaviour of a tester. In each state of a test, a tester may decide to stimulate the SUT, observe its possible outputs or stop the process altogether.

Mathematically, we consider test cases as input-reactive and output-generative probabilistic automata, i.e. Markov automata with $\rightsquigarrow= \emptyset$. This enables us to model the choices of stimulating, observing or stopping probabilistically. Note that, even in the non-probabilistic case, the test cases are often created probabilistically in practice. However, this is rarely ever supported in theory. Thus, our definition fills a small gap here.

Definition 5. *A test over an action signature* (L_i, L_o) *is an IOMA of the form* $t = (S, s_0, L_o \setminus \{\delta\}, L_i \cup \{\delta\}, \{\tau_{stop}, \tau_{stim}, \tau_{obs}\}, \rightarrow, \emptyset)$, *such that*

- *t is internally deterministic and does not contain an infinite path;*
- *t is acyclic and connected;*
- *For every state* $s \in S$, *either*
  - $enabled\{s\} = \emptyset$
  - $enabled\{s\} = \{\tau_{stop}, \tau_{stim}, \tau_{obs}\}$
  - $enabled\{s\} = L_i \cup \{\delta\}$
  - $enabled\{s\} \subseteq L_o \setminus \{\delta\}$

A test for a specification IOMA $\mathcal{M} = \langle S, s_0, L, \rightarrow, \rightsquigarrow \rangle$ *is a test over its action signature.*

Note that the action signature of tests has switched input and output labels. This is to allow for synchronisation in a parallel composition with an implementation IOMA.

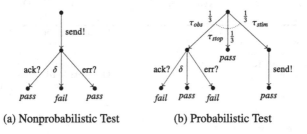

(a) Nonprobabilistic Test   (b) Probabilistic Test

Fig. 2. A regular test and a probabilistic test derived for the specification of Fig. 1.

Example 2. Fig. 2 shows two test cases for the specification IOMA in Fig. 1. The probabilistic test case models the possible behaviour of a tester. Here, a probabilistic choice is made with $\frac{1}{3}$ on whether to stop, stimulate or wait for responses of the system. Traces in the tests are labelled *pass* or *fail* according to Definition 6.

Annotations. To state whether observed functional behaviour is deemed correct, each trace of a test is annotated with a verdict; *pass* for correct and *fail* for erroneous behaviour. The classical **ioco** test case annotation [47] suffices here. Informally, all traces of a test, that are also present in the specification, get annotated as correct.

Definition 6. *For a test t, a test annotation is a function* $a : ctraces(t) \longrightarrow \{pass, fail\}$. *A pair* $\hat{t} = (t, a)$ *consisting of a test and an annotation is called an* annotated test. *If t is a test for a specification* $\mathcal{S}$ *we define the annotation* $a_{\mathcal{S},t} : ctraces(t) \longrightarrow \{pass, fail\}$ *by*

$$a_{\mathcal{S},t}(\sigma) = \begin{cases} fail & if \ \exists \ \varrho \in Traces\,(\mathcal{S})\,, a! \in L_O^\delta : \varrho a! \sqsubseteq \sigma \wedge \varrho a! \notin Traces\,(\mathcal{S})\,; \\ pass & otherwise, \end{cases}$$

where $\sqsubseteq$ denotes the prefix relation for traces.

Algorithms. Algorithm 1 presents the batch test generation according to Definition 5. The inputs are a specification IOMA $\mathcal{M}$ and a history trace, which is initially empty. At each step of the computation, the algorithm decides probabilistically to stop with $p_{\sigma,1}$, stimulate with $p_{\sigma,2}$ or observe with $p_{\sigma,3}$. The latter two choices recursively call the batch-gen algorithm again with updated trace history. Note that $p_{\sigma,1} + p_{\sigma,2} + p_{\sigma,3} = 1$.

Algorithm 2 describes the on-the-fly test case derivation for a given specification $\mathcal{S}$, implementation $\mathcal{I}$ and upper limit for the test length n. It returns a verdict within the first n steps. The verdict is *fail* if unexpected output was encountered and *pass* otherwise. With probability $p_{\sigma,1}$ the algorithm observes the output of the implementation and with probability $p_{\sigma,2}$ it stimulates it with a new input. Note that $p_{\sigma,1} + p_{\sigma,2} = 1$.

Algorithm 1: Batch test generation for *Mar-ioco*.

Input: Specification IOMA $\mathcal{S}$ and history $\sigma \in traces\,(\mathcal{S})$.
Output: A test case t for $\mathcal{S}$.

1 **Procedure** batch$(\mathcal{S}, \sigma)$
2 $\quad p_{\sigma,1}\cdot[\text{true}] \rightarrow$
3 $\quad$ **return** $\{\tau_{stop}\}$
4 $\quad p_{\sigma,2}\cdot[\text{true}] \rightarrow$
5 $\quad$ result $:= \{\tau_{obs}\}$
6 $\quad$ **forall** $b! \in L_o$ **do:**
7 $\qquad$ **if** $\sigma b! \in traces\,(\mathcal{S})$:
8 $\qquad\quad$ result $:=$ result $\cup \{b!\sigma' \mid \sigma' \in$ batch $(\mathcal{S}, \sigma b!)\}$
9 $\qquad$ **else:**
10 $\qquad\quad$ result $:=$ result $\cup \{b!\}$
11 $\qquad$ **end**
12 $\quad$ **end**
13 $\quad$ **return** result
14 $\quad p_{\sigma,3}\cdot[\sigma a? \in traces\,(\mathcal{S})] \rightarrow$
15 $\quad$ result $:= \{\tau_{stim}\} \cup \{a?\sigma' \mid \sigma' \in$ batch $(\mathcal{S}, \sigma a?)\}$
16 $\quad$ **forall** $b! \in L_O$ **do:**
17 $\qquad$ **if** $\sigma b! \in traces\,(\mathcal{S})$:
18 $\qquad\quad$ result $:=$ result $\cup \{b!\sigma' \mid \sigma' \in$ batch $(\mathcal{S}, \sigma b!)\}$
19 $\qquad$ **else:**
20 $\qquad\quad$ result $:=$ result $\cup \{b!\}$
21 $\qquad$ **end**
22 $\quad$ **end**
23 $\quad$ **return** result

Algorithm 2: On-the-fly test case derivation for *Mar-ioco*.

Input: Specification IOMA $\mathcal{S}$, an implementation $\mathcal{I}$ and an upper bound for the test length $n \in \mathbb{N}$.
Output: Verdict pass if Impl. was ioco conform in the first n steps and fail if not.

1 $\sigma := \epsilon$
2 **while** $|\sigma| < n$ **do:**
3 $\quad p_{\sigma,1}\cdot[\text{true}] \rightarrow$
4 $\quad$ *observe next output* $b!$ *(possibly δ) of $\mathcal{I}$*
5 $\quad \sigma := \sigma b!$
6 $\quad$ **if** $\sigma \notin traces\,(\mathcal{S})$:
7 $\qquad$ **return** fail
8 $\quad p_{\sigma,2} \cdot [\sigma a? \in traces\,(\mathcal{S})] \rightarrow$
9 $\quad$ **try:**
10 $\qquad$ **atomic**
11 $\qquad\quad$ *stimulate I with a?*
12 $\qquad\quad \sigma := \sigma a?$
13 $\qquad$ **end**
14 $\quad$ **catch** *an output $b!$ occurs before a? could be applied*
15 $\qquad \sigma := \sigma b!$
16 $\qquad$ **if** $\sigma \notin traces\,(\mathcal{S})$:
17 $\qquad\quad$ **return** fail
18 $\quad$
19 $\quad$ **end**
20 **end**
21 **return** pass

Theorem 7. *All test cases generated by Algorithm 1 are test cases according to Definition 5. All test cases generated by Algorithm 2 assign the correct functional verdict according to Definition 6.*

3.2   Test Execution

Since discrete probabilistic choices and stochastic time delay are integral parts of Markov automata, there is a twofold evaluation process of functional and statistical behaviour. While functional behaviour is assessed via the test annotation as in classic **ioco**-test theory [50], we focus on describing the sampling process to validate statistical correctness.

Sampling. In order to reason about probabilistic correctness, a single test execution is insufficient. Rather, we collect a sample via multiple test runs. The sampling process consists of a push-button experiment in the sense of [34]. Assume a black-box timed trace machine is given with inputs, time and action windows, and a reset button as illustrated in Fig. 3.

At the beginning of the experiment, we set the parameters for sample length $k \in \mathbb{N}$, sample width $m \in \mathbb{N}$ and a level of significance $\alpha \in (0,1)$. That is, we choose the length of individual runs, how many runs should be observed and a limit for the statistical *error of first kind*, i.e. the probability of rejecting a correct implementation.

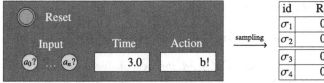

Fig. 3. Black box timed trace machine with input alphabet $a_0?, \ldots, a_n?$, reset button, and time and action windows. Running the machine m times and observing traces of length k yields a sample. The ID together with the trace and the respective number of occurrences are noted down.

We assume that the timer resets to 0 after every visible action and that two consecutive occurrences of the same action are distinguishable. An external observer records each individual execution before the reset button is pressed and the machine starts again. Thus, we collect m traces of length k, which are summarized as a *sample O*.

During each run the black-box $\mathcal{I}$ is governed by a trace distribution $D \in Trd(\mathcal{I})$. In order for any statistical reasoning to work, we assume that D is the same in every run. Thus, the SUT chooses a trace distribution D and D chooses a trace σ to execute.

Frequencies and expectations. We evaluate the deviation of a collected sample to the expected distribution. The latter is given for any underlying trace distribution D of the specification IOMA. Since the trace distribution is assumed to be the same for all runs, the expected probability to observe a trace σ is given by $\mathbb{E}^D(\sigma) = P_D(\sigma)$.

Depending on the accuracy of time measurement, it is unlikely to record the *exact* same timed trace more than once. Therefore, we group traces in classes based on the same visible action behaviour. For a given abstract trace σ, its class Σ_σ is the set of all abstract traces $\varrho \in O$, such that $act(\sigma) = act(\varrho)$. A sample of length k and width m then induces a frequency measure, given by

$$freq(O)(\sigma) = \frac{|\Sigma_\sigma|}{m} \Pi_{i=1}^k \frac{|\{\varrho \in \Sigma_\sigma \mid I_i^\varrho \subseteq I_i^\sigma\}|}{|\Sigma_\sigma|},$$

where I_i^ϱ denotes the i-th time interval of trace ϱ, for any abstract trace σ. The implementation is rejected for statistical reasons, should the deviation of the measure $freq(O)$ to $\mathbb{E}^D$ exceed a certain threshold based on α.

Acceptable outcomes. Conversely, we accept a sample O if $freq(O)$ lies within some distance, say r_α, of the expected distribution $\mathbb{E}^D$. Recall the definition of a closed ball centred at $x \in X$ with radius r as $B_r(x) = \{y \in X \mid dist(x,y) \leq r\}$. All measures deviating at most by r from the expected distribution are contained within the ball $B_r(\mathbb{E}^D)$, where $dist(u,v) := \sup_{\sigma \in (\mathbb{R}_{\geq 0} \times L)^k} \mid u(\sigma) - v(\sigma) \mid$ is the total variation distance of measures.

To limit the error of accepting an erroneous sample, we choose the smallest radius, such that the error of rejecting a correct sample is not greater than the a priori chosen level of significance $\alpha \in (0,1)$ by [2]

$$r_\alpha := \inf\{r \in \mathbb{R}_{>0} \mid P_D(freq^{-1}(B_r(\mathbb{E}^D))) > 1 - \alpha\}.$$

Definition 8. *For $k, m \in \mathbb{N}$ and an IOMA $\mathcal{M}$ the acceptable outcomes under a trace distribution $D \in Trd(\mathcal{M}, k)$ of significance level $\alpha \in (0,1)$ are given by the set*

$$Obs(D, \alpha, k, m) = \left\{ O \in \left((\mathbb{R}_{\geq 0} \times L)^k\right)^m \mid dist(freq(O), \mathbb{E}^D) \leq r_\alpha \right\}.$$

The set of observations of $\mathcal{M}$ of significance level $\alpha \in (0,1)$ is given by

$$Obs(\mathcal{M}, \alpha, k, m) = \bigcup_{D \in Trd(\mathcal{M},k)} Obs(D, \alpha, k, m).$$

The set of observations therefore guarantees two properties, reflecting the error of false rejection and false acceptance respectively:

1. If a sample O was truthfully generated by $\mathcal{M}$ or a behaviourally equivalent IOMA, then there is a trace distribution D such that $P_D(O) \geq 1 - \alpha$; and
2. if a sample O was generated by a behaviourally different MA, then for all trace distributions D' we have $P_{D'}(O) \leq \beta_m$,

---

[2] Note that $freq(O)$ is not a bijection, but used here for ease of notation.

where α is the predefined level of significance and β_m is unknown but minimal by construction. Note that $\beta_m \to 0$ as $m \to \infty$, thus the error of falsely accepting an erroneous sample decreases with increasing sample width. Here, behavioural equivalence is induced by trace distribution equivalence, cf. Definition 4.

Goodness of fit. In order to state whether a given sample O is a truthful observation of $\mathcal{M}$, we need to find a trace distribution $D \in Trd(\mathcal{M})$ such that $O \in Obs(D, m, k, \alpha)$. It guarantees that the error of rejecting a truthful sample is at most α. These sets are crucial for the soundness and completeness proofs. However, they are computationally intractable to gauge for every D, since there are uncountably many.

Instead, we use χ^2 hypothesis testing to assure that a sample is acceptable. The χ^2 score is calculated as:

$$\chi^2 = \sum_{i=1}^{l} \frac{\left(n(\Sigma_{\sigma_i}) - m\mathbb{E}^D(\Sigma_{\sigma_i})\right)^2}{m\mathbb{E}^D(\Sigma_{\sigma_i})} \quad \text{with} \quad l \leq m. \tag{1}$$

To find a trace distribution that gives a high likelihood to an observed sample, we need to find D, such that $\chi^2 < \chi^2_{crit}$. The critical value depends on α and the degrees of freedom in the statistical test. In this case the degrees of freedom are given by the number of trace classes minus one, i.e. the probability of one class is determined, if we know all others. The critical value for χ^2 tests can be calculated or universally looked up in a table.

By construction of adversaries, cf. Definition 2, we are interested in the resolution of the nondeterministic choices. Consequently, (1) turns into a satisfaction problem over a probability vector p in a rational function of two polynomials f and g as $f(p)/g(p)$. As [36] shows, optimization over rational functions and inequality constraints is **NP-hard**.

Since (1) neglects time stamps, we need to assure that the recorded time intervals correspond to the α confidence intervals of specified Markovian actions. That is

$$\forall \lambda \in \mathbb{R}_{\geq 0} \text{ with } (s, \lambda, s') \in \rightsquigarrow \text{ for } s, s' \in S : \lambda \in \left[\frac{2\sum_{i=1}^{n} t_i}{\chi^2_{2n}(1 - \alpha/2)}, \frac{2\sum_{i=1}^{n} t_i}{\chi^2_{2n}(\alpha/2)} \right],$$

The confidence intervals depend on a scheduler that solves the satisfaction problem.

3.3 Test Evaluation and Verdicts

An implementation should pass the test suite, if it passes the two verdicts for functional behaviour and probabilistic behaviour. This is reflected in the mathematical verdicts.

Definition 9. *Given a specification $\mathcal{S} = \langle S, s_0, L, \rightarrow, \rightsquigarrow \rangle$, an annotated test $\hat{t}$ for $\mathcal{S}$, $k, m \in \mathbb{N}$ where k is given by the trace length of $\hat{t}$ and a level of significance $\alpha \in (0, 1)$, we define the* functional verdict *as the function $v_{func} : IOMA \longrightarrow \{pass, fail\}$, with*

$$v_{func}(\mathcal{I}) = \begin{cases} pass & if\ \forall \sigma \in ctraces\,(\mathcal{I}\,||\,t) \cap ctraces\,(t) : a\,(\sigma) = pass \\ fail & otherwise, \end{cases}$$

and the probabilistic verdict as the function $v_{prob} : IOMA \longrightarrow \{pass, fail\}$, with

$$v_{prob}(\mathcal{I}) = \begin{cases} pass & if\ \exists D \in Trd\,(\mathcal{S}, k) : P_D\,(Obs\,(\mathcal{I}\,||\,t, \alpha, k, m)) \geq 1 - \alpha \\ fail & otherwise, \end{cases}$$

where $||$ denotes the parallel composition. The overall verdict is pass, iff an implementation passes both verdicts.

A note on quiescence. A test case needs to assess if an SUT is allowed to be unresponsive when output was expected [45]. Quiescence δ models the absence of output for indefinite time. Therefore, it should be regarded with caution in practical test scenarios. Earlier work assumes a global fixed time-out value set by a user [6].

Time progress of Markov automata is exponentially delayed, hence, a global time-out value has two disadvantages: 1. a time-out might occur, before a specified Markovian action takes place and 2. a *global* time-out value might unnecessarily prolong the test process. Therefore, our interest is to minimize the probability of erroneously declaring quiescence, while keeping the overall testing time as low as possible.

Assume a level of significance $\alpha \in (0,1)$ is given. Let λ be the exit rate of a state s. Then the exit rate of s is a random variable T that is exponentially distributed with parameter λ. The probability, that a Markovian action is executed before a state-specific maximum waiting time t_{max} expires should be greater than $(1 - \alpha)$, i.e.

$$P\,(T < t_{max}) > 1 - \alpha$$

Hence, choosing $t_{max} > -\frac{\log \alpha}{\lambda}$ minimizes the probability of assigning quiescence, when the SUT makes progress. Since the sum of exponential distributions is not exponentially distributed, we resort to less sharper bounds for consecutive Markovian transitions.

Example 3. Fig. 4 shows a simplistic specification of a file exchange protocol. An exponential distribution is used to model the time delay between sending a file and acknowledging its reception. Note that different expected delays are associated with sending a small or a large file respectively.

After a file was send, there is a chance that it gets lost and we do not receive the *acknowledge!* output. In this case the system is judged as quiescent, and therefore faulty. However, since $\nu \ll \lambda$ a test should wait at least $-\frac{\log \alpha}{10}$ time units in s_1 and $-\log \alpha$ in s_2, to minimize the probability to erroneously judge the system as quiescent, while also keeping the testing time as low as possible.

Regardless, for a sufficiently large sample size, an MBT-tool eventually erroneously observes quiescence. The right hand side of Fig. 4 therefore allows for some amount of quiescence observations depending on α.

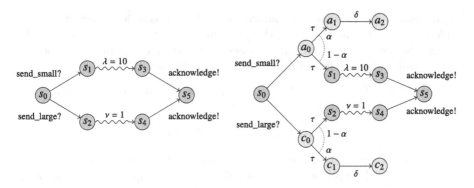

Fig. 4. Specification of a file exchange protocol. Sending a small file is expected to take less time. The right hand side models the possibility to erroneously declare quiescence probabilistically.

4   Conformance, Soundness and Completeness

A fundamental result of our work is the correctness of our framework, phrased as soundness and completeness. *Soundness* ensures that test cases assign the correct verdict. *Completeness* postulates that the framework is powerful enough to discover each deviation from the specification. In order to formulate these properties, we require a formal notion of conformance that we define as the **Mar-ioco** relation [18].

4.1   The Mar-Ioco Relation

The **ioco** relation as defined in [50] states, that an implementation conforms to a specification, if it never provides any unspecified output or quiescence. Mathematically, for two input-output transition systems $\mathcal{I}$ and $\mathcal{S}$, with $\mathcal{I}$ *input enabled*, we say $\mathcal{I} \sqsubseteq_{ioco} \mathcal{S}$, iff

$$\forall \sigma \in \textit{Traces} \, (\mathcal{S}) : \textit{out}_{\mathcal{I}} \, (\sigma) \subseteq \textit{out}_{\mathcal{S}} \, (\sigma) \, .$$

This restricts the theory to functional behaviour in the case of classic transition systems. To generalize **ioco** to Markov automata, we need two auxiliary concepts:

Trace Distribution Prefix. Given a trace distribution D of length k and a trace distribution D' of length greater or equal than k, we say D is a *prefix* of D', written $D \sqsubseteq_k D'$, if both assign the same probability to all traces of length k.

Output Continuation. Given a trace distribution D of length k, its *output continuation* is the set of trace distributions of length $k+1$ such that $D \sqsubseteq_k D'$, assigning probability zero to traces of length $k + 1$ ending in inputs. This set is denoted by $\textit{outcont}_{\mathcal{M}} \, (D)$.

We are now able to define the conformance relation **Mar-ioco**. Intuitively, an implementation is conforming, if the probability of every output trace can be matched by the specification. This includes the three factors: 1. functional behaviour, 2. probabilistic behaviour and 3. stochastic timing.

Definition 10. *Let $\mathcal{I}$ and $\mathcal{S}$ be IOMA with $\mathcal{I}$ input-enabled. We write $\mathcal{I} \sqsubseteq_{Mar-ioco} \mathcal{S}$, if for all $k \in \mathbb{N}$*

$$\forall D \in Trd\,(\mathcal{S}, k) : outcont_{\mathcal{I}}\,(D) \subseteq outcont_{\mathcal{S}}\,(D)\,.$$

The **Mar-ioco** relation conservatively extends the **ioco** relation to Markov automata. That is, both relations coincide for classic input output transition systems (IOTSs).

Theorem 11. *For two IOTSs $\mathcal{I}, \mathcal{S}$ with $\mathcal{I}$ input enabled, we have*

$$\mathcal{I} \sqsubseteq_{ioco} \mathcal{S} \Longleftrightarrow \mathcal{I} \sqsubseteq_{Mar-ioco} \mathcal{S}.$$

In **ioco** theory, the implementation is always assumed to be input enabled, to model that a tester can give any input at any moment. If the specification is input enabled too, **ioco** coincides with trace inclusion [50]. Assuming an input enabled specification, our results show, that **Mar-ioco** coincides with trace distribution inclusion. Moreover, the relation is transitive, just like **ioco** [50].

Theorem 12. *Let $\mathcal{A}, \mathcal{B}$ and $\mathcal{C}$ be IOMAs and let $\mathcal{A}$ and $\mathcal{B}$ be input enabled, then*

- $\mathcal{A} \sqsubseteq_{Mar-ioco} \mathcal{B}$ *if and only if* $\mathcal{A} \sqsubseteq_{TD} \mathcal{B}$.
- $\mathcal{A} \sqsubseteq_{Mar-ioco} \mathcal{B}$ *and* $\mathcal{B} \sqsubseteq_{Mar-ioco} \mathcal{C}$ *imply* $\mathcal{A} \sqsubseteq_{Mar-ioco} \mathcal{C}$.

4.2   Soundness and Completeness

Since the underlying model is probabilistic, there remains a degree of uncertainty known as the *errors of first and second kind*. For MBT of probabilistic systems this translates to the likelihood to reject a correct implementation, and to accept an erroneous one respectively. Hence, a test suite can only be considered sound and complete with a guaranteed (high) probability.

Soundness expresses for a given $\alpha \in (0, 1)$, that there is a $(1 - \alpha)$ probability, that a correct system passes the test suite for sufficiently large sample width m.

Theorem 13. *Each annotated test for an IOMA $\mathcal{S}$ is sound for every level of significance $\alpha \in (0, 1)$ with respect to **Mar-ioco**.*

Completeness of a test suite is inherently a theoretical result. Possible loops and infinite behaviour in the SUT require a test suite of infinite size. Further, there is the chance of accepting an erroneous implementation, i.e. the error of second kind. However, the latter is bound from above and decreases with larger sample size.

Theorem 14. *The set of all annotated tests for an IOMA $\mathcal{S}$ is complete for every level of significance $\alpha \in (0, 1)$ with respect to **Mar-ioco**.*

5 Experiments on the Bluetooth Device Discovery Protocol

Bluetooth is a wireless communication technology standard [41] specifically aimed at low-powered devices that communicate over short distances. To cope with inference, the protocol uses a frequency hopping scheme in its initialisation period. Before any communication can take place, Bluetooth devices organise themselves into small networks called *piconets* consisting of one *master* and up to seven *slave* devices.

To illustrate our framework, we study the discovery phase for one master and one slave device. We give a high level overview of the protocol in this case. The reader is referred to [15] for a detailed description on the protocol in a more general setting.

To resolve possible interference, the master and slave device communicate on a previously agreed sequence of 32 frequencies. Both devices have a 28-bit clock that ticks every $312.5\mu s$. Every two consecutive ticks, the master device sends packages on two frequencies, followed by a two-tick listening period on the same frequencies. It picks the broadcasting frequency according to the formula:

$$freq = [CLK_{16-12} + off + (CLK_{4-2,0} - CLK_{16-12}) \bmod 16] \bmod 32,$$

where CLK_{i-j} marks the bits $i, \ldots, j$ of the clock and $off \in \mathbb{N}$ is an offset. The master device chooses one of two tracks and switches to the other every $2.56s$. Moreover, every $1.28s$, i.e. every time the 12th bit of the clock changes, a frequency is swapped between the two tracks. For simplicity, we chose $off = 1$ for track one and $off = 17$ for track two, such that the two tracks initially comprise frequencies $1, \ldots, 16$ and $17, \ldots, 32$.

Conversely, the slave device periodically scans on the 32 frequencies and is either in a sleeping or listening state. To ensure the eventual connection, the hopping rate of the slave device is much slower. Every $0.64s$ it listens to one frequency in a window of $11.25ms$ and sleeps during the remaining time. It cycles to the next frequency after $1.28s$. This is enough for the master device to broadcast on 16 different frequencies.

We implemented the protocol and two mutants in Java 7; 1. the *master mutant* never switches between tracks one and two, therefore covering far less different frequencies than the correct protocol in the same time and 2. the *slave mutant* only listens for $5.65ms$ every $1.28s$ and therefore has a much longer sleeping period.

Since the time to connect two devices is deterministic for any initial state, we assumed that the clocks are desynchronized, i.e. the master sends out packages, while the slave starts listening after a uniformly chosen random waiting time. The expected waiting time $1/\lambda$ for an established connection is therefore estimated as $1.325s$, i.e. $\lambda \approx 0.755$.

Figure 5a shows the high level specification of the protocol. The request for both devices to synchronise is either followed by an acknowledgement or a time-out. Note that the amount of allowed time-outs is part of the specification and depends on α. A collected sample therefore consisted of the traces

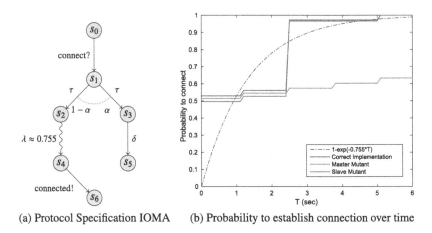

(a) Protocol Specification IOMA   (b) Probability to establish connection over time

Fig. 5. High level specification of the Bluetooth device discovery protocol for one master and one slave device. The time to establish a connection for a correct implementation and two mutants is compared to the assumed underlying exponential distribution with parameter $\lambda \approx 0.755$.

$\sigma_1 = 0$ *connect? t connected!* and $\sigma_2 = 0$ *connect? t δ*. Figure 5b shows the cumulative probability distribution to connect within T seconds of the assumed underlying distribution $1 - exp\left(-0.755T\right)$ and sample data collected for 10^3 runs of the correct implementation and the two mutants.

To mitigate statistical deviations, we collected 10^3 samples of the size 10^3 to calculate the average confidence intervals for $\alpha = 0.05$. The confidence interval of the correct implementation resulted in $[0.721, 0.824]$, containing the assumed value $\lambda = 0.755$ and was therefore judged as correct. The average connection time of the master mutant was $30.2s$ with a confidence interval of $[0.030, 0.034]$ and was therefore rejected. Dividing the listening time of the slave mutant into half had a less significant impact and gave a confidence interval of $[0.781, 0.887]$. It was consequently rejected with a small margin.

6   Conclusions and Future Work

We presented a sound and complete framework to test probabilistic systems with sotchastic-time delays based on a model. We defined a conformance relation in the **ioco** tradition called **Mar-ioco** pinning down precisely what *correctness* means. Our algorithms provide test cases that are sound with respect to this notion. Probabilistic correctness is assessed after a sampling process that counts frequencies of traces and compares them to statistical requirements.

Future work should comprise the practical aspects of our work: more powerful statistical methods facilitating efficient tool support. Lastly, we plan to apply our framework to a case study of larger size.

Acknowledgements. We would like to thank David Huistra for his aid on the case study.

References

1. Beyer, M., Dulz, W.: Scenario-based statistical testing of quality of service requirements. In: Leue, S., Systä, T.J. (eds.) Scenarios: Models, Transformations and Tools. LNCS, vol. 3466, pp. 152–173. Springer, Heidelberg (2005). doi:10.1007/11495628_9
2. Bohnenkamp, H., Belinfante, A.: Timed testing with TorX. In: Fitzgerald, J., Hayes, I.J., Tarlecki, A. (eds.) FM 2005. LNCS, vol. 3582, pp. 173–188. Springer, Heidelberg (2005). doi:10.1007/11526841_13
3. Bohnenkamp, H., Stoelinga, M.: Quantitative testing. In: Proceedings of the 8th International Conference on Embedded Software, (EMSOFT), pp. 227–236. ACM (2008)
4. Böhr, F.: Model-based statistical testing of embedded systems. In: IEEE 4th International Conference on Software Testing, Verification and Validation, pp. 18–25 (2011)
5. Bozga, M., David, A. Hartmanns, H., Hermanns, H., Larsen, K.G., Legay, A., Tretmans, J.: State-of-the-art tools and techniques for quantitative modelling and analysis of embedded systems. In: DATE, pp. 370–375 (2012)
6. Briones, L.B., Brinksma, E.: A test generation framework for *quiescent* real-time systems. In: Grabowski, J., Nielsen, B. (eds.) FATES 2004. LNCS, vol. 3395, pp. 64–78. Springer, Heidelberg (2005). doi:10.1007/978-3-540-31848-4_5
7. Briones, L.B., Brinksma, E., Stoelinga, M.: A semantic framework for test coverage. In: Graf, S., Zhang, W. (eds.) ATVA 2006. LNCS, vol. 4218, pp. 399–414. Springer, Heidelberg (2006). doi:10.1007/11901914_30
8. Cheung, L., Stoelinga, M., Vaandrager, F.: A testing scenario for probabilistic processes. J. ACM **54**(6), 29:1–29:45 (2007). Article 29
9. Choi, S.G., Dachman-Soled, D., Malkin, T., Wee, H.: Improved non-committing encryption with applications to adaptively secure protocols. In: Matsui, M. (ed.) ASIACRYPT 2009. LNCS, vol. 5912, pp. 287–302. Springer, Heidelberg (2009). doi:10.1007/978-3-642-10366-7_17
10. Cleaveland, R., Dayar, Z., Smolka, S.A., Yuen, S.: Testing preorders for probabilistic processes. Inf. Comput. **154**(2), 93–148 (1999)
11. Cohn, D.L.: Measure Theory. Birkhäuser, Basel (1980)
12. D'Argenio, P.R., Katoen, J.-P.: A theory of stochastic systems part I: stochastic automata. Inf. Comput. **203**(1), 1–38 (2005)
13. Deng, Y., Hennessy, M.: On the semantics of Markov automata. Inf. Comput. **222**, 139–168 (2013)
14. Deng, Y., Hennessy, M., van Glabbeek, R.J., Morgan, C.: Characterising testing preorders for finite probabilistic processes. CoRR (2008)
15. Duflot, M., Kwiatkowska, M., Norman, G., Parker, D.: A formal analysis of bluetooth device discovery. Int. J. Softw. Tools Technol. Transf. **8**(6), 621–632 (2006)
16. Eisentraut, C., Hermanns, H., Zhang, L.: On probabilistic automata in continuous time. In: IEEE 25th Annual Symposium on LICS, pp. 342–351 (2010)
17. Gerhold, M., Stoelinga, M.: Model-based testing of probabilistic systems. In: Stevens, P., Wąsowski, A. (eds.) FASE 2016. LNCS, vol. 9633, pp. 251–268. Springer, Heidelberg (2016). doi:10.1007/978-3-662-49665-7_15

18. Gerhold, M., Stoelinga, M.: Model-based testing of stochastic systems with IOCO theory. In: A-TEST 2016, Proceedings of the 7th International Workshop on Automating Test Case Design, Selection, and Evaluation, pp. 45–51. ACM (2016)
19. Guiotto, A., Acquaroli, B., Martelli, A.: MaTeLo: automated testing suite for software validation. In: DASIA, vol. 532 (2003)
20. Hartmanns, A., Hermanns, H.: The Modest Toolset: An Integrated Environment for Quantitative Modelling and Verification. In: Ábrahám, E., Havelund, K. (eds.) TACAS 2014. LNCS, vol. 8413, pp. 593–598. Springer, Heidelberg (2014). doi:10.1007/978-3-642-54862-8_51
21. Hermanns, H., Chains, I.M.: Interactive Markov Chains: and the Quest for Quantified Quality. Springer, Heidelberg (2002)
22. Hessel, A., Larsen, K.G., Mikucionis, M., Nielsen, B., Pettersson, P., Skou, A.: Testing real-time systems using UPPAAL. In: Hierons, R.M., Bowen, J.P., Harman, M. (eds.) Formal Methods and Testing. LNCS, vol. 4949, pp. 77–117. Springer, Heidelberg (2008). doi:10.1007/978-3-540-78917-8_3
23. Hierons, R.M., Merayo, M.G.: Mutation testing from probabilistic and stochastic finite state machines. J. Syst. Softw. **82**(11), 1804–1818 (2009)
24. Hierons, R.M., Núñez, M.: Testing probabilistic distributed systems. In: Hatcliff, J., Zucca, E. (eds.) FMOODS/FORTE -2010. LNCS, vol. 6117, pp. 63–77. Springer, Heidelberg (2010). doi:10.1007/978-3-642-13464-7_6
25. Hierons, R.M., Núñez, M.: Implementation relations and probabilistic schedulers in the distributed test architecture. J. Syst. Softw. (2017)
26. Hwang, I., Cavalli, A.R.: Testing a probabilistic FSM using interval estimation. Comput. Netw. **54**(7), 1108–1125 (2010)
27. Jegourel, C., Legay, A., Sedwards, S.: A Platform for High Performance Statistical Model Checking – PLASMA. In: Flanagan, C., König, B. (eds.) TACAS 2012. LNCS, vol. 7214, pp. 498–503. Springer, Heidelberg (2012). doi:10.1007/978-3-642-28756-5_37
28. Krichen, M., Tripakis, S.: Conformance testing for real-time systems. Form. Methods Syst. Des. **34**(3), 238–304 (2009)
29. Kwiatkowska, M., Norman, G., Parker, D.: PRISM: probabilistic symbolic model checker. In: Field, T., Harrison, P.G., Bradley, J., Harder, U. (eds.) TOOLS 2002. LNCS, vol. 2324, pp. 200–204. Springer, Heidelberg (2002). doi:10.1007/3-540-46029-2_13
30. Larsen, K.G., Mikucionis, M., Nielsen, B.: Online testing of real-time systems using UPPAAL. In: Grabowski, J., Nielsen, B. (eds.) FATES 2004. LNCS, vol. 3395, pp. 79–94. Springer, Heidelberg (2005). doi:10.1007/978-3-540-31848-4_6
31. Larsen, K.G., Skou, A.: Bisimulation through probabilistic testing, pp. 344–352. ACM Press (1989)
32. Lohrey, M., D'Argenio, P.R., Hermanns, H.: Axiomatising Divergence. In: Widmayer, P., Eidenbenz, S., Triguero, F., Morales, R., Conejo, R., Hennessy, M. (eds.) ICALP 2002. LNCS, vol. 2380. Springer, Heidelberg (2002)
33. Marsan, M.A., Balbo, G., Conte, G., Donatelli, S., Franceschinis, G.: Modelling with Generalized Stochastic Petri Nets. Wiley, Hoboken (1994)
34. Milner, R.: A Calculus of Communicating Systems. Springer, Heidelberg (1980)
35. Mostowski, W., Poll, E., Schmaltz, J., Tretmans, J., Wichers Schreur, R.: Model-based testing of electronic passports. In: Alpuente, M., Cook, B., Joubert, C. (eds.) FMICS 2009. LNCS, vol. 5825, pp. 207–209. Springer, Heidelberg (2009). doi:10.1007/978-3-642-04570-7_19
36. Nie, J., Demmel, J., Gu, M.: Global minimization of rational functions and the nearest GCDs. J. Glob. Optim. **40**(4), 697–718 (2008)

37. Puterman, M.L.: Markov Decision Processes: Discrete Stochastic Dynamic Programming. Wiley, Hoboken (2014)
38. Kwiatkowska, M., Norman, G., Parker, D.: Stochastic model checking. In: Bernardo, M., Hillston, J. (eds.) SFM 2007. LNCS, vol. 4486, pp. 220–270. Springer, Heidelberg (2007). doi:10.1007/978-3-540-72522-0_6
39. Russell, N., Moore, R.: Explicit modelling of state occupancy in hidden markov models for automatic speech recognition. In: IEEE International Conference on Acoustics, Speech, and Signal Processing ICASSP, vol. 10, pp. 5–8 (1985)
40. Segala, R.: Modeling and verification of randomized distributed real-time systems. Ph.D. thesis, Cambridge, MA, USA (1995)
41. B. SIG. Bluetooth Specification, version 1.2 (2003). www.bluetooth.com
42. Song, L., Zhang, L., Godskesen, J.C., Hermanns, H., Eisentraut, C.: Late weak bisimulation for Markov automata. CoRR, abs/1202.4116 (2012)
43. Stoelinga, M.: Alea jacta est: verification of probabilistic, real-time and parametric systems. Ph.D. thesis, Radboud University of Nijmegen (2002)
44. Stoelinga, M., Vaandrager, F.: Root contention in IEEE 1394. In: Katoen, J.-P. (ed.) ARTS 1999. LNCS, vol. 1601, pp. 53–74. Springer, Heidelberg (1999). doi:10.1007/3-540-48778-6_4
45. Stokkink, W.G.J., Timmer, M., Stoelinga, M.I.A.: Divergent quiescent transition systems. In: Veanes, M., Viganò, L. (eds.) TAP 2013. LNCS, vol. 7942, pp. 214–231. Springer, Heidelberg (2013). doi:10.1007/978-3-642-38916-0_13
46. Thrun, S.: Probabilistic robotics. Commun. ACM 45(3), 52–57 (2002)
47. Timmer, M., Brinksma, H., Stoelinga, M., Testing, M.-B., Software, I., Safety, S.: Specification and verification, Volume 30 of NATO Science for Peace and Security, pp. 1–32. IOS Press (2011)
48. Timmer, M., Katoen, J.-P., Pol, J., Stoelinga, M.I.A.: Efficient modelling and generation of Markov automata. In: Koutny, M., Ulidowski, I. (eds.) CONCUR 2012. LNCS, vol. 7454, pp. 364–379. Springer, Heidelberg (2012). doi:10.1007/978-3-642-32940-1_26
49. Timmer, M., van de Pol, J., Stoelinga, M.I.A.: Confluence reduction for Markov automata. In: Braberman, V., Fribourg, L. (eds.) FORMATS 2013. LNCS, vol. 8053, pp. 243–257. Springer, Heidelberg (2013). doi:10.1007/978-3-642-40229-6_17
50. Tretmans, J.: Test generation with inputs, outputs and repetitive quiescence. Softw. - Concepts Tools 17(3), 103–120 (1996)
51. Veanes, M., Campbell, C., Grieskamp, W., Schulte, W., Tillmann, N., Nachmanson, L.: Model-based testing of object-oriented reactive systems with spec explorer. In: Hierons, R.M., Bowen, J.P., Harman, M. (eds.) Formal Methods and Testing. LNCS, vol. 4949, pp. 39–76. Springer, Heidelberg (2008). doi:10.1007/978-3-540-78917-8_2
52. Whittaker, J.A., Rekab, K., Thomason, M.G.: A Markov chain model for predicting the reliability of multi-build software. Inf. Softw. Technol. 42(12), 889–894 (2000)

Test Suite Reduction in Idempotence Testing of Infrastructure as Code

Katsuhiko Ikeshita[1], Fuyuki Ishikawa[2(✉)], and Shinichi Honiden[1,2]

[1] The University of Tokyo, Bunkyō, Japan
[2] National Institute of Informatics, Chiyoda, Japan
f-ishikawa@nii.ac.jp

Abstract. Infrastructure as Code, which uses machine-processable code for managing, provisioning, and configuring computing infrastructure, has been attracting wide attention. In its application, the idempotence of the code is essential: the system should converge to the desired state even if the code is repeatedly executed possibly with failures or interruptions. Previous studies have used testing or static verification techniques to check whether the code is idempotent or not. The testing approach is impractically time-consuming, whereas the static verification approach is not applicable in many practical cases in which external scripts are used. In this paper, we present a method for efficiently checking idempotence by combining the testing and static verification approaches. The method dramatically decreases the number of test cases used to check code including external scripts by applying the static verification approach.

1 Introduction

1.1 Idempotence in Infrastructure as Code

Infrastructure as Code is one of the promising disciplines to support DevOps, which is an approach to increase agility and reliability in software systems by unifying the previously-separate processes of software development (Dev) and system operations (Ops) [15,19]. Infrastructure as Code uses machine-processable code for managing, provisioning, and configuring computing infrastructure, which we call *infrastructure code*. It thus aims at enabling effective and efficient engineering of the operation procedures in the same way as the application code. The essential foundations of Infrastructure as Code are Domain-Specific Languages (DSLs) dedicated to specifying the operation procedures, such as Chef [4], Ansible [17], and Puppet [16].

In practices of Infrastructure as Code, operators use a continuous integration tool and execute the infrastructure code frequently to keep the newest version deployed. Therefore, the infrastructure code is supposed to be executed many times, sometimes suffering failures or interruptions, and in any case make the system converge into the desired state. This expectation has been considered as *idempotence* of the infrastructure code. Instead of idempotence as a property of

S. Gabmeyer and E.B. Johnsen (Eds.): TAP 2017, LNCS 10375, pp. 98–115, 2017.
DOI: 10.1007/978-3-319-61467-0_6

functions [13], idempotence here is a property of automated operations that can be repeated and work robustly [1,8]. Without idempotence, we need to take the cost to execute the code exactly once by initializing the servers and other targets every time failures or interruptions occur.

Listing 1.1 is an example of a non-idempotent program in Chef [4], which is one of the most common DSLs for Infrastructure as Code. This program includes the sequential execution of two *resources*, which define the desired states of configuration items (files this time) and actions to reach the states. Both resources state a file to be created on the specified path by using the specified content (if there is not already one that matches). Suppose the content of a.txt is initially "XXX". By reading this content, the first resource writes "copied: XXX" on /tmp/a.txt. Then the second resource overwrites a.txt with it. If we repeat the execution of the program, we obtain "copied: copied: XXX" and more "copied:" on a.txt. Thus the program is considered non-idempotent even though both resources are idempotent. Engineers needs to ensure their code is idempotent by considering not only the whole execution this way but also failures or interruptions in the middle. In addition to repeated execution as in the above example, we need to consider cases such as when the execution is interrupted after the first resource and resumed from the beginning.

Listing 1.1. Non-idempotent chef program

```
file '/tmp/a.txt' do
  content ("copied:" + IO.read('/a.txt'))
  action :create
end
file '/a.txt' do
  content IO.read('/tmp/a.txt')
  action :create
end
```

In addition, infrastructure code can include external legacy scripts. In the case of Chef, there is a type of resource called script resources that state execution of string commands passed to other script engines such as bash, perl, and python. According to Hummer et al. [12], 364 (more than 50%) cookbooks (code artifacts), out of all 665 publicly available cookbooks in the Chef community [5], use one or more script resources. This fact imposes further difficulties in ensuring idempotence because various notations need to be handled including lower-level ones, e.g., a *for* loop that writes each byte to copy a file.

1.2 Existing Approaches

There have been two approaches in research on checking of idempotence of infrastructure code: testing and static verification. Hummer et al. [12] applied the testing approach. They proposed a model-based testing framework for Infrastructure as Code. By considering different input parameters and every possible restart patterns, their testing framework generates all the test cases to check idempotence up to a specified maximum iteration count. They found that several open-source Chef code artifacts have unknown idempotence bugs. However, in their experiment, test case execution took 44.07 CPU days and roughly five days (sped up by parallel execution) even though they took advantage of lightweight virtual machine environments.

On the other hand, Collard et al. [7] applied the static verification approach. Their tool first tries to prove that the code behaves deterministically because Puppet, the DSL they target, has adopted non-deterministic semantics, which means the interpreter of Puppet can execute the program in an arbitrary order as long as it satisfies given dependencies. Then the tool tries to prove idempotence by using static verification mechanisms. Their approach has an inherent limitation: it cannot be applied to infrastructure code including script resources written in various languages.

1.3   Contributions

As we have discussed, the static verification approach is not applicable to many infrastructure code artifacts that include script resources. In other words, the dynamic testing approach is inevitably used to handle the unknown or heterogeneous aspects of (legacy) scripts. On the other hand, the testing approach requires large cost in trying various test cases with different timings and numbers of restarts due to failure or interruption.

In response to this problem, we propose a method for test suite reduction: eliminating test cases that use script resources. This method applies the static verification technique to the non-script resources to find prunable test cases. Specifically, we first convert the source program, e.g., in Chef, into a formal model for ease of analysis and construct a graph that has paths representing all the necessary test cases. Then we apply heuristics to judge which path of the execution graph is likely to be redundant and apply the static verification technique to check whether some test cases on the path can actually be skipped. After iterating those steps, we eventually obtain a reduced test suite, with a much smaller number of test cases. We evaluate our method by using real-world infrastructure code artifacts and show that it effectively reduces the cost in idempotence testing in spite of the existence of external scripts.

In the remainder of this paper, we first define notations used in the subsequent sections (Sect. 2). Then we describe our method in detail (Sect. 3) and evaluate it and discuss the result (Sect. 4). Finally, we discuss related work (Sect. 5) and give concluding remarks (Sect. 6).

2   Preliminaries

In this section, we explain notations and supplementary notions used in the subsequent sections.

Definition 1. A labeled directed graph G is an ordered pair that consists of a set of nodes V and a set of edges $E \subseteq V \times L \times V$. Each edge $e = (u, l, v) \in E$

has the source node $\mathrm{from}(e) := u$, the label $\mathrm{label}(e) := l$, and the destination node $\mathrm{to}(e) := v$.

Given a labeled directed graph $G = (V, E)$ and a node v in V, $\mathrm{incoming}_G(v)$ and $\mathrm{outgoing}_G(v)$ are the sets of incoming and outgoing edges of v.

$$\mathrm{incoming}_G(v) := \{(u, l, v) \in E\}, \mathrm{outgoing}_G(v) := \{(v, l, w) \in E\}$$

Definition 2. Given a labeled directed graph $G = (V, E)$, a path on G is a sequence of edges $p = (e_1, e_2, ..., e_n)$ in which adjacent edges are connected at a node, that is, for any $i \in \{1, ..., n - 1\}$ $\mathrm{to}(e_i) = \mathrm{from}(e_{i+1})$.

For each path $p = (e_1, e_2, ..., e_n)$, we may focus on its label sequence as follows.

$$\mathrm{labels}(p) := (\mathrm{label}(e_1), \mathrm{label}(e_2), ..., \mathrm{label}(e_n))$$

Given a labeled directed graph $G = (V, E)$, $\mathrm{labelseq}(G)$ is the set of label sequences forw paths that starts from an entry node.

$$\mathrm{labelseq}(G) := \{\mathrm{labels}(p) \mid p = (e_1, e_2, ..., e_n) \text{ is a path on } G$$
$$\wedge \mathrm{incoming}_G(\mathrm{from}(e_1)) = \varnothing\}$$

Definition 3. Labelseq-equivalence is an equivalence relation over labeled directed graphs. G_1 and G_2 are labelseq-equivalent if and only if $\mathrm{labelseq}(G_1) = \mathrm{labelseq}(G_2)$.

Let us call a sequence $s = (s_1, s_2, ..., s_m)$ a front sub-sequence of a sequence $t = (t_1, t_2, ..., t_n)$ if and only if $m \le n$ and for any $i \in \{1, ..., m\}$ $s_i = t_i$. Note that if a sequence of labels in a path $s = (l_1, l_2, ..., l_n)$ is in $\mathrm{labelseq}(G)$, its front sub-sequence $t = (l_1, l_2, ..., l_m)$ (where $m \le n$) is also in $\mathrm{labelseq}(G)$. This is because t also represents a path and shares the entry node with s. We call this property as $\mathrm{labelseq}(G)$ is closed under taking a front sub-sequence.

Since $\mathrm{labelseq}(G)$ is closed under taking a front sub-sequence, it does not break labelseq-equivalence to add a path labels of which are a front sub-sequence of labels of an existing path. For example, the two graphs in Fig. 1 are labelseq-equivalent.

Fig. 1. Two labeled directed labelseq-equivalent graphs

In our method (Sect. 3), we use this graph structure as a compact representation for a set of test cases. Each edge represents an action, and thus each path represents a test case. We introduce the concept of labelseq-equivalence as later we manipulate the graph structure without changing the set of test cases represented by the graph.

3 Method

3.1 Overview

Our objective in this paper is to reduce the cost of testing, which is necessary to check idempotence when the target infrastructure code includes script resources. Thus, we follow the approach of [12] for testing idempotence. For example, suppose there are three sequential actions (a, b, c) in the target code. Using their approach, we consider all possible sequences with repetitions and interruptions, such as (a, b, c, a, b, c) and (a, a, b, c). We consider each sequence as a test case and compare the system states after its execution with those after execution of the original sequence (a, b, c). Our method aims to eliminate redundant test cases by finding equivalent sequences by using the static verification approach.

Here we overview the whole workflow of our proposed method. First we translate a source program, e.g., in Chef, into an internal language (Sects. 3.2 and 3.3). We then transform it into an execution graph, which represents all the test cases to be considered (Sect. 3.4). The core of our method works on this graph. We use heuristics to find a sequence of actions that is likely to be prunable and then check whether it is actually prunable by using an SMT (Satisfiability Modulo Theories) solver (Sect. 3.5). We rewrite the graph to eliminate the prunable sequences, being careful to keep other sequences and not to break what we call a simplicity property (Sect. 3.6). We repeat this pruning procedure until no prunable sequence is found. Finally we obtain the reduced test suite from the reduced execution graph (Sect. 3.7).

3.2 Intermediate Language

Source languages have a variety of syntax to write many types of resources and actions, and their behavior may change depending on flags or between versions. To isolate our method from this complexity, we define an intermediate language to model the behavior of the source artifact of infrastructure code.

The intermediate language is a simple imperative language of programs that manipulate the file-system. This language is almost the same as the language defined by Collard et al. [7] but has two additional actions *havoc* and *clear*. The *havoc* action is introduced to model effects of external programs or parts of the program that cannot be analyzed. The *clear* action represents the error recovery behavior when restarting the execution.

In this paper, we adopt deterministic semantics, which is also adopted by Chef and Ansible, for the sake of simplicity. There are source languages that adopt non-deterministic semantics, such as Puppet, which uses declaration of dependencies rather than that of execution orders. Our method can be extended to apply such semantics, though testing idempotence in such languages is more costly as test cases increase when considering possible execution orders.

Programs written in the intermediate language manipulate the file system. We consider the state space, or the set of possible environmental states, as $Env = \Sigma : P \to C$ in our language. Here the file system is modeled as a function $\sigma \in \Sigma$

that maps a path $p \in P$ to file contents $\in C$. The file content may be a regular file $File(str)$ with a certain text str, a directory Dir or a nonexistent file $None$.

An action a in the intermediate language corresponds to a function of $\Sigma \rightarrow \Sigma \times Status$. Here the set $Status = \{success, failure\}$ represents whether the action is succeeded or failed.

The intermediate language includes atomic actions as described below.

- The intermediate language has primitive actions to manipulate the file system in deterministic manners. mkdir(p) creates a directory at the path p, createFile(p, str) creates a file $File(str)$ at the path p, cp(p, q) copies a file at p into a nonexistent file at q, and rm(p) removes a regular file or an empty directory at p.
- The skip action does nothing on Σ and results in the *success* status.
- The err action does nothing on Σ and results in the *failure* status.
- There is a non-deterministic action havoc(p) that reads or modifies a file at p arbitrarily and results in either the *success* or *failure* status. This action is introduced to model script resources or any other constructs in the original language when their semantics cannot be analyzed and we need to pessimistically consider any effects for them.

These actions are recursively combined by composite actions as follows.

- There is a sequencing operator $a; b$ that executes a, and then b. Its status is the conjunction of those of a and b.
- There is a conditional syntax if (π) a else b end if that executes a if π holds, or b otherwise. Its status is that of a or b depending on the evaluation of π. The condition π is specified as any combination of predicates $Test(p, c)$ and with logical operators $\wedge$, $\vee$, and $\neg$. Here the predicate $Test(p, c)$ checks whether a file path p meets a certain condition c. The condition c can be whether a file at p is a regular file ($IsFile$), a regular file with a certain content ($Contains(str)$), a directory ($IsDir$), an empty directory ($IsEmptyDir$), or a nonexistent file ($None$).

For each action that works on the file system, we follow typical definitions of the semantics. For example, mkdir results in the *failure* status if there is already a directory. In any case, we follow the semantics of the original DSLs for infrastrucutre such as Chef. For example, suppose we want to encode the "mkdir"-like feature that does nothing and results in the *success* status if there is already a directory. In that case, we can use the "if" conditional branch with our mkdir to encode this semantics.

The whole program consists of a sequence of top-level actions $\in TopAction = \Sigma \times Status \rightarrow \Sigma \times Status$. A top action may be an action a described above, which executes if it is success and does nothing otherwise, or *clear*, which always results in the *success* status. This *clear* top-level action is just a label without any effect and represents an occurrence of interruption, which leads to re-execution from the beginning.

We did not include syntax elements to represent loops. This is because we assume that in infrastructure code loops are used to have the same processing on a set of files or other system elements and the loops can be unrolled. In other words, we do not consider use of loops such as computing a value by repeatedly mutating the value until it satisfies some condition, which requires more careful consideration.

3.3 Translation into Intermediate Language

Due to space limitations, we briefly describe how source languages can be translated into the intermediate language through examples using Chef as the source language.

Files and directories can be manipulated directly by primitive actions. For example, `directory` and `cookbook_file` in Chef can be translated as shown below.

```
directory"/d" do
   action :create
end
cookbook_file '/foo' do
   source 'foo.txt' # "bar"
   action :create
end
```

```
if Test(/d, None) mkdir(/d)

if !Test(/foo, Contains(bar))
   if Test(/foo, IsFile) rm(/foo)
   createFile(/foo, bar)
end if
```

Variables and loops are not supported in the internal language. Therefore, we have to unroll the loops and expand the variables into their values. For example, a Chef program that creates directories `"a"` and `"b"` under `p` by using an iterating method `array.each` can be simply translated into *if*s and *mkdir*s in the following ways.

```
p = "/app"
["a", "b"].each {|c|
   directory "#{p}/#{c}" do
      action :create
   end
}
```

```
if Test(/app/a, None) mkdir(/app/a)
if Test(/app/b, None) mkdir(/app/b)
```

Structured files. Configuration files such as /etc/hosts or SSH authorized keys are usually structured, so there are actions defined in source languages to add, edit or remove part of the files. In this case, instead of manipulating the file as it is, individual parts of the file should be treated as a file in the intermediate language. For example, a chef program that adds or updates an entry in /etc/hosts file can be translated into an intermediate program that adds or updates a corresponding file as shown below.

```
hostsfile_entry '1.2.3.4' do
   hostname 'host'
   action :create
end
```

```
if Test(/etc/hosts:d, None) mkdir(/
   etc/hosts:d)
if !Test(/etc/hosts:d/1.2.3.4, None)
   rm(/etc/hosts:d/1.2.3.4)
createFile(/etc/hosts:d/1.2.3.4, '
   host')
```

Services. In Chef, services control whether a specified external daemon program is running or not. Although they do not really manipulate files, the states of services should also be represented as files in an internal language.

3.4   Construction of Execution Graph

As described in Sect. 3.1, we consider test cases that represent repeated execution with interruptions (*clear* actions). For example, given the intermediate program $a; b$ and the iteration count 3, the set of test cases to be considered, i.e., the test suite, is as follows:

- *clear*; a; *clear*; a; *clear*; a; b
- *clear*; a; *clear*; a; b; *clear*; a; b
- *clear*; a; b; *clear*; a; *clear*; a; b
- *clear*; a; b; *clear*; a; b; *clear*; a; b

Note that we listed test cases with the exactly three iterations. In the actual setting, we also need to consider test cases with one iteration and those with two iterations (and sometimes more than three if necessary to increase the confidence). In this paper, we focus on a graph for a certain value of the iteration count as in [12]. We can repeat the same process for different values of the iteration count. Rather than just repeating, our method allows to reuse (cache) the results of equivalence checking (Sect. 3.5), e.g., *clear*; a; *clear*; a; is equivalent to *clear*; a;, for different values of the iteration count.

Because it would require too much memory to have this set naively, we represent this set as a labeled directed acyclic graph $G = (V, E)$ called an execution graph, where the set of nodes and that of edges satisfy the following:

- A node is represented by a natural number. $V \subset \mathbb{N}$
- An edge is directed and labeled with a *TopAction*. $E \subseteq V \times TopAction \times V$
- There is only one node called the entry node that has empty incoming edges. $|\{v \in V | \text{incoming}_G(v) = \emptyset\}| = 1$
- For each node, its outgoing edges must have distinct labels. We call this a simplicity property. $\forall v \in V. |\text{outgoing}(v)| = |\{l | \exists w.(v, l, w) \in \text{outgoing}(v)\}|$
- The graph must be acyclic. $\exists r \in V \to \mathbb{N}. \forall e \in E. r(\text{from}(e)) < r(\text{to}(e))$

Given an iteration count i, this graph is constructed straightforwardly as described by Hummer et al. [12]. For example, from an internal program $A; B; C$, an execution graph shown in Fig. 2 is constructed.

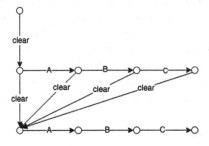

Fig. 2. Construction of execution graph with $i = 2$

3.5   Search for Prunable Action Sequences

To prune actions, first we search for a sequence of top-level actions that can be pruned. There are $O(n^{i+1})$ many paths in the execution graph for n actions and the iteration count i. However, only a small number of them may be pruned. Thus we expect and use typical patterns of prunable action sequences. For instance, the following is an apparently prunable action sequence that ensures a path p_1 is a directory twice, only one of which is sufficient.

```
if (is_dir(p1)) skip; else mkdir(p1)
if (is_dir(p1)) skip; else mkdir(p1)
```

It is inefficient to try to prove prunability of randomly chosen sub-sequences. Instead, to determine which sub-sequences to check, we use the heuristics that a sub-sequence matching one of the following patterns is likely to be prunable.

- $a_1; a_2; ...a_n; a_k$ may be equivalent to $a_1; a_2; ...a_n$ where $k - 1 \leq n$
- $clear; a_1; a_2; ...a_n; clear; a_1; a_2; ...a_n$ may be equivalent to
  $clear; a_1; a_2; ...a_n$ where $a_1, a_2, ..., a_n$ does not contain havoc

The above example of an internal program matches the first pattern. We introduced this pattern because the internal program is supposed to be the result of the inline expansion of function calls in a modularized infrastructure code and should contain many redundant actions. Whereas the first pattern is for redundancy in the internal program, the second pattern is for statically verifiable idempotence. We have to treat these two patterns separately because *clear* behaves differently from other actions. For example, an internal program $clear; mkdir(p1); clear$ would match the first pattern if $a_1, a_2, ...a_n$ could be *clear*. However, that match would falsely suggest that the program is equivalent to a program $clear; mkdir(p1)$. Whereas the former always succeeds, the latter fails if the path $p1$ already has a directory. Thus, they are not equivalent. Therefore, $a_1, a_2, ...a_n$ in the first pattern cannot be *clear*.

We use an SMT solver to try to prove that the action sequence can in fact be pruned. Since the internal language can only manipulate paths that appear in the program, the set of states the SMT solver must maintain is finite. However, this does not mean it suffices to store the state of files only at paths that appear in the intermediate program. Since a file and a directory cannot exist without ancestor directories, the states of every ancestor directory must be tracked. Moreover, the semantics of $rm(p)$ and $emptydir(p)$ requires extra variables for maintaining whether each directory has any children that do not appear in the intermediate program. In our implementation, we realized this by adding an extra child file under each path. We omit the explanation of how we constructed expressions for an SMT solver because it is straightforward.

3.6   Graph Rewriting

Matching of Prunable Action Sequences. Next, we find a path in the execution graph with known prunable action labels. We match edges of the execution graph with known prunable action sequences to find prunable paths.

Algorithm 1. splitNode: Calculate a graph G_r labelseq-equivalent to G, where incoming edges of to(e) other than e are removed

---

Require: $e = (u, l, v) \in E \wedge G$ is acyclic
Ensure: labelseq$(G) =$ labelseq$(G_r) \wedge V(G)\backslash\{v\} \cup \{v_r\} \subseteq V(G_r) \wedge$ incoming$_{G_r}(v_r) = \{(u, l, v_r)\}$
Ensure: $|V(G)|+1 \geq |V(G_r)| \wedge \forall v \in V.|$outgoing$(v)| = |\{l|\exists w.(v, l, w) \in$ outgoing$(v)\}$

    if $|$incoming$_G(v)| \leq 1$ **then**
        $G_r \leftarrow G$
        $v_r \leftarrow v$
    else
        $v_r, v_r' \leftarrow$ fresh nodes
        $V_2 \leftarrow V\backslash\{v\} \cup \{v_r, v_r'\}$
        $E_2 \leftarrow E\backslash$incoming$_G(v)\backslash$outgoing$_G(v) \cup \{(u, l, v_r)\} \cup \{(t, l', v_r')|(t, l', v) \in$ incoming$_G(v)\backslash\{e\}\} \cup \{(v_r, l', w), (v_r', l', w)|(v, l', w) \in$ outgoing$_G(v)\}$
        $G_r \leftarrow (V_2, E_2)$
    end if

Rewriting of Execution Graph. We may not be able to immediately rewrite the prunable path, because there may be incoming edges in the middle of the path. In that case, we have to rewrite the graph labelseq-equivalently so that there is no incoming edge.

We start with a significant sub-algorithm called splitNode, shown in Algorithm 1. The objective of this algorithm is to prepare for modification on an edge $e = (u, l, v)$. The destination node v may have incoming edges other than e. To separate the effect of modification, the algorithm splits v into v_r and v_r' so that e is connected to v_r and the other incoming edges of v are connected to v_r' in the output graph G_r. The paths, or labels of paths, are preserved by this transformation from G to G_r, i.e., G and G_r are labelseq-equivalent.

The algorithm rewritePath is the core of our method and tries to replace a certain path with another path (equivalent action sequence), e.g., (a, b, a, b) with (a, b). This replacement is easy if the target path does not have any incoming or outgoing edges that go out of the path. In that case, we can simply replace the path with the new one. However, because this is not generally the case, we need to be careful in removing a path so that we do not lose paths other than the target of replacement.

Algorithm 2 describes how we handle this point in the algorithm rewritePath. Below we explain how the algorithm works.

1. Thanks to the previous Algorithm 1 (splitNode), we can transform the graph so that there is no incoming edge that merges into a node on the target path. Thus the algorithm starts by applying Algorithm 1 (splitNode) to each node of the target path
2. Then we worry about whether there is an outgoing edge that splits from a node on the target path. For example, suppose we want to replace (a, b, c, d) with (e, f). If b has an outgoing edge to a node g other than c, we need to

---

Algorithm 2. rewritePath: Rewrite a path $((v_1, l_1, v_2), ..., (v_{n-1}, l_{n-1}, v_n))$ in $G = (V, E)$ so that the sequence of the labels on the path will be $l'_1, l'_2, ..., l'_{k-1}$

Require: $((v_1, l_1, v_2), ..., (v_{n-1}, l_{n-1}, v_n))$ is a path in an execution graph G
Require: $\{l'_1, l'_2, ..., l'_{k-1}\} \subseteq T$
  for $j = 1$ to $n - 1$ **do**
    $(v_{j+1}, G) \leftarrow \text{splitNode}(G, (v_j, l_j, v_{j+1}))$
  end for
  $(V', E') \leftarrow G$
  $E' \leftarrow E' \setminus \{(v_{n-1}, l_{n-1}, v_n)\}$
  $j \leftarrow n - 1$
  while $j > 0 \wedge \text{outgoing}_{(V', E')}(v_j) = \emptyset$ **do**
    $V' \leftarrow V' \setminus \{v_j\}$
    $E' \leftarrow E' \setminus \{(v_{j-1}, l_{j-1}, v_j)\}$
    $j \leftarrow j - 1$
  end while
  $v'_1 \leftarrow v_1$
  for $j = 1$ to $k - 1$ **do**
    if $j = k - 1$ **then**
      $v'_{j+1} \leftarrow v_n$
    else
      $v'_{j+1} \leftarrow \text{freshnode}$
      $V' \leftarrow V' \cup \{v'_{j+1}\}$
    end if
    $E' \leftarrow E' \cup \{(v'_j, l'_j, v'_{j+1})\}$
  end for
  $G \leftarrow \text{simplify}((V', E'))$

---

preserve the paths $(..., a, b, g, ...)$ and cannot simply replace the target path (a, b, c, d) with (e, f). Suppose c does not have an outgoing edge that splits from the path. In this case, we delete only c and d to replace the paths $(..., a, b, c, d, ...)$ with $(..., e, f, ...)$ but preserve the paths $(..., a, b, g, ...)$. In this way, the algorithm goes backward to remove nodes and edges on the path to be replaced until it finds a node with an outgoing edge that splits from the path.

3. In any case, we add the new path $((e, f)$ in the above example) to the graph at the same point of the target path (i.e., sharing the incoming edges to the first node).

At the end of Algorithm 2, we use another algorithm called simplify. Because we added new edges, the simplicity property

$$\forall v \in V.|\text{outgoing}(v)| = |\{l|\exists w.(v, l, w) \in \text{outgoing}(v)\}|$$

may not be satisfied. The simplify algorithm is used for this purpose (Algorithm 3). This runs a depth-first search from the entry node, and checks the nodes in a reverse postordering. If the node under consideration u has two or more outgoing edges $\in E'$ with the same label l between u and every node in V',

---

Algorithm 3. simplify: Recover the simplicity property

Require: $G = (V, E)$ is an execution graph but the simplicity property may not hold
Ensure: (V, E) is an execution graph that satisfies the simplicity property and is labelseq-equivalent to G
   for all $u \in V$ in a reverse postordering **do**
      for all (l, V', E') where $V' = \{v|(u, l, v) \in E\} \wedge E' = \{(u, l, v)|v \in V\} \wedge |V'| > 1$ **do**
         $v' \leftarrow$ fresh node
         $V \leftarrow V \backslash V' \cup \{v'\}$
         $E \leftarrow E \backslash E' \cup \{(u, l, v')\} \cup \{(v', l', w)|\exists v \in V'.(v, l', w) \in E\}$
      end for
   end for

---

the nodes in V' are replaced with a fresh node v' and all incoming and outgoing edges of the old nodes in V' are properly replaced. Through this algorithm, two paths, or test cases, can be unified into one if they have a common front sub-sequence, as shown in Fig. 3.

Fig. 3. Unification of two test cases (upper side) into one (bottom side) by simplify

The computational cost of the whole rewriting procedure (Algorithm 2, rewritePath) resides primarily in the simplify (Algorithm 3). The rewritePath algorithm focuses on the target path and simply iterates on each node on it. It uses the splitNode algorithm, but this algorithm has an iteration only over incoming and outgoing edges on the target node. On the other hand, the simplify algorithm has iterations over the whole graph to have some processing for each node if it has multiple edges with the same label. Thus, its computational order is $O(|V||L|)$ where $|V|$ is the number of nodes in the graph and $|L|$ is the number of labels.

3.7 Test Case Generation

When searchCandidateForPruning and Algorithm 2 are executed a sufficient number of times and candidates for pruning can no longer be found, we transform the execution graph into test cases (enumerateTestCases, Algorithm 4). The algorithm collects into $R(u) \subset seq(TopAction)$ for each node u a set of sequences of labels on the path from u to the exit nodes by running a depth-first search from the entry node and visiting all the nodes in a postordering. At the end, $R(s)$ contains all the test cases, where s is the entry node.

Algorithm 4. enumerateTestCases: Enumerate all the test cases represented by the execution graph

---

Require: $G = (V, E)$ is an execution graph
  $R \leftarrow \emptyset$
  for all $u \in V$ in a postordering **do**
    $C \leftarrow \{(l, ...rest) | (u, l, v) \in \text{outgoing}_G(u) \wedge rest \in R(v)\}$
    if $\text{outgoing}_G(u) = \emptyset$ **then**
      $C \leftarrow \{()\}$
    end if
    $R \leftarrow R \cup \{u \mapsto C\}$
  end for
  $\{s\} \leftarrow \{s \in V | \text{incoming}_G(s) = \emptyset\}$
  return $R(s)$

---

4 Evaluation

4.1 Setup

We implemented our method in Scala with the Z3 Theorem Prover [9] as an underlying SMT solver. We prepared three Chef programs for the evaluation and added three variants to investigate characteristics of our method, as described below.

The `package installer` program on the list is a simple Chef program that installs a MySQL server. We implemented a program that executes an apt-file command in a virtual machine (called Docker for Mac) so that we can enumerate which files are touched during the installation process. Therefore, the number of files and their file paths are realistic.

The `mysql cookbook` program is one of the most popular (and the most frequently downloaded) public Chef programs of the main Chef community, which supports tasks for MySQL servers (version 7.1.1). In this evaluation, database operation was translated into a *havoc* action.

The `tomcat6` program is based on a Chef program found to be nonidempotent by Hummer et al. [12]. Because its problem was caused by file permissions, we represented permissions as files in the translation. Although the original Chef program contains a bash script resource, we translated the inside of the script into the intermediate language rather than using the *havoc* action to observe effects of non-idempotent actions. Thus, this `tomcat6` program is the only one with no *havoc* action.

Three variants are obtained from the above programs. The programs of `worst case` and `worst case`' are variants of the `package installer` program with *havoc* moved from the end to the beginning. This prevents the prover from proving prunability in many paths. In `worst case`', all the recursive *mkdir* actions are preserved, while in `worst case` duplicate *mkdir* actions are removed. The `wrong package installer` program is a variant of the `package installer` program. We changed the order of directory creations randomly so that we can investigate how potential errors in an internal program affect our method.

Table 1. Results for test suite reduction

Target program	Iteration	Top actions	Initial test cases	Final test cases
Package installer	3	12	169	1
Mysql cookbook	3	38	1521	1
tomcat6	3	11	144	24
Worst case	3	12	169	144
Worst case'	3	22	529	144
Wrong package installer	3	12	169	1

Table 2. Results for execution time

Target program	searchCandidate ForPruning (ms)	isPrunable (ms)	rewritePath (ms)	Simplify (ms)	Total running time (ms)
Package installer	246	2067	1379	7444	13376
Mysql cookbook	9690	7847	51393	368802	592651
tomcat6	859	6441	1210	5127	18651
Worst case	162	99	262	1510	9877
Worst case'	2723	2341	7233	100644	159109
Wrong package installer	370	1847	1599	6884	13943

To reduce variance due to context switch and caches, we executed our method five times with three iterations and measured the initial (before pruning) number of test cases and the final test cases (Table 1). We also measured the execution time of our method, for the whole method and each constituent algorithm, in milliseconds. The results for execution times are the averages of five run-times (Table 2).

4.2 Overall Results

Tables 1 and 2 show the evaluation result for the test suite reduction and execution time, respectively.

Table 1 shows that the number of test cases always decreased. This was true even with the **worst case** and **worst case'** programs, which were prepared as the cases in which our method would not work effectively. This is because all the test cases with a repetition count $n - 1$ times or fewer were absorbed into test cases with repetition count of n. The reduction always includes reduction of redundant *clear; clear* into *clear*. This reduction is trivial if we consider each test case but requires careful processing not to lose paths in the graph representation for a set of test cases (as explained in Sect. 3.6). In the other programs, our method succeeded in dramatically decreasing the number of test cases, even into just one test case for the three practical programs of **package installer** and **mysql cookbook**. This is because in these programs we had *havoc* actions at the latter part of them. Repetitions of the preceding part were eliminated as it and its sub-sequence are idempotent: for a sequence $a_1; a_2; ...$, the repetition

a_1, a_1 was equivalent to a_1, a_1, a_2, a_1, a_2 was equivalent to a_1, a_2, and so on. We confirmed that this actually happened by carefully checking the results (the remaining test cases and some eliminated test cases).

Table 2 shows that the majority of the execution time was consumed in simplify. This algorithm occupies 55% to 61% of the execution time, with the exception of the tomcat program. This result was contrary to our expectation that the execution time of isPrunable would be dominant (it was actually only 1% to 15%). The present SMT solver is quite efficient for our problem setting in which idempotence of short sub-sequences is checked. On the other hand, we found that simplify is time-consuming by updating the whole graph by adding and removing edges very frequently, which suggests an important direction for future improvement.

4.3   Individual Results

In the case of the package installer program, our method was able to eliminate the most test cases. This was because the program was made of actions for package file installation and an action of external script invocation (translated into a *havoc* action). The sub-sequences that consist of installation actions were idempotent and thus pruned effectively.

The mysql cookbook program was the most complicated program in the evaluation. Although its longest execution time (about 10 min) suggests future improvement, it is still practically effective given the much greater saving in execution time by eliminating test cases. This program also benefited from our method with a long prunable sequence by having the *havoc* action at the end of the program.

The tomcat6 program was the case that includes non-idempotent sequences. Remember that this case does not include the *havoc* action and was prepared in order to investigate effects of non-idempotent action sequences, though the static verification approach works for this case. As expected, the test cases cannot be reduced into one as there are non-idempotent actions. The distribution of the execution time is different from those for the other programs. Execution time of isPrunable or simplify is not dominant and is almost the same as the time of "others" omitted in Table 2, mainly the time of test case generation.

The programs of worst case and worst case' were prepared as the cases in which our method does not work effectively. Only obvious pruning of *clear*; *clear* occurred as the minimum effect of our method. The worst case' had more redundancy than the worst case program, which allowed our method to prune them. The execution time of isPrunable is very short for the worst case program because the findPrunablePaths algorithm avoids trying to prune a path with *havoc* on one of its edges.

The results for the wrong package installer were similar to those for the package installer program. Our method is not sensitive to internal errors.

4.4 Evaluation Summary

We have confirmed that our method effectively reduces teh test suite. What affects the effectiveness is the position of the *havoc* action. In the extreme (worst) case, when the *havoc* action is at the beginning, the remaining factor affecting how many test cases can be reduced is mostly only whether duplicate or redundant actions exist. As in the programs used in the evaluation, there are practical programs that use *havoc* actions (database operations, custom file operations, etc.) in the late part of the program. The execution time of our method is acceptable given its saving in the time of test execution, though future work should improve the execution time of the graph manipulation part (i.e., simplify) of the method.

If there is no *havoc* but the number of test cases is more than one, this means isPrunable failed for some sequence $clear; a_1; a_2; ...; a_n; clear; a_1; a_2; ...; a_n$. The result suggests broken idempotence, and reporting such a case would be helpful to a user. The problem when it comes to practical use is execution time. The running times of isPrunable and the underlying SMT solver seem negligible compared with those of graph rewriting algorithms. This problem would be solved by improving graph rewriting algorithms, because the final execution graph contained redundancy.

5   Related Work

Our work is motivated by the two existing approaches discussed in Sect. 1.2. In this section, we briefly discuss other related studies.

There have been test frameworks that allow a programmer to write test code for infrastructure code. For example, Test Kitchen [11] is a testing framework for Chef. It usually creates virtual environments where test cases can be run within various platforms and environment settings. It then runs the infrastructure code till it converges and runs test cases against the converged environment to verify their state. Such frameworks are complementary with our work as they support efficient execution of generated test cases while needing our work (or its ancestor [12]) to avoid costly and error-prone manual definitions of test cases.

Test suite reduction has been considered important in the field of testing. In a general setting, a typical approach to evaluate and select test cases is to consider what requirements are covered by each test case. Heuristics with this approach has long been investigated and evaluated [6] but is still being actively improved recently by using search-based methods or metaheuristics [20]. Heuristics for test suite reduction can explore aspects other than requirements. Specifically, bug finding capability is also essential so that we do not weaken it by reducing test cases [14] and so that similar test cases may be eliminated more aggressively [3]. In this paper, we instead rely on an approach to logically judge redundant test cases, though we used a kind of heuristics in searching the prunable paths. In this sense, similar directions can be found in the literature such as the work of Vaysburg et al. [18]. In their approach, they judge whether two test cases are redundant by dependency analysis based on state machine analysis. In this paper, we presented heuristics dedicated for idempotence testing given the increasing demand for Infrastructure as Code.

6 Concluding Remarks

In application of Infrastructure as Code, the idempotence of the code is essential: the system should converge into the desired state even if the code is executed repeatedly possibly with failures or interruptions. Checking idempotence is not trivial because combining idempotent snippets does not necessarily lead to idempotent programs and external legacy scripts are often used that are written in various languages. Previous studies have used testing or static verification techniques to check whether code is idempotent or not. The testing approach is impractically time-consuming, whereas the static verification approach is not applicable in many practical cases in which external scripts are used.

In this paper, we presented a method for efficiently checking idempotence by combining the testing and static verification approaches. The method dramatically decreases the number of test cases used to check code including external scripts by applying the static verification approach. We demonstrated the effectiveness of the method in terms of test suite reduction as well as the acceptability of its execution time through experiments.

6.1 Future Directions

There are several directions for our future work, primarily in terms of practical implementations. First, we should improve the implementation of the graph manipulation part in the method, as suggested by the experiment results. Second, we should establish a robust mechanism to generate executable test cases. This task contains a kind of view-update problem or bidirectional transformation problem [2,10], as we first have executable test cases in the source language, then conduct the reduction method after translation into the intermediate language, and finally want to have reduced test cases in the source language. Finally, we should release a practical toolset based on this work for a wide range of uses as well as a large set of experiments.

Acknowledgment. This work was partially supported by ERATO HASUO Metamathematics for Systems Design Project (No. JPMJER1603), Japan Science and Technology Agency (JST).

References

1. Burgess, M.: Testable system administration. Commun. ACM **54**(3), 44–49 (2011)
2. Caroprese, L., Trubitsyna, I., Truszczynski, M., Zumpano, E.: The view-update problem for indefinite databases (2012). CoRR, abs/1205.4655
3. Cartaxo, E.G., Machado, P.D.L., Oliveira Neto, F.G.: On the use of a similarity function for test case selection in the context of model-based testing. Softw. Test. Verif. Reliab. **21**(2), 75–100 (2011)

4. Chef Software, Inc.: Chef Embrace DevOps - Chef. https://www.chef.io/
5. Chef Software, Inc.: Welcome - The Resource for Chef cookbooks - Chef Super-market. https://supermarket.chef.io/
6. Chen, T.Y., Lau, M.F.: A simulation study on some heuristics for test suite reduction. Inf. Softw. Technol. **40**(13), 777–787 (1998)
7. Collard, J.M., Gupta, N., Shambaugh, R., Weiss, A., Guha, A.: On static verification of puppet system configurations (2015). CoRR, abs/1509.05100
8. Couch, A., Sun, Y.: On the algebraic structure of convergence. In: Brunner, M., Keller, A. (eds.) DSOM 2003. LNCS, vol. 2867, pp. 28–40. Springer, Heidelberg (2003). doi:10.1007/978-3-540-39671-0_4
9. de Moura, L., Bjørner, N.: Z3: an efficient SMT solver. In: Ramakrishnan, C.R., Rehof, J. (eds.) TACAS 2008. LNCS, vol. 4963, pp. 337–340. Springer, Heidelberg (2008). doi:10.1007/978-3-540-78800-3_24
10. Foster, J.N., Greenwald, M.B., Moore, J.T., Pierce, B.C., Schmitt, A.: Combinators for bidirectional tree transformations: a linguistic approach to the view-update problem. ACM Trans. Program. Lang. Syst. (TOPLAS) **29**(3), 17 (2007)
11. Heavy Water Operations, LLC (OR): Welcome to Test Kitchen - KitchenCI. http://kitchen.ci/
12. Hummer, W., Rosenberg, F., Oliveira, F., Eilam, T.: Testing idempotence for infrastructure as code. In: Eyers, D., Schwan, K. (eds.) Middleware 2013. LNCS, vol. 8275, pp. 368–388. Springer, Heidelberg (2013). doi:10.1007/978-3-642-45065-5_19
13. Kolokoltsov, V., Maslov, V.P.: Idempotent Analysis and Its Applications. Mathematics and Its Applications. Springer, Netherlands (1997)
14. Lin, J.-W., Huang, C.-Y.: Analysis of test suite reduction with enhanced tie-breaking techniques. Inf. Softw. Technol. **51**(4), 679–690 (2009)
15. Nelson-Smith, S.: Test-Driven Infrastructure with Chef: Bring Behavior-Driven Development to Infrastructure as Code. O'Reilly Media Inc., Sebastopol (2013)
16. Puppet: Puppet - the shortest path to better software. https://puppet.com/
17. Red Hat, Inc.: Ansible is Simple IT Automation. https://www.ansible.com/
18. Vaysburg, B., Tahat, L.H., Korel, B.: Dependence analysis in reduction of requirement based test suites. In: Proceedings of the 2002 ACM SIGSOFT International Symposium on Software Testing and Analysis, ISSTA 2002, pp. 107–111. ACM, New York (2002)
19. Wittig, A., Wittig, M.: Amazon Web Services in Action, 1st edn. Manning Publications Co., Greenwich (2015)
20. Zhong, H., Zhang, L., Mei, H.: An experimental study of four typical test suite reduction techniques. Inf. Softw. Technol. **50**(6), 534–546 (2008)

Short Contributions and Tool Demonstrations

Checking UML and OCL Model Behavior with Filmstripping and Classifying Terms

Martin Gogolla[(✉)], Frank Hilken, Khanh-Hoang Doan, and Nisha Desai

Database Systems Group, University of Bremen, Bremen, Germany
{gogolla,fhilken,doankh,nisha}@informatik.uni-bremen.de

Abstract. This tool paper discusses how model behavior expressed in a UML and OCL model can be analysed with filmstrips and classifying terms in the tool USE. Classifying terms are a means for systematic construction of test cases. In the case of behavior models these test cases correspond to testing the model with different sequence diagrams. We explain how behavior analysis can be carried out in the tool. We discuss lessons learnt from the case study and how conceptual and technical support can be improved.

1 Introduction

Models are the cornerstones in Model-Driven Engineering (MDE). Therefore model analysis and quality improvement techniques like validation and verification of properties are crucial for the success of MDE.

We here employ the UML (Unified Modeling Language) and OCL (Object Constraint Language) for formulating models and focus on analysis techniques for model properties regarding behavior in the context of the tool USE (UML-based Specification Environment) [8]. In particular, USE allows the developer to automatically construct test cases in form of system states (object diagrams) for UML and OCL models. This opens the option to validate models against informal expectations and to verify essential properties like model consistency. Behavior is expressed in our approach by OCL operation contracts, i.e., pre- and postconditions. In our approach, behavioral models are transformed into so-called filmstrip models [9] that explicitly express behavior through operation call objects. Behavior in filmstrip models is formulated with multiple snapshot objects being part of a single system state. Our approach offers a high degree of test automation through the use of so-called classifying terms [10] that partition the test input space into relevant equivalence classes and allow to select equivalence class representatives. We have not yet studied an approach that combines filmstripping with classifying terms.

One main contribution of this paper is introducing the option to prove behavioral consistency of a UML and OCL model through the construction of a test case: the operations contracts (pre- and postconditions) together with the invariants are shown to be satisfiable. The notion behavioral consistency is understood here in the sense that there exists a sequence of operation calls, in which all

© Springer International Publishing AG 2017
S. Gabmeyer and E.B. Johnsen (Eds.): TAP 2017, LNCS 10375, pp. 119–128, 2017.
DOI: 10.1007/978-3-319-61467-0_7

operations occur, and in which all invariants and all pre- and postconditions are satisfied. To the best of our knowledge, showing consistency of operation contracts considered together with class invariants has not been studied so far.

The rest of this paper is organized as follows. Section 2 explains the basics of our approach to behavior modeling. Section 3 sketches behavior validation and verification options. Section 4 discusses the lessons learnt from our example case. The paper is closed with related work and a short conclusion.

2   Filmstripping UML and OCL Models

2.1   Application Model

Our starting example model MarriageWorld is a toy model as displayed in the grey part of Fig. 1. We call this grey part the *application model* as we will later use a transformation of it, the so-called *filmstrip model*. This application model comprises invariants and operation contracts including operation frame conditions that express which model parts are left unchanged by a particular operation. These complete operation contracts may be seen as an alternative to an imperative operation implementation which is not needed in our approach.

The application model encompasses one set-valued OCL query operation and OCL invariants and operation contracts. We show the single invariant and the marry contract. The divorce contract is formulated analogously.

2.2   Filmstrip Model

The filmstrip model results from a transformation of the application model where classes and associations are added (the non-grey part in Fig. 1) and in particular pre- and postconditions are transformed into invariants. An application model sequence of operation calls and intermediate object diagrams correspond to a single object diagram in the filmstrip model. Operation calls in the application model are represented as operation call objects in the filmstrip model. For example, the top right sequence diagram in Fig. 2 corresponds to the top left object diagram. The transformation is realized through a USE plugin. The resulting filmstrip model is a plain UML class model with invariants only.

The filmstrip model organizes application model object diagram sequences into a linear sequence of so-called snapshots (the Snapshot objects in Fig. 2) encompassing the respective objects from the different application model object diagrams. The filmstrip model introduces further operations on class Person not shown in Fig. 1: succPlus(), succStar(), predPlus() and predStar() for the transitive closure and transitive-reflexive closure of the roles succ and pred, respectively. The role succ, for example, points from one object to its next reincarnation in the following snapshot. These operations employ the OCL operation closure and are essential to navigate forward and backward between different 'points in time from the application model point of view'. Generated invariants take care that the filmstrip model object diagrams behave correctly, e.g., that an object and its reincarnations build a cycle-free pred-succ chain (for example, in the left top part of Fig. 2 the reincarnations of person4 are person12 and then person2).

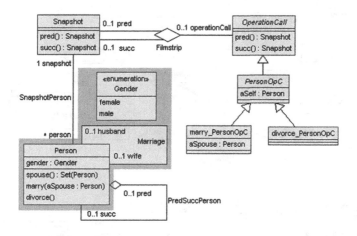

```
spouse():Set(Person)=
  if wife->notEmpty and husband->notEmpty then Set{wife,husband} else
  if wife->notEmpty then Set{wife} else
  if husband->notEmpty then Set{husband} else Set{} endif endif endif
context Person inv traditionalRoles:
  (gender=#female implies wife->isEmpty) and
  (gender=#male implies husband->isEmpty)
context Person::marry(aSpouse:Person)
  pre unmarried:
    self.spouse()->isEmpty and aSpouse.spouse()->isEmpty and
    Set{self.gender,aSpouse.gender}=Set{#female,#male}
  post married:
    Set{aSpouse}=self.spouse() and Set{self}=aSpouse.spouse()
  post personUnchangedExceptSet: let x=self.spouse()->including(self) in
    Person.allInstances@pre=Person.allInstances and
    Person.allInstances->forAll(p|
      (p.gender@pre=p.gender) and
      (x->excludes(p) implies p.wife@pre=p.wife) and
      (x->excludes(p) implies p.husband@pre=p.husband))
```

Fig. 1. Example application model (grey) and filmstrip model.

3 Analysing Model Behavior

3.1 Configurations and Classifying Terms

The USE model validator [12] constructs object diagrams for a UML class diagram enriched by OCL invariants and is based on relational logic [11]. The validator has to be instructed by a so-called *configuration* that determines how the classes and associations are *populated*. For every class a mandatory upper bound and an optional lower bound for the number of objects is given. For every association optional lower and upper bounds can be stated.

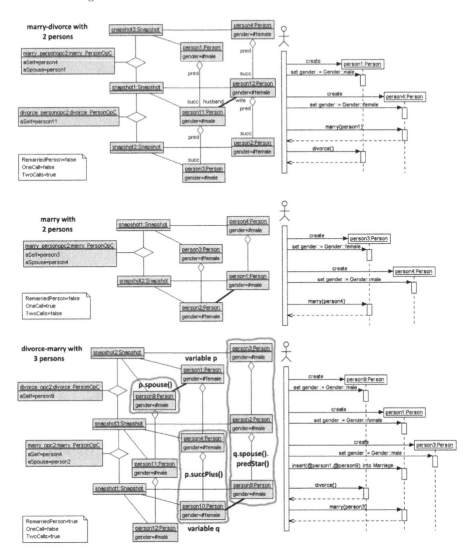

Fig. 2. Generated behavior scenarios.

Figure 3 shows the used configuration (association bounds with grey background) in the example. The configuration determines scenarios having (a) two snapshots with one operation call in between or (b) three snapshots with two operation calls in between. In each snapshot two, three or four persons can be present. The kind of operation call (marry or divorce) is left open as both operation call classes are allowed to have 0, 1 or 2 elements.

A central ingredient in our approach are so-called classifying terms that allow the developer to construct test cases for a UML and OCL model in a systematic way. They classify and determine test equivalence partitions. The test cases

	Three Sequence Diagrams [min..max]	Application model: APP Filmstrip model: FS
Snapshot	2..3	FS
Filmstrip	1..2	FS
marry_PersonOpC	0..2	FS
divorce_PersonOpC	0..2	FS
Person	4..12	APP
SnapshotPerson	4..12	FS
PredSuccPerson	2..8	FS
Marriage	0..*	APP

Classes: White background	Associations: Gray background	

Fig. 3. Used model validator configuration.

are specified by a set of OCL query expressions on the UML class model, the classifying terms, and are manifested in form of object diagrams. The constructed object diagrams will show *differences* with respect to at least one *classifying term*. The classifying terms used here are as follows.

```
[RemarriedPerson]
  Person.allInstances->exists(p | p.spouse()->size=1 and
    p.succPlus()->exists(q | q.spouse()->size=1 and
      q.spouse().predStar()->excludesAll(p.spouse()))))
[OneCall]  OperationCall.allInstances->size=1
[TwoCalls] OperationCall.allInstances->size=2
```

The classifying terms refer to the filmstrip model. The three boolean typed classifying terms ask for scenarios where the terms either yield false or true and can be understood as follows: [RemarriedPerson] one person exists that is married differently in two different snapshots; the variable p fixes that person, and the variable q contains a later incarnation of p; the two snapshots are p.snapshot and q.snapshot; furthermore the previous incarnations of the spouses of q must be disjoint from the spouses of p; [OneCall] there is exactly one operation call; [TwoCalls] there are exactly two operation calls.

The classifying terms [OneCall] and [TwoCalls] cannot both be true at the same time. As the configuration allows one or two operation calls, the classifying terms [OneCall] and [TwoCalls] assert that at least one scenario with one operation call and at least one scenario with two operation calls will be constructed. As three boolean terms are given here, potentially $2^3 = 8$ scenarios will be constructed, but not all options can be realized.

3.2 Constructing Sequence Diagrams

In Fig. 2 the found three solutions for the configuration and the classifying terms are shown: in the left in form of the found filmstrip object diagram and in the right in form of a sequence diagram from the application model corresponding to the filmstrip object diagram. The links from the application model (the Marriage links) are displayed with fat lines. From the 8 possible combinations of the 3 boolean terms only 3 are feasible.

The found scenarios illustrate the behavior of the UML and OCL model with concrete behavior manifestations. Thus configurations and classifying terms support the developer in exploring model behavior. The construction of sequence diagrams with two operation calls employing different operations (marry and divorce) furthermore verifies the consistency of the invariants and the operation contracts taken together, because a scenario has been found where all invariants and all pre- and postconditions are valid.

The classifying term [RemarriedPerson] is true only in the third generated scenario in Fig. 2. In the figure, the distinguishing classifying term values are shown in the comment nodes. In addition, the objects that must be substituted for the OCL variables p and q are indicated. Furthermore, the values of the central OCL expressions from [RemarriedPerson] are marked: p.succPlus() and q.spouse().predStar() are disjoint collections.

Figure 4 gives an overview on the approach taken in this contribution. First the application model is filmstripped which results in the filmstrip model. Then the classifying terms and the model validator configuration (possessing parts for the application and for the filmstrip model) are used to generate object diagrams. The filmstrip parts of the configuration can guarantee, for example, that all (application model) operations calls occur exactly once. Note that all

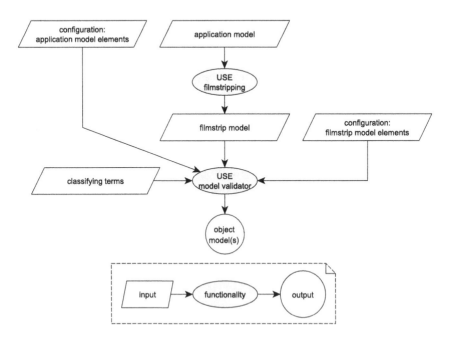

Fig. 4. Overview on combination of filmstripping with classifying terms.

OCL quantifications (for example in the invariants or the classifying terms) range over finite domains, e.g., over classes or over constructed finite collections of datatype values. Thus a mapping into SAT solvers is feasible.

As already mentioned, in our approach verification of properties like consistency considering invariants and operation contracts together is possible. We are not aware of approaches that explore behavioral consistency focussing on the interplay of operation contracts and invariants.

4   Lessons Learnt

The small study shows that with the already existing options interesting results can be obtained, but the study also revaled topics for future work.

- The access to objects and their incarnations is rather involved through complicated OCL expressions. More standard filmstrip operations are needed to simplify such expressions. Currently, there is also only a rather involved access to the operations in which the objects occur. Again, more standard filmstrip operations can help to make the expressions easier.
- Filmstrip configurations should distinguish between application objects (e.g. from class Person) and filmstrip objects (from classes Snapshot or OpC). Dependencies between configuration items should be handled automatically (e.g. [Number of Snapshot objects] $- 1 =$ Number of OpC objects).
- An automatic layout for filmstrip object diagrams (in which OpC objects are placed between snapshots, and snapshots are placed above application model objects) would be helpful. The automatic representation of filmstrip object diagrams as application model sequence diagrams is needed.
- The approach scales to achieve larger scenarios. There is large potential for optimization in the filmstrip model through the construction of (Snapshot,ApplicationModelObject) templates that only need to be completed by the model validator. For example, if n operation calls on m application model objects are wanted, one can pre-compute the needed $n + 1$ snapshot objects each connected to m application objects and one could establish the proper links automatically. Figure 5 sketches an example with 7 operation calls and 64 Person objects. The scenario was obtained by creating the snapshots and the application objects explicitly with a script; then the model validator had only to find the proper operation call objects and the attribute values.

5   Related Work

Many approaches and tools have been proposed to support UML validation and verification. Using Constraint Logic Programming as the underlying formalism, *UMLtoCSP* [5] can automatically check several correctness properties of a UML class diagram enriched with OCL constraints. That approach also handles OCL contracts [4], however operation call and snapshot sequences are not treated.

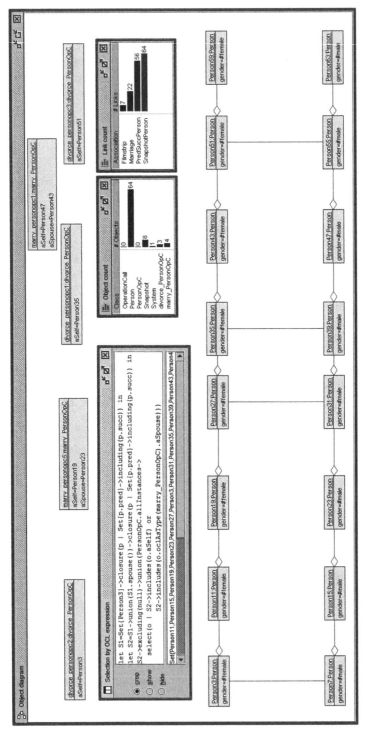

Fig. 5. Large example with 8 snapshots and 7 operation calls; irrelevant objects hidden with an OCL expression; 'Object count' and 'Link count' indicate the complete state.

In [6], *DresdenOCL* is employed as a tool for OCL constraints verification. The *HOL-TestGen* tool presented in [3] is able to automatically generate test cases based on a transformation of UML class models enhanced with OCL constraints into higher-order logic. In [16], an approach for the validation both static and dynamic aspects, e.g., class liveness property, of a UML model is introduced using a toolset based on Abstract State Machines. The approach in [15] describes a transformation of class diagrams and OCL constraints into first-order logic and methods for verifying properties such as class liveliness. As presented in [1], *UML2Alloy* can automatically transform UML model into Alloy, and then test models for consistency using the Alloy analyzer. Another approach is presented in [13], which uses a deep embedding strategy to allow for a transformation of more UML class diagram features. The approach in [2] studies model tests based on (positive and negative) UML sequence diagrams in connection with state charts. The work in [14] describes an approach to transform structural properties of class diagrams into Alloy and then verifies OCL constraints by finding valid snapshots of models. Details of the example model of this contribution, e.g., the complete filmstripped USE model, can be found in [7]. In contrast to the other mentioned approaches, our approach is the only one supporting systematic test case construction with classifying terms.

6 Conclusion and Future Work

We have presented an approach for automatically validating and verifying behavioral model features. In our approach it is possible to check behavioral model consistency and, in principle, behavioral model equivalence on the basis of generated test cases. The implementation of our model validator is based on the relational model finder Kodkod which in turn is translating into SAT solvers.

Future work will address a number of topics. Optimizing our translation and providing more SAT solvers could improve validation and verification efficiency. Further state space reduction techniques have to be considered. The current user interface in our tool for behavioral feature support is minimal. Advanced user feedback in the case that a verification task could not be successfully finished is desirable. Support for building frame conditions, automatic transformation into the filmstrip model as well as advice and proposals for configuration settings for the filmstrip model configuration are needed. Templates for verification tasks could minimize the developer interaction and inspire the developer for checking crucial properties. Expressing properties in an OCL version with temporal operators would increase readability and expressiveness of behavioral properties. Last but not least, larger case studies should give more feedback on the practicability of the approach.

References

1. Anastasakis, K., Bordbar, B., Georg, G., Ray, I.: On challenges of model transformation from UML to Alloy. Softw. Syst. Model. **9**(1), 69–86 (2010)
2. Brosch, P., et al.: Towards scenario-based testing of UML diagrams. In: Brucker, A.D., Julliand, J. (eds.) TAP 2012. LNCS, vol. 7305, pp. 149–155. Springer, Heidelberg (2012). doi:10.1007/978-3-642-30473-6_12
3. Brucker, A.D., Krieger, M.P., Longuet, D., Wolff, B.: A specification-based test case generation method for UML/OCL. In: Dingel, J., Solberg, A. (eds.) MODELS 2010. LNCS, vol. 6627, pp. 334–348. Springer, Heidelberg (2011). doi:10.1007/978-3-642-21210-9_33
4. Cabot, J., Clarisó, R., Riera, D.: Verifying UML/OCL operation contracts. In: Leuschel, M., Wehrheim, H. (eds.) IFM 2009. LNCS, vol. 5423, pp. 40–55. Springer, Heidelberg (2009). doi:10.1007/978-3-642-00255-7_4
5. Cabot, J., Clarisó, R., Riera, D.: On the verification of UML/OCL class diagrams using constraint programming. J. Syst. Softw. **93**, 1–23 (2014)
6. Demuth, B., Wilke, C.: Model and object verification by using dresden OCL. In: Proceedings of the Russian-German WS Innovation Information Technologies: Theory and Practice, pp. 687–690 (2009)
7. Gogolla, M., Hilken, F., Doan, K.H., Desai, N.: Addendum to checking UML and OCL model behavior with filmstripping and classifying terms. Technical report, University of Bremen (2017). http://www.db.informatik.uni-bremen.de/publications/intern/GHDD2017ADD.pdf
8. Gogolla, M., Büttner, F., Richters, M.: USE: a UML-based specification environment for validating UML and OCL. Sci. Comput. Program. **69**, 27–34 (2007)
9. Gogolla, M., Hamann, L., Hilken, F., Kuhlmann, M., France, R.B.: From application models to filmstrip models: an approach to automatic validation of model dynamics. In: Fill, H., Karagiannis, D., Reimer, U. (eds.) Proceedings of the Modellierung (Modellierung 2014), GI, LNI, vol. 225, pp. 273–288 (2014)
10. Gogolla, M., Vallecillo, A., Burgueno, L., Hilken, F.: Employing classifying terms for testing model transformations. In: Cabot, J., Egyed, A. (eds.) Proceedings of the 18th International Conference on Model Driven Engineering Languages and Systems (MoDELS 2015), pp. 312–321. ACM (2015)
11. Jackson, D.: Software Abstractions - Logic, Language, and Analysis. MIT Press, Cambridge (2006)
12. Kuhlmann, M., Gogolla, M.: From UML and OCL to relational logic and back. In: France, R.B., Kazmeier, J., Breu, R., Atkinson, C. (eds.) MODELS 2012. LNCS, vol. 7590, pp. 415–431. Springer, Heidelberg (2012). doi:10.1007/978-3-642-33666-9_27
13. Maoz, S., Ringert, J.O., Rumpe, B.: CD2Alloy: class diagrams analysis using alloy revisited. In: Whittle, J., Clark, T., Kühne, T. (eds.) MODELS 2011. LNCS, vol. 6981, pp. 592–607. Springer, Heidelberg (2011). doi:10.1007/978-3-642-24485-8_44
14. Massoni, T., Gheyi, R., Borba, P.: A UML class diagram analyzer. In: 3rd International Workshop Critical Systems Development with UML, pp. 143–153 (2004)
15. Queralt, A., Teniente, E.: Reasoning on UML class diagrams with OCL constraints. In: Embley, D.W., Olivé, A., Ram, S. (eds.) ER 2006. LNCS, vol. 4215, pp. 497–512. Springer, Heidelberg (2006). doi:10.1007/11901181_37
16. Shen, W., Compton, K., Huggins, J.: A toolset for supporting UML static and dynamic model checking. In: Proceedings of the Computer Software and Applications Conference (COMPSAC 2002), pp. 147–152 (2002)

Skolem Function Continuation for Quantified Boolean Formulas

Katalin Fazekas[1], Marijn J.H. Heule[2(✉)], Martina Seidl[1], and Armin Biere[1]

[1] Johannes Kepler University, Linz, Austria
{katalin.fazekas,martina.seidl,armin.biere}@jku.at
[2] The University of Texas at Austin, Austin, USA
marijn@cs.utexas.edu

Abstract. Modern solvers for quantified Boolean formulas (QBF) not only decide the satisfiability of a formula, but also return a set of Skolem functions representing a model for a true QBF. Unfortunately, in combination with a preprocessor this ability is lost for many preprocessing techniques. A preprocessor rewrites the input formula to an equi-satisfiable formula which is often easier to solve than the original formula. Then the Skolem functions returned by the solver represent a solution for the preprocessed formula, but not necessarily for the original encoding.

Our solution to this problem is to combine Skolem functions obtained from a QRAT trace as produced by the widely-used preprocessor Bloqqer with Skolem functions for the preprocessed formula. This approach is agnostic of the concrete rewritings performed by the preprocessor and allows the combination of Bloqqer with any Skolem function producing solver, hence realizing a smooth integration into the solving tool chain.

1 Introduction

Quantified Boolean formulas (QBFs) [1] extend propositional logic with existential and universal quantifiers over the Boolean variables. This extension allows a compact formalization of PSPACE-hard problems, thus QBFs can be remarkably beneficial in applications of formal verification [2], synthesis [3], and artificial intelligence [4], driving the demand for efficient and reliable QBF solving tools.

Modern QBF solvers not only decide the satisfiability of a formula, but also produce *certificates* [5–14]. Such a certificate is either syntactical or semantical. A syntactical certificate is basically a trace of the individual steps taken by a solver to derive either a conflict in the case of unsatisfiability or to derive the empty formula in the case of satisfiability. The correctness of the individual steps has to be checkable efficiently, i.e., in polynomial time by an external tool that independently confirms the correctness of the solving result. Examples of such syntactical certificates are Q-resolution proofs [15], the QBF variant of resolution

This work has been supported by the Austrian Science Fund (FWF) under projects W1255-N23 and S11408-N23, and by the National Science Foundation (NSF) under grant number CCF-1618574.

© Springer International Publishing AG 2017
S. Gabmeyer and E.B. Johnsen (Eds.): TAP 2017, LNCS 10375, pp. 129–138, 2017.
DOI: 10.1007/978-3-319-61467-0_8

proofs produced by solvers based on conflict/solution-driven clause/cube learning (QCDCL) [16], and QRAT proofs [12]. *Quantified Asymmetric Tautologies* (QRAT) is a redundancy criterion allowing for the safe addition/deletion/update of clauses with this property. A semantic certificate is a model (counter-model) of a satisfiable (unsatisfiable) QBF. Usually such certificates are represented as so-called Skolem (Herbrand) functions, encoding a strategy to set the existential (universal) variables to satisfy (falsify) the QBF. Skolem functions are of particular interest when solving application problems, because they contain information about the solution. For example, if a verification approach based on bounded model checking reports that an error state is reachable by the program to be verified, then the Skolem function encodes a program trace showing the erroneous behavior. Checking the correctness of a Skolem (Herbrand) function is a coNP-complete (NP-complete) problem, because the validity (satisfiability) of a propositional formula has to be checked. Skolem functions are either efficiently extracted from syntactic certificates like Q-resolution and QRAT proofs [7,12], or they are produced directly by a solver [17].

QBF solving tool chains often involve an additional *preprocessing* phase in which the original QBF is rewritten to an equi-satisfiable formula that is then passed to the solver. In many cases, solvers are only able to solve the preprocessed formula, but not the original one [18,19]. Then, however, the found set of Skolem functions is only a solution and witness for the preprocessed formula, because in general, the preprocessing techniques are not model-preserving. To enable both preprocessing and certification at the same time, Janota et al. [20] showed how to obtain Skolem functions for a subset of the preprocessing techniques implemented in the widely-used preprocessor Bloqqer [21] by establishing a solution reconstruction rule for each of the considered preprocessing technique.

In this paper, we present a general approach to obtain Skolem functions with *all* preprocessing techniques implemented in Bloqqer enabled. Therefore, we use the QRAT trace produced by Bloqqer together with the Skolem function produced by state-of-the-art QBF solvers like DepQBF [22] or Caqe [17]. The QRAT trace is not a full syntactical certificate if the formula is not solved by Bloqqer, but it only justifies the rewriting steps from the original QBF to the preprocessed formula. We show that it is nevertheless sufficient to build an incomplete Skolem function which—when continued with the Skolem function provided by the solver—yields a complete Skolem function for the original problem.

This paper is structured as follows. First we review the basic concepts of QBFs and Skolem functions in Sect. 2, then in Sect. 3 we present the formal foundation of our procedure and illustrate the approach on a simple example. In Sect. 4 we describe the main steps of our general tool chain to construct valid Skolem functions for true QBFs in presence of preprocessing. Finally, the paper ends with the experimental evaluation in Sect. 5 and concludes in Sect. 6.

2   Preliminaries

In this section, we introduce concepts and terminology used in the rest of the paper. A *literal* is a variable (x) or the negation of a variable ($\bar{x}$). The negation of a literal l is denoted by $\bar{l}$ and $var(l) := x$ if $l = x$ or $l = \bar{x}$. A *clause* is a disjunction of literals and (possibly negated) truth constants $\top$ (verum) and $\perp$ (falsum). A propositional formula in *conjunctive normal form* (CNF) is a conjunction of clauses. A QBF in *prenex conjunctive normal form* (PCNF) has the form $\Pi.\psi$ where ψ is a propositional CNF formula defined over the variables of prefix $\Pi :=$ $Q_1 X_1 \ldots Q_n X_n$ with $Q_i \in \{\forall, \exists\}$, $Q_i \neq Q_{i+1}$, and $X_i \cap X_j = \emptyset$. The set of all variables occurring in prefix Π is denoted by $vars(\Pi)$. The quantifier $\mathsf{quant}(\Pi, l)$ of literal l is Q_i if $var(l) \in X_i$. If $\mathsf{quant}(\Pi, l) = Q_i$ and $\mathsf{quant}(\Pi, k) = Q_j$, then $l <_\Pi k$ if $i < j$. A QBF $\forall x \Pi.\psi$ is satisfiable iff both $\Pi.\psi[x/\top]$ and $\Pi.\psi[x/\perp]$ are satisfiable where $\psi[x/t]$ denotes the replacement of x by t in ψ. Dually, a QBF $\exists x \Pi.\psi$ is satisfiable iff $\Pi.\psi[x/\top]$ or $\Pi.\psi[x/\perp]$ is satisfiable. The truth constants $\top$ and $\perp$ as well as the Boolean connectives follow the standard propositional semantics. Two QBFs ϕ_1 and ϕ_2 are equivalent (written as $\phi_1 \sim \phi_2$) iff they have the same truth value. The expression $ite(c, b_1, b_2)$ stands for $(c \rightarrow b_1) \wedge (\bar{c} \rightarrow b_2)$.

The *Skolem function* of an existential variable x w.r.t. QBF $\phi = \Pi.\psi$ is a propositional formula $f(y_1, \ldots, y_n)$ where $y_1, \ldots, y_n$ are all the universal variables of ϕ with $y_i <_\Pi x$. A Skolem function f_x for variable x of QBF $\Pi.\psi$ is valid iff $\Pi.\psi \sim \Pi.\psi[x/f_x]$. A *Skolem set* F of QBF ϕ maps each existential variable x of ϕ to a Skolem function $\mathsf{F}(x)$ of x. A Skolem set is valid if it maps existential variables only to valid Skolem functions. By $\phi[\mathsf{F}]$ we denote $\phi[x_1/\mathsf{F}(x_1), \ldots, x_n/\mathsf{F}(x_n)]$ where $x_1, \ldots, x_n$ are the existential variables of ϕ. If clear from the context, we sometimes speak about Skolem functions when referring to a complete Skolem set.

3   Skolem Function Continuation

Skolem functions as introduced above yield a strategy for assigning truth values to the existential variables based on the truth values of the universal variables such that the QBF under consideration evaluates to true. Some solvers are able to directly produce Skolem functions [6,8,17] while for others it is possible to extract the Skolem functions from proofs produced during the search [7,10,12]. In [12] we showed how to extract a Skolem function if the preprocessor Bloqqer is able to solve a true formula. In that case the produced QRAT proof of Bloqqer provides all the necessary information to construct a Skolem function. Now we reuse this technique for the case that not Bloqqer solves the formula, but another solver finds the solution for the preprocessed formula produced by Bloqqer.

In particular, we consider the following scenario: Given a satisfiable QBF ϕ, a QRAT trace T produced by a preprocessor rewriting ϕ to a QBF ϕ', and a valid Skolem set F' of ϕ', we show how to obtain a valid Skolem set F for ϕ.

Definition 1. *A* QRAT *trace T of a QBF $\Pi.\psi$ is a sequence of clause additions and clause deletions in the form of $(p_1, C_1), \ldots, (p_n, C_n)$, where prefix $p_i \in \{+, -\}$[1] indicates if clause C_i is added $(p_i = +)$ or deleted $(p_i = -)$ justified by the rules of the* QRAT *proof system [12].*

---

[1] In the QRAT format, clause deletion lines start with "d".

For the detailed definitions of the QRAT rules and soundness arguments, we kindly refer to [12]. Note that the QRAT proof system also contains rules for modifying clauses. We omit these rules here because for satisfiable formulas a modification rule always can be expressed by a clause addition and a clause deletion rule. Basically, a QRAT trace of a QBF $\Pi.\psi$ compactly describes the sequence $\psi_T^0, \ldots, \psi_T^n$ of propositional formulas as follows:

$$\psi_T^i := \begin{cases} \psi & \text{if } i = 0 \\ \psi_T^{i-1} \cup \{C_i\} & \text{if } p_i = + \\ \psi_T^{i-1} \setminus \{C_i\} & \text{if } p_i = - \end{cases}$$

A clause addition step may even introduce new variables. We follow the convention of the QRAT proof format that such variables are existentially quantified and that they are appended right-most to the quantifier prefix. By Π_T^i we therefore refer to the quantifier prefix of ψ_T^i. A QRAT trace T with $|T| = n$ of a QBF $\Pi.\psi$ is a satisfaction proof if $\psi_T^n = \emptyset$. To construct a valid Skolem set from a QRAT satisfaction proof, a randomly initialised Skolem set is refined by traversing the proof backwards until it is valid [12]. For the case that the formula has not been solved by the preprocessor, i.e., $\psi_T^n \neq \emptyset$, we use the Skolem functions of the preprocessed formula for this initialization.

Definition 2. *Let $\phi = \Pi.\psi$ be a satisfiable QBF that is transformed to an equi-satisfiable QBF $\phi' = \Pi'.\psi'$ with valid Skolem set F'. Further, let T be a QRAT trace, with $|T| = n$, that describes the transformation of ψ to ψ' by the sequence $(\psi_T^0, \ldots, \psi_T^n)$ of propositional formulas where $\psi = \psi_T^0$, $\psi' = \psi_T^n$, and $\Pi' = \Pi_T^n$ as above.*

Then a sequence of Skolem sets $(F_T^0, \ldots, F_T^n)$ for $(\psi_T^0, \ldots, \psi_T^n)$ is defined as follows. The Skolem sets F_T^i for $0 \leq i < n$ are constructed as in [12] and

$$F_T^n(x) := \begin{cases} F'(x) & x \in vars(\Pi') \\ \bot & x \in \bigcup_{j=0}^{n-1} vars(\Pi_T^j) \setminus vars(\Pi'). \end{cases}$$

Variables not occurring in ϕ', but somewhere in the QRAT trace are assigned an arbitrary value in F_T^n ($\bot$ in our case). Next, we argue that each F_T^i is a valid Skolem set for $\Pi_T^i.\psi_T^i$ and so F_T^0 is a valid Skolem set for ϕ, the formula for which we want to construct the Skolem set.

Theorem 3. *Let $\phi = \Pi.\psi$ be a satisfiable QBF that is transformed to an equi-satisfiable QBF $\phi' = \Pi'.\psi'$ with valid Skolem set F'. Further, let T be a QRAT trace that describes the transformation of ψ to ψ'. Then the Skolem set $F_T = F_T^0$ obtained from $(F_T^0, \ldots, F_T^n)$ as described above, is valid on ϕ.*

Proof. We show by reverse induction that Skolem set F_T^i is valid on $\Pi_T^i.\psi_T^i$, i.e., $\psi_T^i[F_T^i] \sim \top$, for all $0 \leq i \leq |T|$. Since F' is a valid Skolem set on ϕ', the base case ($i = n = |T|$) trivially holds. The induction step is the same as in [12]. □

QBF ϕ	QRAT trace T of ϕ	ϕ': preprocessed ϕ	QRP trace of ϕ'
$\forall x \exists y.(x \vee \bar{y}) \wedge (\bar{x} \vee y)$	delete $\bar{x} \vee y$	$\forall x \exists y.(x \vee \bar{y})$	Q-resolution proof

<table>
<tr><td>
<pre>
p cnf 2 2
a 1 0
e 2 0
1 -2 0
-1 2 0
</pre>
</td><td>
<pre>
d -2 1 0
</pre>
</td><td>
<pre>
p cnf 2 1
a 1 0
e 2 0
-1 2 0
</pre>
</td><td>
<pre>
p qrp 2 1
a 1 0
e 2 0
1 -1 2 0 0
2 2 0 0
3 0 2 0
r SAT
</pre>
</td></tr>
</table>

| (a) | (b) | (c) | (d) |

Fig. 1. (a) original QBF ϕ in QDIMACS format, (b) QRAT trace, (c) preprocessed formula ϕ' in QDIMACS format, (d) Q-resolution satisfaction proof in QRP format.

As a consequence of Theorem 3 we can reuse the Skolem function extraction algorithm of [12] and extract partial Skolem functions which we then continue with the Skolem functions of the preprocessed formula resulting in a valid Skolem set of the original formula. The approach is illustrated by the following example.

Example 4. Let ϕ be the true QBF $\forall x \exists y.(x \vee \bar{y}) \wedge (\bar{x} \vee y)$ (the QDIMACS representation is shown in Fig. 1(a)). Assume that a simple preprocessor removes the first clause because it is a blocked clause [21] producing the QRAT trace T shown in Fig. 1(b). The preprocessed formula $\phi' = \forall x \exists y.(\bar{x} \vee y)$ (see Fig. 1(c)) is then passed to a QBF solver that decides its satisfiability. A solver like DepQBF also produces a Q-resolution proof in the QRP format [10] as shown in Fig. 1(d). From this proof, a Skolem set F' can be extracted for ϕ' with $\mathsf{F}'(y) = f'_y(x) = \top$ [7]. Note that F' is not a valid Skolem set for ϕ because $\phi\,[y/\top] \sim \bot$. In order to get a valid Skolem set for ϕ, we use the extraction algorithm of [12] and get $\mathsf{F}^0_T(y) = f_y(x) = ite(\bar{x}, \bot, I)$, where we plug in f'_y for I. After simplifications, we get $f_y(x) = x$ which is a valid Skolem function for ϕ.

4   Architecture

We implemented the Skolem function continuation approach described above in a tool called extract, which is available on http://fmv.jku.at/sk-extract. The full tool chain is shown in Fig. 2. The upper part shows the typical QBF evaluation process involving preprocessing. The lower part shows the extension with our new tool. Given a satisfiable QBF problem ϕ in PCNF, it is first simplified by the preprocessor Bloqqer, that employs different rewritings on the formula and produces a QRAT trace in order to ensure the correctness of these simplification steps. We modified the qrat-trim tool for checking QRAT traces (the original version only checks full QRAT proofs). The simplified formula ϕ' is then passed to a QBF solver that decides its truth value. The solver also generates (maybe with the help of further tools) a valid Skolem set F' on ϕ'. This Skolem set

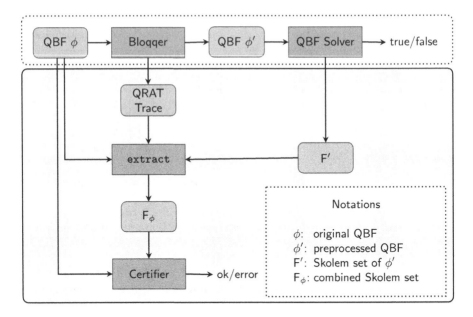

Fig. 2. Overview of our Skolem function continuation tool chain. The upper part of the figure shows a standard QBF evaluation process including preprocessing with Bloqqer, while the lower part presents the Skolem function combination steps.

is assumed to be represented as an And-Inverter-Graph (AIG) in the AIGER format (see http://fmv.jku.at/aiger/). Note that the AIG is the only interface to the QBF solver, hence the approach can be used with any solver that produces Skolem functions in AIGER format.

Given QBF ϕ, the QRAT trace, as well as the Skolem set of the preprocessed formula in AIGER format as input, extract constructs a valid Skolem function set F_ϕ of the original QBF ϕ. In a final step, we check if the produced Skolem set is valid. Therefore, the Certifier of Fig. 2 (1) checks the structural correctness of the Skolem set with the tool cheskol and (2) builds $\phi\,[F_\phi]$ that is a universally quantified formula. For evaluating it with a SAT solver, its negation is translated to a CNF formula that must be unsatisfiable if F is valid.

5   Experimental Evaluation

To evaluate our approach we consider 367 formulas of the QBF Eval 2016 main track that was claimed to be satisfiable by at least one QBF solver participating in the competition. All experiments were run on a cluster of computers with Intel Q9550 2.83 GHz CPUs equipped with 8 GB of memory. We set the memory limit to 7 GB and the time limit to 900 s for the full solving tool chain.

For preprocessing with QRAT tracing, we use the preprocessor Bloqqer version v038 in configurations FULL (all options enabled), noMS (miniscoping for universal expansion disabled), and noCCE (covered clause elimination disabled).

Table 1. Comparison of different Skolem function extraction tool chains

Solver	pre-#	sol-#	ext-#	che-#	MO-#	TO-#	che-t	tot-t
DepQBF	–	160	151	123	10	234	21	30
Caqe	–	148	148	111	186	70	31	40
Bloqqer-BP-DepQBF	114	273	268	251	12	104	14	48
Bloqqer-noCCE-QRAT-DepQBF	150	282	275	258	7	102	18	39
Bloqqer-FULL-QRAT-DepQBF	178	289	275	257	9	101	14	28
Bloqqer-noMS-QRAT-DepQBF	136	281	266	247	11	109	21	35
Bloqqer-noCCE-QRAT-Caqe	150	270	268	236	53	78	18	35

pre-#: formulas solved by preprocessor, sol-#: formulas solved in total, MO-#: memory-outs, ext-#: extracted Skolem functions, che-#: checked Skolem functions, TO-#: timeouts, ch-t: average checking time (s), tot-t: average total time without time/memoryouts (s)

Miniscoping is a syntactic-based technique relaxing the quantifier ordering and is the only technique currently not supported by the qrat-trim checker which verifies that all steps of the QRAT trace are correct. If we keep miniscoping enabled, we currently lose this additional check. CCE is a preprocessing technique that often considerably increases the size of the Skolem functions. For comparison, we also include the version of Bloqqer modified by Janota et al. [20] (called Bloqqer-BP in the following) that performs only a subset of preprocessing techniques for which solution reconstruction is implemented in a tool called backport. Checking the extracted Skolem functions is done with the checker king-cc. In all other tool chains, we use the SAT solver Lingeling version ayv for verifying that the extracted Skolem functions are valid. We further checked syntactical correctness of the Skolem functions generated by our approach with the tool cheskol. As complete QBF solvers, we integrated the two recent tools Caqe [17] and DepQBF [22] into the framework as shown in Fig. 2. Both of them provide Skolem functions represented as AIG. The solver Caqe directly produces Skolem functions during solving, while DepQBF dumps Q-resolution proofs from which Skolem functions are extracted by qbfcert [10].

The results of our experiments are summarized in Table 1. Timeouts and memory outs are given in columns TO-# and MO-#. Column sol-# shows the number of solved formulas. Out of them pre-# formulas are directly solved by the preprocessor. The column che-# shows the number of formulas that passed the complete solving flow, i.e., for these formulas Skolem functions could be extracted that were successfully checked. We did not encounter any formulas where the check failed except for timeouts or memoryouts. With preprocessing enabled more than 100 further formulas pass the whole solving flow. We also observe that our general approach based on QRAT traces performs in the same order of magnitude as the specialized approach based on the traces produced by Bloqqer-BP. Detailed runtime comparisons between all solvers and a comparison of Skolem function sizes produced by the Bloqqer-BP-DepQBF and the Bloqqer-noCCE-QRAT-DepQBF configurations are shown in Fig. 3. Scripts and log-files of the experiments are available on http://fmv.jku.at/sk-extract.

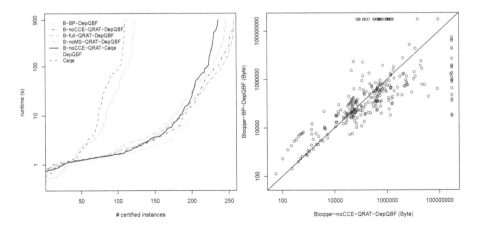

Fig. 3. Runtime comparison of full tool chains (left) and size comparison of Skolem functions by Bloqqer-BP-DepQBF and Bloqqer-noCCE-QRAT-DepQBF (right).

6   Conclusion

In this paper we described a general approach to obtain valid Skolem functions for a quantified Boolean formula that has been preprocessed by a QRAT trace producing preprocessor like Bloqqer. The described method reuses and modifies a previously presented approach for extracting Skolem functions from QRAT proofs [12]. We showed how to continue the incomplete Skolem functions extracted from the QRAT trace with the Skolem functions of the preprocessed formula. We implemented this method in a new Skolem function extraction tool and performed an extensive evaluation on formulas of the QBF Eval 2016 main track. We observed that our general method performs similarly well as the only available specialized approach for that purpose. Thus, our tool can be smoothly integrated into typical QBF solving tool chains in order to find semantic certificates of true QBFs. Such certificates are witnesses for the correctness of the solving results as solutions of the application problem encoded in QBF.

Potential future work is the extraction of Herbrand functions as witnesses of unsatisfiable QBFs as well as the optimization of extracted Skolem functions. For obtaining a tighter integration of preprocessing and solving, we consider to directly integrate proofs of different proof systems.

Acknowledgements. We would like to thank Luca Pulina for providing us with the list of satisfiable instances of the QBF Eval 2016.

References

1. Kleine Büning, H., Bubeck, U.: Theory of quantified Boolean formulas. In: Handbook of Satisfiability, pp. 735–760. IOS Press (2009)

2. Benedetti, M., Mangassarian, H.: QBF-based formal verification: experience and perspectives. JSAT 5(1–4), 133–191 (2008)
3. Bloem, R., Könighofer, R., Seidl, M.: SAT-based synthesis methods for safety specs. In: McMillan, K.L., Rival, X. (eds.) VMCAI 2014. LNCS, vol. 8318, pp. 1–20. Springer, Heidelberg (2014). doi:10.1007/978-3-642-54013-4_1
4. Egly, U., Kronegger, M., Lonsing, F., Pfandler, A.: Conformant planning as a case study of incremental QBF solving. In: Aranda-Corral, G.A., Calmet, J., Martín-Mateos, F.J. (eds.) AISC 2014. LNCS, vol. 8884, pp. 120–131. Springer, Cham (2014). doi:10.1007/978-3-319-13770-4_11
5. Balabanov, V., Jiang, J.R., Scholl, C.: Skolem functions computation for CEGAR based QBF solvers. In: QBF (2015)
6. Rabe, M.N., Seshia, S.A.: Incremental determinization. In: Creignou, N., Le Berre, D. (eds.) SAT 2016. LNCS, vol. 9710, pp. 375–392. Springer, Cham (2016). doi:10.1007/978-3-319-40970-2_23
7. Balabanov, V., Jiang, J.R.: Unified QBF certification and its applications. Form. Methods Syst. Des. 41(1), 45–65 (2012)
8. Benedetti, M.: Extracting certificates from quantified Boolean formulas. In: IJCAI, pp. 47–53. Professional Book Center (2005)
9. Narizzano, M., Peschiera, C., Pulina, L., Tacchella, A.: Evaluating and certifying QBFs: a comparison of state-of-the-art tools. AI Commun. 22(4), 191–210 (2009)
10. Niemetz, A., Preiner, M., Lonsing, F., Seidl, M., Biere, A.: Resolution-based certificate extraction for QBF. In: Cimatti, A., Sebastiani, R. (eds.) SAT 2012. LNCS, vol. 7317, pp. 430–435. Springer, Heidelberg (2012). doi:10.1007/978-3-642-31612-8_33
11. Jussila, T., Biere, A., Sinz, C., Kröning, D., Wintersteiger, C.M.: A first step towards a unified proof checker for QBF. In: Marques-Silva, J., Sakallah, K.A. (eds.) SAT 2007. LNCS, vol. 4501, pp. 201–214. Springer, Heidelberg (2007). doi:10.1007/978-3-540-72788-0_21
12. Heule, M.J.H., Seidl, M., Biere, A.: Solution validation and extraction for QBF preprocessing. J. Autom. Reason. 58(1), 97–125 (2017)
13. Goultiaeva, A., Van Gelder, A., Bacchus, F.: A uniform approach for generating proofs and strategies for both true and false QBF formulas. In: IJCAI/AAAI, pp. 546–553 (2011)
14. Van Gelder, A.: Certificate extraction from variable-elimination QBF preprocessors. In: QBF, pp. 35–39 (2013)
15. Kleine Büning, H., Karpinski, M., Flögel, A.: Resolution for quantified Boolean formulas. Inf. Comput. 117(1), 12–18 (1995)
16. Giunchiglia, E., Marin, P., Narizzano, M.: Reasoning with quantified Boolean formulas. In: Handbook of Satisfiability, pp. 761–780. IOS Press (2009)
17. Rabe, M.N., Tentrup, L.: CAQE: a certifying QBF solver. In: FMCAD, pp. 136–143 (2015)
18. Lonsing, F., Seidl, M., Van Gelder, A.: The QBF gallery: behind the scenes. Artif. Intell. 237, 92–114 (2016)
19. Marin, P., Narizzano, M., Pulina, L., Tacchella, A., Giunchiglia, E.: Twelve years of QBF evaluations: QSAT is PSPACE-hard and it shows. Fundam. Inform. 149(1–2), 133–158 (2016)
20. Janota, M., Grigore, R., Marques-Silva, J.: On QBF proofs and preprocessing. In: McMillan, K., Middeldorp, A., Voronkov, A. (eds.) LPAR 2013. LNCS, vol. 8312, pp. 473–489. Springer, Heidelberg (2013). doi:10.1007/978-3-642-45221-5_32

21. Biere, A., Lonsing, F., Seidl, M.: Blocked clause elimination for QBF. In: Bjørner, N., Sofronie-Stokkermans, V. (eds.) CADE 2011. LNCS, vol. 6803, pp. 101–115. Springer, Heidelberg (2011). doi:10.1007/978-3-642-22438-6_10
22. Lonsing, F., Egly, U.: DepQBF: an incremental QBF solver based on clause groups. CoRR abs/1502.02484 (2015)

WSCLim: A Tool for Model-Based Testing of WS-BPEL Compositions Under Load Conditions

Afef Jmal Maâlej[1]([✉]), Moez Krichen[1,2], and Mohamed Jmaïel[1,3]

[1] ReDCAD Laboratory, National School of Engineers of Sfax, University of Sfax,
B.P. 1173, 3038 Sfax, Tunisia
{afef.jmal,moez.krichen,mohamed.jmaiel}@redcad.org
[2] Faculty of CSIT, Al-Baha University, Al Baha, Saudi Arabia
[3] Digital Research Center of Sfax, B.P. 275, Sakiet Ezzit, 3021 Sfax, Tunisia

Abstract. Web services compositions must provide different utilities to hundreds even thousands of users simultaneously. An important challenge of testing these applications is load testing. For this purpose, we proposed in a previous work a test architecture aiming to study the limitations of WS-BPEL compositions under load conditions. We also concretized our solution by implementing a tool support (WSCLim). We introduce in this paper a case study on Hospital Blood Ordering for Transfusion Purposes in order to best illustrate our solution.

Keywords: Web services composition · Timed Automata · Load testing · Log analysis · Performance monitoring

1 Introduction

Clearly, not all service is able to respond the need of a user. In this case, it is possible to combine existing services together in order to fulfil this need. The act of combining these services is called Web service composition. Although much researches have been focused on the discovery, selection and composition of Web services, research areas such as testing of Web services (especially Web service compositions) are still new and immature [1]. Some surveys on Web services testing can be found in [2,3]. Furthermore, Bucchiarone and Severoni [4] and Zakaria et al. [5] provided surveys focusing on testing of web service compositions.

Nowadays, Web services compositions (particularly BPEL[1] [6] compositions) are still considered as a major player in the implementation of distributed architectures. Such applications must offer different services to hundreds even thousands of users instantaneously. An important challenge of testing these applications is load testing [7], which is frequently performed in order to ensure that a system satisfies a particular performance requirement under a heavy load. In this context and in addition to conventional functional testing procedures, load testing is an important procedure that reveals programming errors which would not

---

[1] Business Process Execution Language.

S. Gabmeyer and E.B. Johnsen (Eds.): TAP 2017, LNCS 10375, pp. 139–151, 2017.
DOI: 10.1007/978-3-319-61467-0_9

appear if the SUT[2] is executed with a limited workload or for a short time. Such errors emerge when the system is executed under a heavy load or over a long period of time. On the other hand, a given process may be correctly implemented but fails under some particular load conditions because of external causes (e.g. misconfiguration, hardware failures, etc.) [8]. Consequently, it is important to identify and remedy these different problems. For that, we investigated in [9] the opportunities as well as challenges of load testing in general.

The motivation of our work is to help practitioners to study the limitations of BPEL compositions, in particular under load conditions. For that, we provided a complete approach dedicated to BPEL compositions, that combines functional and load testing [10]. The added value in this work is the treatment/use of *switch* activity within the BPEL flow in order to choose between two actions. In fact, conditional branching introduces decision points to control the flow of execution of a BPEL process service component. Consequently, the treatment of such activity needs the implementation of additional programming code in the WSCLim core. Thus, our tool becomes more agile and generic so different other case studies, particularly business processes containing *switch* activities, could be tested under load conditions thanks to our tool.

We also concentrate on the combination of test and proof by the use of a formal model for the testing. To explain, we highlight that in our work we deal with model-based testing, so we check/verify some constraints of a BPEL implementation with regard to a formal model (Timed Automata) considering load conditions. Our WSCLim tool automatically executes the corresponding random load tests on the implementation. At the end, test results are exhaustively analyzed, with regard to specified constraints in the model, and advanced information is provided, which permits to detect different natures and causes of problems. For that, we take into consideration the execution context (connections with partner services, SUT environment, etc.) of the application under test while periodically capturing, under load, some performance metrics of the system such as CPU usage, memory usage, etc. To detail, our test solution is performed based on two steps. The first one is to run a load test during which the process under test is monitored and performance data are recorded. The second step is to analyze the resulting test logs in order to identify problems under load. Besides the theoretical framework, we have developed a tool, called WSCLim[3] (WS-BPEL Compositions Limitations), that helps in the automation of our testing approach [10].

The remainder of this paper is organized as follows. Section 2 discusses some existing works on load testing. In Sect. 3, we describe the inputs and outputs of our proposed WSCLim tool. In Sect. 4, we introduce a Hospital Blood Ordering for Transfusion Purposes (HBO-TP) case study, its corresponding reference specification expressed in Timed Automata [11] and a BPEL Implementation of a HBO-TP Scenario. Section 5 is dedicated to validate our approach by means of the introduced case study and using our WSCLim tool. Finally, Sect. 6 provides a conclusion that summarizes the paper and discusses items for future work.

---

[2] System Under Test.
[3] http://www.redcad.org/members/afef.jmal/WSCLim/Overview.html.

2   Comparison of Existing Works on Load Testing

Yang and Pollock [12] proposed a technique to identify the load sensitive parts in sequential programs based on a static analysis of the code. They also illustrated some load sensitive programming errors, which may have no damaging effect under small loads or short executions, but cause a program to fail when it is executed under a heavy load or over a long period of time. In addition, Zhang and Cheung [13] described a procedure for automating stress test case generation in multimedia systems. For that, they identify test cases that can lead to the saturation of one kind of resource, namely CPU usage of a node in the distributed multimedia system. Furthermore, Grosso et al. [14] proposed to combine static analysis and program slicing with evolutionary testing, in order to detect buffer overflow threats. For that purpose, the authors used of Genetic Algorithms in order to generate test cases. Garousi et al. [15] presented a stress test methodology that aims at increasing chances of discovering faults related to distributed traffic in distributed systems. The technique uses as input a specified UML 2.0 model of a system, extended with timing information. Moreover, Jiang et al. [16] and Jiang [17] presented an approach that accesses the execution logs of an application to uncover its dominant behaviour and signals deviations from the application basic behaviour.

Comparing the previous works, we notice that load testing concerns various fields such as multimedia systems [13], network applications [14], etc. Furthermore, all these solutions focus on the automatic generation of load test suites. Besides, most of the existing works aim to detect anomalies which are related to resource saturation or to performance issues as throughput, response time, etc. Only Yang and Pollock [12] proposed a solution that allows to verify functional errors in programs/implementations under load conditions. In fact, detected faults according to Yang and Pollock [12] are related to dynamic memory allocation, and may occur because of memory leaks, incorrect dynamic memory allocation, etc. Besides, few research efforts, such as Jiang et al. [16] and Jiang [17], are devoted to the automated analysis of load testing results in order to uncover potential problems. Indeed, it is hard to detect problems in a load test due to the large amount of data which must be analyzed. Current industrial practice mainly involves time-consuming manual checks which, for instance, search through the logs of the application for error messages. We also notice that the identification of problem cause(s) (application, network or other) is not the main goal behind load testing, rather than studying performance of the application under test, this fact explains why few works address this issue. However, in our work, we are able to recognize if the detected problem under load is caused by implementation anomalies, network or other causes. Indeed, we defined and validated our approach based on interception of exchanged messages between the composition under test and its partner services. That way it would be possible to monitor exchanged messages instantaneously, and to recognize what is the cause behind their loss or probably their reception delay, etc. To conclude, we underline that the main contribution of our work is the verification of Web service compositions requirements (which are supposed to be formally modeled) under diverse load conditions. Moreover, final results about abnormal behaviours and observed error rates are also provided with the aim to identify and address detected problems under load. Definitely all that makes our solution richer and more interesting than existing ones.

3   Overview of Our WSCLim Tool

Java is the programming language used to implement our proposed WSCLim tool. Our test solution is performed based on two steps. The first one is to run a load test during which the process under test is monitored and performance data are recorded. The second step is to analyze the resulting test logs, with regard to specified constraints in the model (Timed Automata), in order to identify problems under load. For that, the tool user is firstly asked to specify (1) the path of the specification (Timed Automata) used as a reference in the test, (2) the path of the composition WSDL specification, (3) the number of BPEL concurrent instances, and (4) the delay between each two successive invocations of the BPEL process under test. During the test execution, details are stored in log files. At the end of a test, the analysis of results is launched and the interface containing test verdicts is displayed. In fact, different errors' natures and causes are considered in our study of BPEL compositions limitations under load conditions [10]. In particular, our WSCLim tool is able to detect problems caused by (1) the application (BPEL implementation) such as (i) non specified behaviours adding or required behaviours omission in addition to (ii) erroneous delays. Another problem cause could be (2) the test environment either (i) a problem of connection to a partner service or (ii) a problem of getting a response from a partner service. The last possible cause is (3) the SUT Node (delay in treatment of a partner service response).

4   Description of Our Illustrative Case Study

In this section, we introduce a HBO-TP (Hospital Blood Ordering for Transfusion Purposes) case study for a better illustration of our solution later.

4.1   HBO-TP Case Study

The transfusion of blood or its components (plasma, platelets, etc.) has an important role in modern medicine and surgery. In this context, we show our approach by means of a case study consisting of a hospital ordering blood components for transfusion purposes.

We suppose that the required business process (written in BPEL) composes services of: local blood search (LBS), local blood ordering (LBO), hospital maintenance (HM) and unsatisfactory customer (UC). We also assume that the two first partner services (LBS) and (LBO) are connected to a local blood bank which is situated in the involved hospital. In fact, the blood bank is mainly responsible for rapid response to urgent requests for blood components and for selection of suitable blood component for each clinical condition.

Once a hospital unit (such as emergency, surgery, etc.) sends a request to the HBO-TP process, the (LBS) service is invoked to search for required blood component from the local blood bank. This search is conditioned by a waiting time. Indeed, the process should receive a response from (LBS) within maximum 60 s (for example). Otherwise, the process sends a connection problem report to the (HM) service. In case of getting a blood search response before reaching 60 s, obtained search results are analyzed. If the conditions related to the needed blood component are satisfied, then the (LBO) service is invoked to order blood from the local blood bank. Otherwise, an unsatisfactory customer report is sent to (UC) service for information about unavailable required blood component. Thus, responsibles are put in charge to answer quickly the hospital unit need for blood. Finally, a detailed reply informing about final results is sent to the concerned hospital unit.

4.2 Reference Specification Expressed in Timed Automata

As a first input of our WSCLim tool, one should provide a written specification in Timed Automata, which is an abstraction that expresses appropriately functional requirements besides timing delays when modeling particularly Web service compositions. For this reason, we first modeled the described HBO-TP scenario using Uppaal[4], an integrated tool environment for modeling, validation and verification of systems modeled as networks of Timed Automata.

In Uppaal, synchronous communication between the Timed Automata is performed by hand-shake synchronization using input and output actions. Output and input actions are denoted with an exclamation mark and a question mark respectively, e.g., a! and a?. Asynchronous communication is achieved by means of shared variables.

Throughout the paper we use Uppaal syntax to illustrate Timed Automata. The graph in Fig. 1 is directly exported from Uppaal, where x is a local clock. In addition, initial locations are marked using a double circle. Edges are by convention labeled by the triple: guard, action, and assignment in that order (possible but not necessary annotation). Finally, bold-faced clock conditions placed under locations are location invariants.

Before referring to the elaborated specification expressed in Timed Automata for testing different HBO-TP BPEL implementations, we should be sure that this model respects both functional and non-functional system requirements. For that, Uppaal proposes a simulation module of systems modeled in Timed Automata which enables to follow how the built model can evolve in time. The realized simulations allowed us to detect and correct some errors when modeling our considered HBO-TP scenario in Timed Automata. Furthermore, we used Uppaal's verification module which enables to check various properties (safety, liveness, deadlock, etc.) of our created model. That way, we obtain at the end a checked and valid specification expressed in Timed Automata as a reference for testing later.

---

[4] http://uppaal.org/.

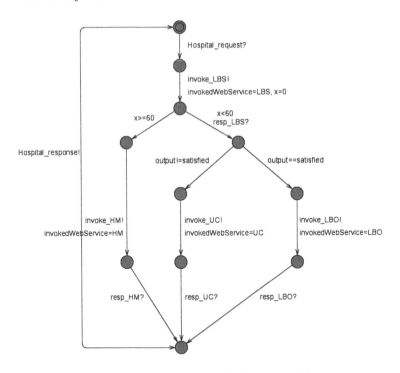

Fig. 1. The HBO-TP process modeled in Timed Automata

4.3   BPEL Implementation of the HBO-TP Scenario

The WSCLim tool requires, as a second input, a given BPEL implementation which corresponds in our case to the previously described HBO-TP scenario. This implementation is then tested; with regard to the provided Timed Automata for our tool; under various load conditions.

A BPEL model can be described in form of a graphical representation. In Fig. 2, we illustrate a correct BPEL process corresponding to our considered HBO-TP case study. It uses a *pick* activity for one of the following cases: (1) to receive a response from (LBS) within 60 s maximum and to continue its execution, or (2) to send a connection problem report to (HM) service if there is no received response from (LBS) after a delay of 60 s.

Besides, a *switch* activity is used to choose between two actions : (1) if the branch condition is satisfied then the (LBO) service is invoked to order blood from the local blood bank, else (2) an unsatisfactory customer report is sent to (UC) service to inform about required blood component unavailability.

In order to validate our approach in a way that one has an idea of its fault-detection effectiveness, we used mutation testing, i.e., we produced mutated versions of our HBO-TP BPEL process by seeding artificial defects that can cause load testing faults, such as the implementation of non specified behaviours (wrt. the model) or the omission of required behaviours in the BPEL flow, we may also

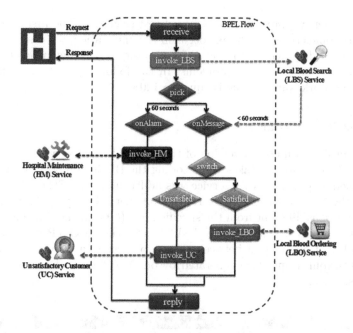

Fig. 2. The HBO-TP process

consider erroneous delays within a *pick* activity of the BPEL process. It consists of an implementation of a synchronous communication conditioned by a timeout response of a partner service which is different from the specified one [10]. We note that we designed BPEL processes using the Oracle JDeveloper environment[5]. In addition, we used Oracle BPEL Process Manager infrastructure[6] for deploying and managing designed processes.

5   Testing Scenarios: Results and Interpretations

In order to study the limitations of the HBO-TP process under load conditions, we defined several test scenarios. We highlight that we made use of our WSCLim tool for different mutated BPEL versions. For instance, we considered wrong delays corresponding to blood search waiting times. That is in this case, the implemented delay value (*pick* activity) is different from the specified one (which is equal to 60 s according to the timed automaton in Fig. 1). Besides, we considered the addition of some non required behaviours (e.g., new service invocation), and in other altered BPEL processes, we omitted some specified requirements. Other possible mutation may be the implementation of a wrong branch condition (*switch* activity) which affects normal behaviour of the BPEL process.

---

[5] http://www.oracle.com/technetwork/developer-tools/jdev/.
[6] http://www.oracle.com/technetwork/middleware/bpel/.

In this paper, we present two proposed test scenarios. The first one is used to illustrate some errors which may occur in the application, whereas the second test scenario is designed to subject the composition to a higher load in order to identify the non-functional problems. In the following, we assume that the maximum network waiting time is equal to 120 s.

5.1 First Test Scenario

First, we consider a mutated version of the HBO-TP process where we suppose that a developer made mistakes while coding the BPEL composition. In fact, a non specified/required partner service was added in the BPEL implementation just after the (UC) service. Moreover, the implemented timeout (30 s) of service (LBS) response is different from the specified one (60 s) in the timed automaton (see Fig. 1). In this scenario, we invoked 30 times the HBO-TP process considering a delay of one second between each two successive invocations. Figure 3 shows the graphical interface generated by our WSCLim tool according to the first test scenario.

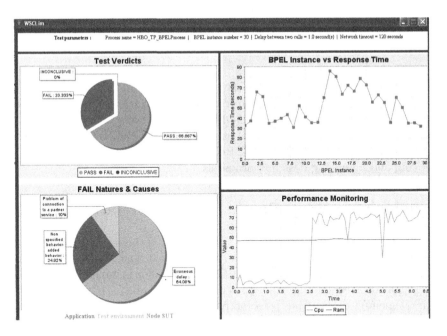

Fig. 3. Graphical interface generated by WSCLim tool - scenario 1 (Color figure online)

We notice that, for this scenario, the percentage of FAIL verdict is equal to 33.33% (red-coloured zone of *Test Verdicts* block), which means that 10 BPEL instances among 30 ones failed during load testing. Concerning the *FAIL natures and causes* of this execution, there are problems at the application level (problem cause) (24,92% of errors (magenta-coloured zone) correspond to non specified added behaviours; first application FAIL nature; and 64.08% of errors (salmon-coloured zone) are about erroneous delays; second application FAIL nature). The source/cause of the rest of problems (10%) is test environment (cyan-coloured zone) and their nature relates to problems of connection to a partner service.

According to the test report depicted in Listing 1.1, the BPEL instance of identifier 450480 follows a path which does not exist in the specification. In fact, it illustrates the invocation of an unexpected partner service (HM) at the level of *Switch* activity in case where the response of (LBS) service is non satisfied, while according to the specification, only the service (UC) should be invoked. This added behaviour shows clearly the presence of an error while implementing the BPEL process.

Listing 1.2 depicts an example which shows a problem of connection to partner services. Concerning the BPEL instance 450469, the (LBS) service responded to the composition before the implemented response delay (30 s). Thus, the (LBO) service should be invoked. However, we did not observe this invocation in the test report. Thus, we conclude that the (LBO) service could not be invoked by the BPEL process. This problem of connection to service (LBO) under load conditions is definitely caused by the test environment.

Listing 1.1. Test report corresponding to BPEL instance 450480

```
450480:Hospital_request?,(123),Thu Sep 15 18:55:20 GMT+01:00 2014
450480:Invoke_LBS!,(123)
450480:random1
450480:typeInput=PASS
450480:cAttente= 17452.3002696788
450480:resp_LBS?,(FuzSM),x=17
450480:Invoke_UC!,(FuzSM)
450480:random17
450480:typeInput=PASS
450480:resp_UC?,(jZYZ3),0ms
450480:Invoke_HM!,(jZYZ3)
450480:random19
450480:typeInput=PASS
450480:resp_HM?,(ulHzX),16ms
450480:Hospital_response!,(ulHzX),Thu Sep 15 19:20:57 GMT+01:00
     2014
```

Listing 1.2. Test report corresponding to BPEL instance 450469

```
450469:Hospital_request?,(123),Thu Sep 15 18:54:50 GMT+01:00 2014
450469:Invoke_LBS!,(123)
450469:random4
450469:typeInput=PASS
450469:cAttente= 4867.44407152456
450469:resp_LBS?,(Tnt2E),x=4
450469:Hospital_response!,(Tnt2E),Thu Sep 15 18:56:00 GMT+01:00
     2014
```

5.2   Second Test Scenario

In this case, we invoked 50 times the HBO-TP process considering a delay of
one second between each two successive invocations. In addition, we consider
a BPEL implementation that complies with the specification. Consequently, we
do not suspect load sensitive faults within the application. Figure 4 shows the
graphical interface generated by our WSCLim tool according to the second test
scenario.

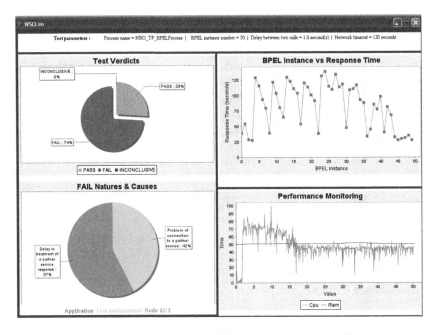

Fig. 4. Graphical interface generated by WSCLim tool - scenario 2 (Color figure online)

The analysis of the corresponding execution results shows that there is a
FAIL percentage of 74% (37 instances among 50). As explained in Fig. 4, 57%
of problems (purple-coloured zone) are located in the SUT node and 42% ones
(cyan-coloured zone) correspond to problems of connection to partner services
caused by the test environment.

According to the observed behaviour in the test report corresponding to
BPEL instance 330265 (see Listing 1.3), we notice that the (LBS) service was
invoked and it answered the BPEL process in a time less than the specified period
(60 s). However, the BPEL process follows the branch onAlarm. This could be
interpreted by a delay in treatment of the response sent from the (LBS) service
caused essentially by the load increase (particularly from the SUT node side).

Listing 1.3. Test report corresponding to BPEL instance 330265

```
330265:Hospital_request?,(123),Thu Aug 06 19:08:37 GMT+01:00 2014
330265:Invoke_LBS!,(123)
330265:typeInput=PASS
330265:resp_LBS?,(TBUhZ),x=9
330265:Invoke_HM!,(TBUhZ)
330265:typeInput=PASS
330265:resp_HM?,(34Fem),16ms
330265:Hospital_response!,(34Fem),Thu Aug 06 19:08:48 GMT+01:00
    2014
330265:typeOutput=PASS
```

Listing 1.4 illustrates an example that shows a problem of connection to partner services. Concerning the BPEL instance 330277, the (LBS) service answered
the BPEL process in a time less than the specified period (60 s). Thus, the (LBO)
service should be invoked. However, we did not observe this invocation in the
test report. Thus, we conclude that the (LBO) service could not be invoked
by the BPEL process. This problem of connection to (LBO) service under load
conditions is definitely caused by the test environment.

According to our previous experiments based on seeding various artificial
defects within BPEL processes, the example shows that our proposed WSCLim
tool can detect and identify different BPEL implementation errors, which are
hidden under a certain load and may appear while increasing load placed on
BPEL composition under test.

Listing 1.4. Test report corresponding to BPEL instance 330277

```
330277:Hospital_request?,(123),Thu Aug 06 19:08:54 GMT+01:00 2014
330277:Invoke_LBS!,(123)
330277:typeInput=PASS
330277:resp_LBS?,(MDfyd),x=19
```

5.3 Overhead of Our WSCLim Tool

Aiming to determine the overhead of our proposed WSCLim tool, we represented,
for both cases, the measurement curves of the execution time average while
varying the load conditions. In the first case, tests are performed using our
testing tool. In the second case, test executions are performed directly from the
console of the orchestration server and without turning to our WSCLim tool. To
lead these experiments, we considered again the same HBO-TP process structure
as described in Sect. 4.3.

As shown in Fig. 5, the use of our WSCLim tool does not cause a significant
additional overhead to the average of the process execution time. Indeed, for a
given load, the difference between the two corresponding times is of the order
of a few seconds (3 s on average). This negligible overhead (compared to the
average of one instance execution time) is due to additional activities such as
the verification of variable types, the logging activity, etc., which are carried out
by our tool during the load testing.

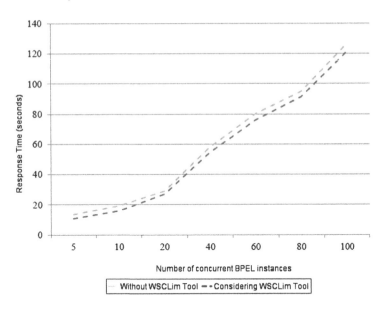

Fig. 5. Evolution of the response time with and without considering the WSCLim Tool

6   Conclusion and Future Work

In this paper we firstly described the inputs and outputs of our WSCLim tool. Then we presented a HBO-TP case study in order to validate the applicability of our load testing approach for the study of BPEL compositions behaviours under various load conditions. For that, we created, simulated and verified the reference model (corresponding to our case study and written in Timed Automata) using the Uppaal test environment. Then, we implemented different mutated versions of the considered BPEL process, and we used our WSCLim tool to automatically execute the corresponding load tests of these implementations. Finally, test results were exhaustively analyzed and advanced information was provided by our tool, which permits to detect different natures and causes of errors.

The provided results are clear evidence of the efficiency of our proposed solution. As these results are based on relatively small scale compositions, case studies with higher complexity are needed to validate the accuracy of our approach. Another future work would be the extension of our testing tool for cloud computing. In fact, we can benefit from this technology to distribute more realistically the components of our test architecture. Besides, it would be possible to support the scalability issue by opting, as an example, for the load balancing concept.

References

1. Canfora, G., Penta, M.: Testing services and service-centric systems: challenges and opportunities. IT Prof. **8**(2), 10–17 (2006)
2. Canfora, G., Penta, M.: Service-oriented architectures testing: a survey. In: De Lucia, A., Ferrucci, F. (eds.) ISSSE 2006-2008. LNCS, vol. 5413, pp. 78–105. Springer, Heidelberg (2009). doi:10.1007/978-3-540-95888-8_4
3. Harman, M., Bozkurt, M., Hassoun, Y.: Testing web services: a survey. Technical report TR-10-01, Department of Computer Science, King's College London, January 2010
4. Bucchiarone, A., Severoni, F.: Testing service composition. In: Proceedings of the 8th Argentine Symposium on Software Engineering (ASSE), Mar del Plata, Argentina, 29–31 August 2007
5. Zakaria, Z., Atan, R., Ghani, A.A., Sani, N.F.: Unit testing approaches for BPEL: a systematic review. In: Proceedings of the 16th Asia-Pacific Software Engineering Conference (APSEC), Washington, DC, USA, pp. 316–322. IEEE Computer Society (2009)
6. Barreto, C., Bullard, V., Erl, T., Evdemon, J., Jordan, D., Kand, K., Knig, D., Moser, S., Stout, R., Ten-Hove, R., Trickovic, I., van der Rijn, D., Yiu, A.: Web services business process execution language version 2.0 primer. OASIS, May 2007
7. Beizer, B.: Software Testing Techniques, 2nd edn. Van Nostrand Reinhold Co., New York (1990)
8. Jiang, Z.M., Hassan, A.E., Hamann, G., Flora, P.: Automatic identification of load testing problems. In: 2008 IEEE International Conference on Software Maintenance, ICSM 2008, pp. 307–316. IEEE (2008)
9. Maâlej, A.J., Krichen, M., Jmaïel, M.: A comparative evaluation of state-of-the-art load and stress testing approaches. Int. J. Comput. Appl. Technol. (IJCAT) **51**(4), 283–293 (2015)
10. Maâlej, A.J., Krichen, M.: Study on the limitations of WS-BPEL compositions under load conditions. Comput. J. **58**(3), 385–402 (2015)
11. Alur, R., Dill, D.L.: A theory of timed automata. Theor. Comput. Sci. **126**(2), 183–235 (1994)
12. Yang, C.D., Pollock, L.L.: Towards a structural load testing tool. SIGSOFT Softw. Eng. Notes **21**(3), 201–208 (1996)
13. Zhang, J., Cheung, S.C.: Automated test case generation for the stress testing of multimedia systems. Softw. Pract. Exp. **32**(15), 1411–1435 (2002)
14. Grosso, C., Antoniol, G., Penta, M., Galinier, P., Merlo, E.: Improving network applications security: a new heuristic to generate stress testing data. In: Proceedings of the Genetic and Evolutionary Computation Conference (GECCO), Washington DC, USA, 25–29 June 2005, pp. 1037–1043. ACM (2005)
15. Garousi, V., Briand, L.C., Labiche, Y.: Traffic-aware stress testing of distributed systems based on UML models. In: 28th International Conference on Software Engineering (ICSE), Shanghai, China, 20–28 May 2006, pp. 391–400. ACM (2006)
16. Jiang, Z.M., Hassan, A.E., Hamann, G., Flora, P.: Automatic identification of load testing problems. In: Proceedings of ICSM 2008, Beijing, China, 28 September - 4 October 2008, pp. 307–316. IEEE (2008)
17. Jiang, Z.M.: Automated analysis of load testing results. In: Proceedings of ISSTA 2010, Trento, Italy, 12–16 July 2010, pp. 143–146. ACM (2010)

Testing a Saturation-Based Theorem Prover: Experiences and Challenges

Giles Reger[1], Martin Suda[2(✉)], and Andrei Voronkov[1,3]

[1] University of Manchester, Manchester, UK
`giles.reger@manchester.ac.uk`
[2] TU Wien, Vienna, Austria
`msuda@forsyte.tuwien.ac.at`
[3] Chalmers University of Technology, Gothenburg, Sweden

Abstract. This paper attempts to address the question of how best to assure the correctness of saturation-based automated theorem provers using our experience with developing the theorem prover Vampire. We describe the techniques we currently employ to ensure that Vampire is correct and use this to motivate future challenges that need to be addressed to make this process more straightforward and to achieve better correctness guarantees.

1 Introduction

This paper considers the problem of checking that a saturation-based automated theorem prover is *correct*. We consider this question within the context of the Vampire theorem prover [14], but many of our discussions generalise to similar theorem provers such as E [22], SPASS [26], and iProver [13]. We discuss what we mean precisely by correctness, describe how we detect bugs and, as our main contribution, outline the challenges that need to be addressed.

Automated theorem provers (ATPs) are often used as *black boxes* in other techniques (e.g. program verification) and those techniques rely on the results of the theorem prover for the correctness of their own results. Another area that makes use of ATPs is the application of so-called *hammers* [12,15] in interactive theorem proving. These combinations usually provide functionality to reconstruct the proofs of the ATP using their own trusted kernels, although also offer users the option to skip such steps.

It is clear that correctness is important here, so how are we doing? Most theorem provers seem to be generally correct. However, cases of unsoundness are not uncommon. In SMT-COMP 2016 there were 603 conflicts (solvers returning different results) on 73 benchmarks caused by three solvers giving incorrect

This work was supported by EPSRC Grant EP/K032674/1, ERC Starting Grant 2014 SYMCAR 639270, Austrian research projects FWF S11403-N23 and S11409-N23, and the Wallenberg Academy Fellowship 2014 – TheProSE.
Andrei Voronkov—EasyChair

S. Gabmeyer and E.B. Johnsen (Eds.): TAP 2017, LNCS 10375, pp. 152–161, 2017.
DOI: 10.1007/978-3-319-61467-0_10

results for various reasons.[1] In the CASC competition [25], there is a period of testing where soundness is checked and resolved, and there have been a number of solvers later disqualified from the competition due to unsoundness. In our experience, adding a new feature to a theorem prover is a highly complex task and it is easy to introduce unsoundness, or general incorrectness, especially in areas of the code that are encountered during proof search infrequently.

This paper begins by describing what we mean by correctness with respect to saturation-based theorem provers (Sect. 2) and the approach we take to finding and fixing bugs (Sect. 3). This provides sufficient context to present a set of challenges that need to be addressed to produce a better solution to this problem (Sect. 4). Addressing these challenges is part of our current ongoing research. An extended version of this paper containing examples of bugs found in Vampire is available online [20].

2 What Does Correctness Mean for Us?

Broadly there are two ways in which a theorem prover such as Vampire can be incorrect: either it *returns the wrong result*, or it *violates a contract of proper behaviour*.

2.1 Incorrect Result

To understand what a correct and incorrect result mean to Vampire, we need to introduce some of the theoretical foundations of the underlying technique. We note that the approach used by Vampire is the same as that taken by other first-order theorem provers, so these discussions, and the challenges outlined later, generalise beyond Vampire.

Vampire accepts problems (formulas) in the form

$$(Premise_1 \land \ldots \land Premise_n) \rightarrow Conjecture \tag{1}$$

and can give one of three answers:

- *Theorem*, if (1) is true in all models,
- *Non-Theorem*, if there are models in which (1) is false, and
- *Unknown*, if Vampire cannot deduce one of the previous answers.

Providing one of the first two results when that result does not hold is clearly incorrect. Providing *Unknown* as the result is clearly incorrect in the sense that there is a known answer, but, due to the undecidability of first-order-logic and the general hardness of the problem, it is often unavoidable. However, as discussed below, we should understand the different ways in which *Unknown* as a result can be produced. Note that *Unknown* will be returned if Vampire exceeds either the time or memory allotted to it.

---

[1] See http://smtcomp.sourceforge.net/2016/.

More specifically, Vampire is a refutational theorem prover; it establishes the *validity* of problems in the form (1) by detecting *unsatisfiability* of its negation:

$$Premise_1 \wedge \ldots \wedge Premise_n \wedge \neg Conjecture. \qquad (2)$$

This works by translating (2) into a set of *clauses* $\mathcal{S}$ and adding consequences of $\mathcal{S}$ until the contradiction *false* is derived or all possible consequences have been added. This process is called *saturation* and may not terminate in general for a satisfiable set $\mathcal{S}$.

If Vampire derives a contradiction then it has shown that the problem (1) is *valid*, i.e. a theorem. Deriving a contradiction when the problem in (1) is not valid is *unsound* and an *incorrect result*.

If Vampire fails to derive a contradiction and *saturates* the set $\mathcal{S}$ in finitely many steps then there is a result [2] telling us that under certain conditions we can conclude that *false* cannot be a consequence of $\mathcal{S}$ and therefore problem (1) is a non-theorem. These conditions capture the *completeness* of the underlying inference system and generally require that all possible *non-redundant* inferences have been performed.

However, there are many things that Vampire does to heuristically improve proof search that break the completeness conditions. For example, (i) certain well-performing selection functions [10] might prevent inferences that need to be performed for completeness conditions to hold; and (ii) some preprocessing steps and proof search strategies explicitly remove clauses from the search space in an attempt to mitigate search space explosion [11,21]. If the completeness conditions do not hold then upon saturation the result is *Unknown*. Sometimes it is easy to detect when these conditions hold, sometimes it is non-trivial, and sometimes they are erroneously broken. In this last case (when we think the conditions hold but they do not) this will lead to incorrectly reporting non-theorem i.e. this *completeness issue* is another kind of *incorrect result*.

To ensure the requirement that all possible non-redundant inferences will in the end be performed, we impose certain *fairness* criteria on the saturation process. More concretely, we require that no such inference is postponed indefinitely. Notice that this is by nature a tricky condition to deal with as it cannot be seen to have been violated after finitely many steps while the prover is running. And since, due to the semi-decidability of first-order logic, there is no upper bound on the length of the computation required to derive *false*, a non-fair implementation might in certain cases never be able to return *Theorem*, even if it is the correct answer and instead keep computing indefinitely. Thus, this *fairness issue* does not lead to an incorrect result per se, but rather just negatively influences performance. As such it may be extremely hard to detect and deal with.

2.2 Violating the Contract of Proper Behaviour

There are two kinds of contracts of proper behaviour that Vampire can violate: those introduced implicitly by the underlying system, and those introduced explicitly by us in the form of assertions. We discuss both kinds of bug below:

- *Program crash.* A program crash is where Vampire terminates unexpectedly, usually due to an unhandled exception, floating point error (SIGFPE), or segmentation fault (SIGSEG). Unhandled exceptions are bugs as we should handle them. In general, Vampire handles all known classes of exceptions at the top level, but we have recently had issues with integrated tools (MiniSAT and Z3) producing exceptions that we did not handle. Floating point errors and segmentation faults are typical software bugs that should be detected and removed.
- *Assertion violation.* Vampire is developed defensively with frequent use of *assertions*. For example, these are inserted wherever a function makes some assumptions about its input or the results of a nested function call, and wherever we believe a certain line to be unreachable. Vampire consists of roughly 194,000 lines of C++ code with roughly 2,500 assertions, meaning that there is roughly one assertion per 77 lines. The majority of potential errors are detected early as assertion violations.

3   Finding Bugs

In this section we briefly describe how we detect and investigate bugs in Vampire where these two steps can be equally difficult. The search space for Vampire is vast, and finding the combination of inputs that triggers a bug is very difficult. Some bugs are incredibly subtle, particularly soundness bugs or those involving memory errors, and tracking them down can involve hunting through thousands of lines of output.

3.1   The Input Search Space

The two inputs to Vampire are the input problem and a strategy capturing proof search parameters. The space of possible input problems is infinite. However, we do not currently explore this space systematically. Instead we sample from sets of representative benchmarks, e.g. TPTP [24] (~20k problems) and SMT-LIB [4] (~46k relevant problems). Vampire currently uses roughly 75 proof search parameters with more than half of these having more than two possible values and some taking arbitrary numeric values (although in testing we fix these to a predefined sensible set). Therefore, the search space is significantly larger than 2^{75}, i.e. too large to explore systematically.

3.2   The Debug Process

Bug reports come from two sources:

- Users of the Vampire system may report bugs to us. Currently this is an informal process carried out by personal email. Sometimes these bugs are actually feature requests, and other times they can be due to a misuse of Vampire.

- More commonly, they come from randomly sampling the parameter space and sets of available problems (ensuring reasonable diversity in terms of features and status, e.g. theorems and non-theorems). We use a cluster[2] that enables us to carry out around a million checks a day (using varying short time limits).

Once an error is detected, we must diagnose and fix the fault. Below we describe some of our methods for doing this.

- *Tracing.* Vampire has its own library for tracing function calls. A macro is manually inserted at the start of each significant function. This macro enables the tracing library to maintain the current call stack, which is then printed on an assertion violation or during signal handling along with the number of such call points passed so far. This second piece of information can be used to explicitly log function calls for some range of call points, e.g. those just before the erroneous point. This feature is invaluable in quickly locating the cause of an assertion violation.
- *Memory Checking.* Vampire implements its own memory management library, allowing fine-grained control of memory allocation and deallocation and enforcement of soft memory limits. In debug mode, Vampire keeps track of each allocated piece of memory and checks that the corresponding deallocation is as expected. Vampire also reports memory leaks i.e. unallocated memory at the end of the proof search.
- *Segmentation Faults and Silent Memory Issues.* The most difficult bug to debug is a rogue pointer or piece of uninitialised memory. We find that a first step of applying Valgrind[3] will often detect the more straightforward issues. However, such bugs are often only noticed via incorrect results and fixed by much manual effort.
- *Proof Checking.* To detect unsoundness we employ proof checking, which we discuss further below. We do not currently have a corresponding method for checking that a saturated set complies with necessary completeness conditions.

3.3 Proof Checking

The easiest way to confirm a result indicating that the input formula is a theorem is to check that the associated proof only performs sound inference steps. This process is called proof checking and here we briefly describe the capabilities and limitations of the proof checking technique as currently realised in Vampire.

We introduce the idea of proof checking using an example (see [17] for more information about proofs in Vampire). Given the clauses

$$p(a) \qquad \neg p(x) \lor b = x \qquad \neg p(b)$$

Vampire will produce the following proof in TPTP format[4]

---

[2] Consisting of 46 nodes with quad-core Intel Xeon CPUs and 12 GB RAM.

[3] http://valgrind.org.

[4] All TPTP-compliant provers must produce proofs in this format (see http://www.cs.miami.edu/~tptp/TPTP/QuickGuide/Derivations.html). We note that the TPTP project also provides separate proof checking tools [23].

```
1. p(a) [input]
2. ~p(X0) | b = X0 [input]
3. ~p(b) [input]
4. a = b [resolution 2,1]
5. ~p(a) [backward demodulation 4,3]
7. $false [subsumption resolution 5,1]
```

A proof is a directed acyclic graph printed in a linear form where nodes that have no incoming edges are either input formulas or axioms introduced by Vampire, and the single node with no outgoing edges contains the contradiction. In the above proof each derived clause is labelled with the name of the inference and the lines of the premises.

To check a proof we just need to establish that for each inference its conclusion logically follows from its premises. By running vampire -p proofcheck we can produce a series of TPTP problems capturing each proof step. For example the following problem captures step 5 in the above proof.

```
fof(pr4,axiom, a = b ).
fof(pr3,axiom, ~p(b) ).
fof(r5,conjecture, ~p(a) ).
```

We can pass these directly to an independent theorem prover[5] and if a step cannot be independently verified then it should be investigated.

4   Challenges

We now present a discussion of what we have identified as the main challenges left to be solved, or at least addressed, given in order of importance, as we perceive it.

4.1   Full and Automated Proof Checking

As described in Sect. 3.3, there is already reasonable support for independently checking the correctness of proofs. However, this situation could still be improved.

Missing Features. There are parts of proofs that cannot currently be proof checked, the two main parts are:

- *Symbol Introducing Preprocessing.* Certain inference steps of the clausification phase, e.g. Skolemization and formula naming [19], introduce new symbols and as such do not preserve logical equivalence. This means the conclusion of the inference does not logically follow from its premises. What these steps preserve is global satisfiability of the clause set they modify. One necessary

---

[5] Currently we use E [22], iProver [13], and CVC4 [3] as independent provers but could use any accepting TPTP formatted problems.

condition for correctness is that the introduced symbols be *fresh*, i.e. not appearing elsewhere in the input. This requires a non-trivial extension to the described approach.

– *SAT and SMT solving.* Vampire makes use of SAT and SMT solvers in various ways (see [18]). This means that we have some inferences in Vampire that are of the form $P_1 \wedge \ldots \wedge P_n \rightarrow C$ *by SAT/SMT*, or even the argument that some abstraction or grounding of the premises leads to C by SAT or SMT solving. To handle such proof steps we need to collect together the premises (potentially apply the necessary abstraction or grounding) and run a SAT or SMT solver as appropriate.

Extra information may need to be added to proofs to support these checks.

Automating Proof Checking. Having tools able to check the correctness of proofs is irrelevant if those tools are not used. Ideally, theorem provers should provide the functionality to check the proofs that they produce automatically. As the problems produced during proof checking are often easy to solve, one could imagine a situation where, in a certain mode, a theorem prover applied proof checking to its proof output.

Independence. It might not be possible to find an independent solver able to handle the problems produced by proof checking. A solver might not be able to check an individual step, because it is too hard, or not be able to handle the language features the problem contains. A weaker independence could be achieved by making use of a previous version of the original theorem prover that we are more confident in.

4.2 Analysability of Unsound Proofs

Checking whether a proof is correct or not is essential. However, knowing that a proof is incorrect is not, in itself, very useful. Another missing piece to this puzzle are tools that can analyse proofs and extract, summarise or explain the *reason* the proof is incorrect. The proof checking process will reveal the proof step that fails to hold, but the problem of detecting the underlying reason for that proof step to have occurred is non-trivial.

One step in this direction is the application of *delta-debugging* [27] to reduce the input to a simpler form to aid debugging efforts. This approach has been explored for SAT/QBF solvers [1,5] applied to both the input problem and the parameter space.

4.3 Handling Non-theorem Results

So far we have ignored the incorrect result of reporting a problem to be satisfiable when it is not. It is not clear how to practically check whether a saturated set is indeed saturated as the notion of saturation is dependent on the used calculus and its instantiation with parameters such as the term ordering and literal selection methods.

Non-redundant Inferences. A necessary condition for completeness it that proof search never deletes anything that is not redundant. Checking this is significantly more complex than proof checking. In proof checking we must check that each inference of the proof is sound i.e. that we were allowed to perform those inferences to derive a contradiction. If we have a saturated set then we should check that every inference that we chose not to perform was redundant; this is what we often have to do manually, with some intuition about what such inferences might be. The number of such inferences is typically a few orders of magnitude larger than the length of a typical proof.

Monitoring Fairness. To avoid missing a saturated set we need to satisfy the fairness criteria discussed in Sect. 2.1. However, this is not *monitorable* in a formal sense [8,9] as it cannot be satisfied or violated based on a finite number of observations. However, if we were to introduce a *stronger* property of *bounded fairness* [7], e.g. a clause of age A will be processed within kA iterations for some constant k, then this property becomes monitorable (this is now a *response* property).

4.4   Achieving Better Coverage with Random Testing

As previously discussed, due to the enormous variability in proof search parameters and possible problem inputs, the best approach to detecting errors and incorrect results is through random search. However, the current approaches to random search are not optimal. Here we briefly outline areas of improvement.

Code Coverage. Our current approach makes no attempts to ensure that testing covers all lines in the code. Even though this is a very weak notion of coverage, it could be used to detect areas of code that should be tested, or removed if never used.

Coverage of the Parameter Space. Whilst random sampling of the parameter space can be effective at discovering bugs, it is not clear that all areas of the parameter space are of equal interest. Clearly, combinations of features that have not been tested together should have priority, and features added more recently should be tested more thoroughly. In this vein we could borrow from T-wise test case generation strategies for Software Product Lines [16] which aims to test all T-combinations of features.

Coverage of the Problem Space. This is an area where relatively little has been done (in the first-order setting). We currently use libraries of existing problems as possible inputs to the testing process. However, if we do not have a problem that exercises a certain feature sufficiently, we are unlikely to detect bugs related to that feature. For example, the TPTP language contains features that are very rarely used within the TPTP library. This issue is not confined to language features. Proof search is dependent on particular dimensions of the input problem (e.g. size, signature) that are difficult to quantify. If the input problems do not cover these dimensions sufficiently then certain parts of Vampire will not be tested effectively. A useful area of research would be the automatic generation of problems, or *fuzzing* of existing problems, to cover such dimensions. In this direction we could borrow from successful results in SAT/QBF solving [5,6].

5 Conclusion

This paper describes our experience testing the Vampire theorem prover and what we see as the challenges to overcome to help us improve this effort. The ideas we discuss generalise to other theorem provers and some efforts, such as proof checking techniques and better problem coverage, would be widely beneficial. Addressing the challenges set out in this paper is part of our current research and we plan to provide a proof checking tool that can fully and automatically check proofs produced by Vampire.

References

1. Artho, C., Biere, A., Seidl, M.: Model-based testing for verification back-ends. In: Veanes, M., Viganò, L. (eds.) TAP 2013. LNCS, vol. 7942, pp. 39–55. Springer, Heidelberg (2013). doi:10.1007/978-3-642-38916-0_3
2. Bachmair, L., Ganzinger, H.: Resolution theorem proving. In: Handbook of Automated Reasoning, vol. 1, chap. 2, pp. 19–99. Elsevier Science (2001)
3. Barrett, C., Conway, C., Deters, M., Hadarean, L., Jovanovic, D., King, T., Reynolds, A., Tinelli, C.: CVC4. In: Gopalakrishnan, G., Qadeer, S. (eds.) CAV 2011. LNCS, vol. 6806, pp. 171–177. Springer, Heidelberg (2011). doi:10.1007/978-3-642-22110-1_14
4. Barrett, C., Stump, A., Tinelli, C.: The Satisfiability Modulo Theories Library (SMT-LIB) (2010). www.SMT-LIB.org
5. Brummayer, R., Lonsing, F., Biere, A.: Automated testing and debugging of SAT and QBF solvers. In: Strichman, O., Szeider, S. (eds.) SAT 2010. LNCS, vol. 6175, pp. 44–57. Springer, Heidelberg (2010). doi:10.1007/978-3-642-14186-7_6
6. Creignou, N., Egly, U., Seidl, M.: A framework for the specification of random SAT and QSAT formulas. In: Brucker, A.D., Julliand, J. (eds.) TAP 2012. LNCS, vol. 7305, pp. 163–168. Springer, Heidelberg (2012). doi:10.1007/978-3-642-30473-6_14
7. Dershowitz, N., Jayasimha, D.N., Park, S.: Bounded fairness. In: Dershowitz, N. (ed.) Verification: Theory and Practice. LNCS, vol. 2772, pp. 304–317. Springer, Heidelberg (2003). doi:10.1007/978-3-540-39910-0_14
8. Diekert, V., Leucker, M.: Topology, monitorable properties and runtime verification. Theor. Comput. Sci. **537**, 29–41 (2014). Theoretical Aspects of Computing (ICTAC 2011)
9. Falcone, Y., Fernandez, J.C., Mounier, L.: Runtime verification of safety-progress properties. In: Bensalem, S., Peled, D.A. (eds.) RV 2009. LNCS, vol. 5779, pp. 40–59. Springer, Heidelberg (2009). doi:10.1007/978-3-642-04694-0_4
10. Hoder, K., Reger, G., Suda, M., Voronkov, A.: Selecting the selection. In: Olivetti, N., Tiwari, A. (eds.) IJCAR 2016. LNCS, vol. 9706, pp. 313–329. Springer, Cham (2016). doi:10.1007/978-3-319-40229-1_22

11. Hoder, K., Voronkov, A.: Sine qua non for large theory reasoning. In: Bjørner, N., Sofronie-Stokkermans, V. (eds.) CADE 2011. LNCS, vol. 6803, pp. 299–314. Springer, Heidelberg (2011). doi:10.1007/978-3-642-22438-6_23
12. Kaliszyk, C., Urban, J.: Hol(y)hammer: online ATP service for HOL light. Math. Comput. Sci. **9**(1), 5–22 (2015)
13. Korovin, K.: iProver - an instantiation-based theorem prover for first-order logic (system description). In: Armando, A., Baumgartner, P., Dowek, G. (eds.) IJCAR 2008. LNCS, vol. 5195, pp. 292–298. Springer, Heidelberg (2008). doi:10.1007/978-3-540-71070-7_24
14. Kovács, L., Voronkov, A.: First-order theorem proving and vampire. In: Sharygina, N., Veith, H. (eds.) CAV 2013. LNCS, vol. 8044, pp. 1–35. Springer, Heidelberg (2013). doi:10.1007/978-3-642-39799-8_1
15. Paulson, L.C., Blanchette, J.C.: Three years of experience with sledgehammer, a practical link between automatic and interactive theorem provers. In: The 8th International Workshop on the Implementation of Logics, IWIL 2010. EPiC Series in Computing, vol. 2, pp. 1–11. EasyChair (2012)
16. Perrouin, G., Sen, S., Klein, J., Baudry, B., Traon, Y.l.: Automated and scalable t-wise test case generation strategies for software product lines. In: Proceedings of the 2010 Third International Conference on Software Testing, Verification and Validation, ICST 2010, pp. 459–468. IEEE Computer Society (2010)
17. Reger, G.: Better proof output for Vampire. In: Proceedings of the 3rd Vampire Workshop, Vampire 2016. EPiC Series in Computing, vol. 44, pp. 46–60. EasyChair (2017)
18. Reger, G., Suda, M.: The uses of sat solvers in vampire. In: Proceedings of the 1st and 2nd Vampire Workshops. EPiC Series in Computing, vol. 38, pp. 63–69. EasyChair (2016)
19. Reger, G., Suda, M., Voronkov, A.: New techniques in clausal form generation. In: 2nd Global Conference on Artificial Intelligence, GCAI 2016. EPiC Series in Computing, vol. 41, pp. 11–23. EasyChair (2016)
20. Reger, G., Suda, M., Voronkov, A.: Testing a Saturation-Based Theorem Prover: Experiences and Challenges (Extended Version). ArXiv e-prints (2017)
21. Riazanov, A., Voronkov, A.: Limited resource strategy in resolution theorem proving. J. Symb. Comput. **36**(1–2), 101–115 (2003)
22. Schulz, S.: E - a brainiac theorem prover. AI Commun. **15**(2–3), 111–126 (2002)
23. Sutcliffe, G.: Semantic derivation verification: techniques and implementation. Int. J. Artif. Intell. Tools **15**(6), 1053–1070 (2006)
24. Sutcliffe, G.: The TPTP problem library and associated infrastructure. J. Autom. Reason. **43**(4), 337–362 (2009)
25. Sutcliffe, G.: The CADE ATP system competition - CASC. AI Mag. **37**(2), 99–101 (2016)
26. Weidenbach, C., Dimova, D., Fietzke, A., Kumar, R., Suda, M., Wischnewski, P.: SPASS version 3.5. In: Schmidt, R.A. (ed.) CADE 2009. LNCS, vol. 5663, pp. 140–145. Springer, Heidelberg (2009). doi:10.1007/978-3-642-02959-2_10
27. Zeller, A.: Yesterday, my program worked. Today, it does not. Why? In: Nierstrasz, O., Lemoine, M. (eds.) ESEC/FSE 1999. LNCS, vol. 1687, pp. 253–267. Springer, Heidelberg (1999). doi:10.1007/3-540-48166-4_16

Author Index

Printed in the United States
By Bookmasters